W9-BNI-807

"Further evidence—as if any were needed—that Bishop Barron is the best catechist and apologist in English-speaking Catholicism. A book to savor, ponder, and celebrate, *Vibrant Paradoxes* is a treasure chest of insight, informed by a profound Catholic faith and a deep intelligence, and written with the kind of brio that makes the New Evangelization fun."

> —George Weigel
> Distinguished Senior Fellow and William E. Simon Chair in Catholic Studies
> Ethics and Public Policy Center

"We all know Bishop Robert Barron's engaging style as a preacher and teacher. In *Vibrant Paradoxes: The Both/And of Catholicism*, we find this gifted writer at his best. With freshness and insight Bishop Barron explores seemingly opposite realities: sin and mercy, suffering and joy, faith and reason. His profound understanding of the spiritual life guides the reader to discover how the Christian faith is 'permanently fresh, startling, and urgent.' *Vibrant Paradoxes* is a must read for anyone looking for a new presentation of our ancient faith."

> —Cardinal Donald Wuerl
> Archbishop of Washington

"Bishop Robert Barron, like Fulton Sheen before him, speaks with an authority that is more than episcopal. He came by his episcopal authority long after he had won the trust and admiration of a multitude. These short essays show you how he did it. They treat eternal and ephemeral matters in fascinating ways. His methods somehow combine the techniques of Chesterton and Aquinas with a dash of Bob Dylan—and the mix is always exactly right. His Excellency is especially good when he treats biblical themes. His words are wise and luminous. So why are you reading mine when you could be reading his?"

> —Dr. Scott Hahn
> Author of *Rome Sweet Home* and *The Lamb's Supper*

"Bishop Robert Barron is one of the most effective evangelists in the Catholic Church. His new book collects some of his best essays, on a typically wide variety of topics, and is written in his trademark inviting, accessible, and knowledgeable style. He's a real blessing for our Church and his new book will be a real blessing for you."

> —James Martin, SJ
> Author of *Jesus: A Pilgrimage*

"If you've ever wanted to share one of Bishop Robert Barron's fantastic meditations on Christianity but can't quite remember where he said it (or how he said it!), then look no further. This book is for you. *Vibrant Paradoxes* is a cornucopia of wisdom, overflowing with insights into sin and mercy, reason and faith, matter and spirit, suffering and joy."

> —Dr. Brant Pitre
> Author of *The Case for Jesus: The Biblical and Historical Evidence for Christ*

"*Vibrant Paradoxes* is a wonderful collection of clear, accessible, and learned articulations of different aspects of Catholic faith and practice. With the publication of this book, it is evident why Bishop Robert Barron is more and more being recognized as America's premier Catholic priest public intellectual, the likes of which we have not seen since the days of Archbishop Fulton Sheen and Fr. John Courtney Murray."

—Francis J. Beckwith
Professor of Philosophy and Church-State Studies, Baylor University

"In *Vibrant Paradoxes*, Bishop Barron puts to rest the caricature that draws Catholicism as something narrow in thought and discriminating in practice. In one entertaining and accessible essay after another, he demonstrates Catholic thinking as broad, paradoxical, respectful, and much too thorough to demand "either/or" when it can so clearly (and wisely) argue for the sake of "both/and". This book will surprise you, enlighten you, and help you to appreciate the width and breadth of Catholicism."

—Elizabeth Scalia
Author and U.S. Editor-in-Chief at Aleteia.org

"The riches of Catholic moral teaching are like a hidden treasure chest, waiting to be discovered. In *Vibrant Paradoxes*, Bishop Barron cracks open the chest and leaves us standing in awe of the riches it contains. Written in a warm, fatherly tone with straightforward prose that anyone can understand, this is a book that is sure to change a lot of people's lives."

—Jennifer Fulwiler
Author of *Something Other Than God*

"*Vibrant Paradoxes* is a stimulating exploration of contemporary issues via the deep, broad, and inclusive lens of Catholicism. Bishop Barron's essays offer invaluable insights for anyone committed to dialoguing from a place of love and truth in this skeptical, yearning world."

—Amy Welborn
Author of *The Words We Pray: Discovering the Richness of Traditional Catholic Prayer*

"What does our Catholic faith mean practically, generously, daily? Bishop Robert Barron helps us see. *Vibrant Paradoxes* illuminates the opportunities for seeing the light of faith everywhere—in every news story (both those that are well-covered and those that are not), in every cultural moment, in every human encounter. Our mission is integral and eternal, and Bishop Barron is tireless in highlighting the opportunities for mission."

—Kathryn Jean Lopez
Senior fellow, National Review Institute

VIBRANT
PARADOXES
The Both/And of Catholicism

ROBERT BARRON

Second edition published in 2017.
© 2017 by Word on Fire Catholic Ministries
Printed in the United States of America
All rights reserved.
Originally published in 2016.

20   6

ISBN: 978-1-943243-10-5

Cover Image: Ceiling of Basilica de la Sagrada Família in Barcelona, Spain

Library of Congress Control Number: 2016935323
Barron, Robert E., 1959-

www.wordonfire.org

CONTENTS

MATTER AND SPIRIT
131

FREEDOM AND DISCIPLINE
159

SUFFERING AND JOY
227

FOREWORD

Any publisher will tell you that collections of short essays usually sell as well as thread. But this book will be a best seller, because these little gems are pearls.

My most common response when asked to write a Foreword, or a recommendation to a publisher, or a blurb for a book, is a polite "thanks but no thanks." I am a curmudgeon, for I have read so many books that I am bored with most of them. Occasionally I will say yes because the manuscript sent to me is worth publishing; but even then I usually merely do my duty, like a professor reading a term paper, giving it just a good enough read to know it is good enough to publish, but without much passion, love, fire, or enthusiasm, and certainly not reading the whole thing from cover to cover with delight. That is how it is with 90% of the books I'm sent, and 100% of the collections of short essays.

Until now.

Everyone complains about the dullness of Catholic homilies and essays. Nearly all our priests are good priests (their job, of course) and some are good kings (administration), but none are great prophets and preachers. Since Fulton Sheen died, there have been exactly zero Catholic masters in this field.

Until now.

Technically, Bishop Barron's articles are essays, not homilies, because most are not reflections on the Scripture passages assigned in the liturgy of the Mass. They range, like free horses. Some are philosophical, some theological, some ethical, some apologetical, some psychological, some sociological, some personal, some historical, some about current issues, some about perennial issues, some about all of the above. They are "homiletic," though, in that there are pastoral. Pope Francis memorably said that the Church's shepherds ought to smell like the sheep. These do. They point to crucial foods or dangers that the sheep most need to know today.

Bishop Barron is already famous for his blockbuster *CATHOLICISM* film series and is a master of both visual and verbal media. Here he shows another side: he is simply the most readable and delightful Catholic essayist alive.

As a philosopher, I like to prove my claims with logical arguments, especially when they sound outrageous. Here's my proof. Its major premise has 12 parts. It answers the question: What are the most important qualities of a Catholic essay? The minor premise is the data you hold in your hand. Each of these essays do all 12 of these things. The conclusion is my First Place award.

So what should a good essay be?

First, it should be interesting. It should wake us up, not put us to sleep. After it is finished, the reader should spontaneously pray, "Thank God for that!" rather than "Thank God that's over!" If it made him happy, its termination should make him unhappy.

Second, it should have "existential import." It should make a difference to our lives. Life is too precious and time too short to waste it on mere words.

Third, it should be short. Like his hero, St. Thomas Aquinas, Bishop Barron has an amazing ability to put a lot of stuff into a small space without stuffing it. These are bite-sized edibles. Each is just the right size to read and think about over a single cup of coffee in the morning, or a quick trip to the bathroom an hour later.

Fourth, since it is short, it should be concentrated, unified. It should teach just one major point. In the classic Protestant "three-point sermon" the preacher first told you what he was going to say, then said it, then told you what he said. Sermons were invented in an age before all our technological time-saving devices robbed us of leisure. Homiletic essays should not be sermons, not even short sermons.

Fifth, it should be clear. I think it's quite clear what "clear" means. The mind's eye should not have to search for its light.

Sixth, it should make us think, not just feel good. In fact it should make us think deeply. It should be profound.

Being clear is rare, but being clear and profound (points five and six) at the same time is extremely rare. St. Thomas Aquinas did exactly that. So does his disciple and apprentice.

Seventh, it should be surprising. It should tell us something we didn't know, or understand, or appreciate before. (This is almost never true in Catholic essays, except in the sense that I find it always surprising that Catholic essays are never surprising.)

Eighth, although it is short, it should be tall; though small, it should teach a "big idea," an idea that stays with us. We don't have enough space or time in our memory banks to hold millions of little ideas; that's why we remember only a few big ones. We don't have to deal with the moth on the living room rug but we do have to deal with the elephant.

Ninth, it should be apostolic. That is, it should stem from a strong, loving, and enthusiastic personal faith in *The* Faith. When we read it we should hear the authority of Christ and his apostles, to whom he said, "He who hears you, hears me" (Luke 10:16).

Tenth, it is not scholarly but personal, so the tone should not be at all pompous or patronizing. It should reveal that the shepherd has been among his sheep, sensitive and listening to their needs and questions and ignorance and hungers, and that he cares about their souls and minds and lives.

Items nine and ten do not lead in opposite directions, although many people think they do. But Jesus was neither compromising nor insensitive. Truth and love were equally absolute for him.

Eleventh, because it shines eternal truths on temporal things, it should be both old and new. This involves what theologians call a "hermeneutic of continuity" rather than a "hermeneutic of discontinuity." Jesus said it more simply: that every scribe of the Kingdom should take from its storehouse things old and new. St. Augustine called God himself "Beauty ever ancient, ever new." Good essays should make old points in new ways, apply old truths to new events, and show how the Catholic faith is truly "catholic," that is, "universal," like a prism that translates its unitary light into many different colors.

Twelfth, and most important of all, it should bring us closer to God.

These little gems shine brightly from all facets. Enjoy their light and color.

— Dr. Peter Kreeft

INTRODUCTION

One of the books that truly re-arranged the furniture of my mind is G.K. Chesterton's 1908 masterpiece *Orthodoxy*. As many have commented, there are enough rhetorical fireworks and intellectual insights on any page of *Orthodoxy* to last a lifetime. But the idea that particularly struck me and which has stayed with me throughout my life, influencing practically every book and article I've written, is what I would call "bi-polar extremism."

Chesterton said that Catholicism keeps its beliefs "side by side like two strong colors, red and white...It has always had a healthy hatred of pink." What he meant was that Catholicism consistently celebrates the coming together of contraries, not in the manner of a bland compromise, but rather in such a way that the full energy of the opposing elements remains in place. And so, to give just one instance, the communion of saints, which includes the warrior Joan of Arc and the pacifist Francis of Assisi; the towering intellectual Thomas Aquinas and the barely literate Catherine of Siena; Antony, the recluse of the desert, and Thomas More, the Lord Chancellor of England, who, as Chesterton delights in recalling, wore under the splendid vestments of his office a penitential hair shirt.

The deepest ground for this uncompromising celebration of the both/and is, I would argue, the orthodox Christology of the Church. According to the Council of Chalcedon, Jesus is not partly divine and somewhat human, nor partly human and somewhat divine. Instead, he is both fully divine and fully human, each nature non-competitively present to the other in the unity of his person.

Early heresies missed this both/and principle. Monophysitism hyper-stressed the Lord's divinity, and Nestorianism hyper-stressed his humanity; and Arianism presented the apparently reasonable compromise—a blend of divinity and humanity. Yet Chalcedon, with extraordinary finesse, said no to each of these positions, and waved the flag of divinity and the flag of humanity with equal vigor.

Once you grasp this principle, you begin to see it everywhere in the great Catholic tradition. Grace and nature; faith and reason; Scripture and tradition; body and soul; God's immanence and God's transcendence: what the great Protestant theologian Karl Barth called "that damnable Catholic 'and'" is what I would call its vibrant paradox.

The essays collected in this book, written over the course of several years and destined for a variety of audiences, reflect the Chestertonian master idea. They bring together themes and motifs that many would consider mutually exclusive or, at best, awkward in their juxtaposition. I have tried to show that the coming together of opposites, considered according to the deeper logic of the Incarnation, actually causes light to shine in every direction.

—Bishop Robert Barron
Auxiliary Bishop of Los Angeles

SIN AND MERCY

Many receive the message of divine mercy as tantamount to a denial of the reality of sin, as though sin no longer matters. But just the contrary is the case. To speak of mercy is to be intensely aware of sin and its peculiar form of destructiveness.

– BISHOP BARRON

God Joins Our
Dysfunctional Family

The Gospel reading for the Mass of Christmas Day is taken from the prologue of John's Gospel, and it includes what is probably the best-known line of the New Testament: "and the Word became flesh and dwelt among us" (John 1:14). God's Word became flesh, entering into the temporality, finitude, muck and mud of our human condition. This incarnation of God is the hinge on which the whole of Christianity turns. To get a further feel for the texture of it, I would suggest that we turn from the prologue of John to the prologue of Matthew.

The opening lines of Matthew's Gospel—and hence the first words that one reads in the New Testament—are a listing of the genealogy of Jesus, the 42 generations that stretch from Abraham to Christ. If the Word truly became flesh, then God had not only a mother but also a grandmother, cousins, great-aunts, and weird uncles. If the Word truly dwelt among us, then he was part of a family that, like most, was fairly dysfunctional, a mix of the good and the bad, the saintly and the sinful, the glorious and the not so glorious. And this is such good news for us.

Let me highlight just a few figures from Jesus' family tree. Matthew tells us that the Messiah was descended from Jacob, a great patriarch and hero of Israel, and also a man who wrestled with God. In a lyrical passage from the 32nd chapter of the book of Genesis, we hear that Jacob struggled all night with the Lord and was wounded permanently in the process. I imagine that there are some reading these words who have wrestled all their lives with God, questioning, doubting, wondering, struggling mightily with the Lord, perhaps even bearing spiritual wounds as a consequence. Well, the Messiah came forth from Jacob and was pleased to be a relative of this fighter.

Matthew's genealogy informs us that Ruth was an ancestor of the Lord. Ruth was not an Israelite, but rather a Moabite, a foreigner. She married into an Israelite family, and even after her husband died, she remained loyal to her mother-in-law, returning with her to the town of Bethlehem, where she eventually married Boaz and became the mother of Jesse, who in turn became the father of King David. I would be willing to bet that there are some reading these words who have felt all their lives like outsiders, not part of the "in" crowd, perhaps looked at askance by others. Well, the Messiah came forth from Ruth the foreigner and was pleased to be her relative.

And we should say a word about Ruth's famous grandson, who is mentioned prominently in the genealogy. David was, it could be argued, the greatest figure in the Old Testament. He was the slayer of Goliath, the king who united Israel and formed her into a great power, a man of intense prayer and piety, a composer of psalms, and an incomparable warrior. But he was also a murderer and an adulterer. Reread that devastating account of David's seduction of Bathsheba from the second book of Samuel (11-12) to get the details. I'm sure that there are some reading these words who feel a bit like David. Perhaps you're a person of great success, power, and influence...who harbors a secret sin. Perhaps you've abused your power in order to freeze out someone who was threatening you or to demean someone whom you envied. Maybe you've done worse. Well, the Messiah came forth from David and was pleased to be a relative of that deeply ambiguous character.

If preserving Jesus' respectability was Matthew's goal, he would certainly have found a way to eliminate the name of Rahab from the genealogy. As you recall from the book of Joshua (2, 6), Rahab was a prostitute living and working in Jericho at the time of the Israelite conquest of the promised land. When Joshua sent spies into the city, Rahab hid and protected them. As a consequence, when the entire city was destroyed and the people put to the sword, Rahab and her family were spared. Are there people reading these words who feel like Rahab? Who think that their whole lives have been sunk in sin, who have become unrecognizable to themselves? Well, the Messiah came forth from Rahab the prostitute, and he was pleased to be her relative.

And Matthew mentions Abiud, Zadok, and Azor as ancestors of Jesus. Who were they? No one really knows. Their identities and accomplishments are lost in the mists of history. I'd be willing to bet that there are some reading this article who feel like those forgotten figures: unsung, unaccomplished, unknown. Well, the Messiah was pleased to become a relative of those nobodies Abiud, Zadok, and Azor.

The good news of Christmas is that God himself pushed into the dysfunctional and ambiguous family of man. And he continues to join us, even though we, like so many of his Israelite ancestors, are unworthy of him. Like them, we are flawed, compromised, half-finished. But he becomes our brother anyway. That's the amazing grace of the Incarnation.

Extreme Demands,
Extreme Mercy

The Catholic Church is often criticized as rigorist, unrealistic, and unbending, especially in regard to its teaching on sexuality. How could anyone, we hear over and again, possibly live up to the Church's demands concerning masturbation, artificial contraception, or sex outside of marriage? Moreover, every poll that comes out suggests that increasing numbers of Catholics themselves don't subscribe to these moral demands. Few expect the Church to acquiesce to the moral laxity of the surrounding culture, but even many faithful Catholics think that the Church ought at least to soften its moral doctrine, adjusting a bit to the times to become a tad more realistic.

I wonder whether I might address these questions a bit obliquely, shifting the focus from the sexual arena into another area of moral concern. The Church's teaching on just war is just as rigorist as its teaching on sexuality. In order for a war to be considered justified, a number of criteria have to be simultaneously met. These include declaration by a competent authority, a legitimating cause, proportionality between the good to be attained and the cost of the war, that military intervention is a last resort, etc. Furthermore, in the actual waging of a war, the two great criteria of proportionality and discrimination have to be met. The latter means, of course, that those engaged in the war must distinguish carefully between combatants and non-combatants, targeting only the former. If these criteria are strictly applied, it is difficult indeed to find any war that is morally justifiable. Many would hold that the Second World War met most if not all of the criteria for entering into a war, but even its most ardent moral defenders would have a difficult time justifying, in every detail, the waging of that war. For example, the carpet bombings of Dresden, Frankfurt, and Tokyo, which resulted in the deaths of hundreds of thousands of innocents, certainly violated the principles of discrimination and proportionality. Even more egregious examples of this violation, of course, were the atomic bombings of Hiroshima and Nagasaki. Catholic moral theology would characterize all of these actions as intrinsically evil, that is to say, incapable of being justified under any circumstances.

In the wake of the atomic bombings in 1945, the English moral philosopher Elizabeth Anscombe made the Catholic case vociferously in a number of public debates. She went so far as to protest President Harry Truman's reception of an honorary degree at Oxford, on the grounds that a great university should not honor a man responsible for the deaths of hundreds of thousands of innocents. In answer to Anscombe's criticisms, many Americans—Catholics included—used frankly consequentialist forms of moral reasoning, arguing that the atomic bombings undoubtedly saved untold numbers of lives, both American and Japanese, and effectively brought a terrible war to an end. And I am sure that a poll of American Catholics conducted, say, in late 1945 would have revealed overwhelming support for the bombings. But does anyone really think that the Church ought to lower its standards in regard to just war? Does anyone really think that the difficulty of following the Church's norms in this arena should conduce toward a softening of those norms?

Here is the wonderful and unnerving truth: the Catholic Church's job is to call people to sanctity and to equip them for living saintly lives. Its mission is not to produce nice people, or people with hearts of gold or people with good intentions; its mission is to produce saints, people of heroic virtue. Are the moral demands regarding warfare extravagant, over the top, or unrealistic? Well, of course they are! They are the moral norms that ought to guide those striving for real holiness. To dial down the demands because they are hard and most people have a hard time realizing them is to compromise the very meaning and purpose of the Church.

Now let us move back to the Church's sexual morality. Is it exceptionally difficult to live up to all of the demands in this arena? Do the vast majority of people fall short of realizing the ideal? Do polls of Catholics consistently reveal that many if not most Catholics would welcome a softening of sexual norms? Well, of course. But none of these data prove much of anything, beyond the fact that living a heroically virtuous life is difficult. As in regard to just war, a compromising of the ideal here would represent an abdication of the Church's fundamental responsibility of equipping the saints.

However, here is the flip-side. The Catholic Church couples its extraordinary moral demand with an extraordinarily lenient penitential system. Suppose the pilot of the plane that dropped the atomic bomb on Hiroshima (I believe he was a Catholic) came into a confessional box and, in an attitude of sincere repentance, confessed the sin of contributing to the deaths of 100,000 innocent people. The priest would certainly give him counsel and perhaps assign a severe penance, but he would then say, "I absolve you of all your sins, in the name of the Father, and of the Son, and of the Holy Spirit." And that man's sins, before God, would be wiped away. Period.

The Church calls people to be not spiritual mediocrities, but great saints, and this is why its moral ideals are so stringent. Yet the Church also mediates the infinite mercy of God to those who fail to live up to that ideal (which means practically everyone). This is why its forgiveness is so generous and so absolute. To grasp both of these extremes is to understand the Catholic approach to morality.

Evangelizing on the Road to Emmaus

The greatest evangelist is, of course, Jesus himself, and there is no better presentation of Jesus' evangelical technique than Luke's masterful narrative concerning the disciples on the road to Emmaus (24:13-35).

The story opens with two people going the wrong way. In Luke's Gospel, Jerusalem is the spiritual center of gravity: it is the locale of the Last Supper, the cross, the Resurrection, and the sending of the Spirit. It is the charged place where the drama of salvation unfolds. So in walking away from the capital city, these two erstwhile disciples of Jesus are going against the grain.

Jesus joins them on their journey—though we are told that they are prevented from recognizing him—and he asks them what they are talking about. Throughout his ministry, Jesus associated with sinners. He stood shoulder to shoulder in the muddy waters of the Jordan with those seeking forgiveness through the baptism of John; over and over again, he ate and drank with disreputable types, much to the chagrin of the self-righteous; and at the end of his life he was crucified in between two thieves. Jesus hated sin, but he liked sinners and was consistently willing to move into their world and to engage them on their terms.

And this is the first great evangelical lesson. The successful evangelist does not stand aloof from the experience of sinners, passing easy judgment on them, praying for them from a distance; on the contrary, she loves them so much that she joins them and deigns to walk in their shoes and feel the texture of their experience.

Prompted by Jesus' curious questions, one of the travelers, Cleopas by name, recounts all of the "things" concerning Jesus of Nazareth. "He was a prophet mighty in word and deed before God and all the people; our leaders, though, put him to death; we thought he would be the redeemer of Israel; this very morning, there were reports that he had risen from the dead."

Cleopas has all of the "facts" straight; there is not one thing he says about Jesus that is wrong. But his sadness and his flight from Jerusalem testify that he doesn't see the whole picture.

I love the clever and funny cartoons in the New Yorker magazine, but occasionally there is a cartoon I just don't understand. I've taken in all of the details; I've seen the main characters and the objects around them; I've understood the caption. Yet I don't see why it's funny. And then there comes a moment of illumination: though I haven't seen any further detail, though no new piece of the puzzle has emerged, I discern the pattern that connects them together in a meaningful way. In a word, I "get" the cartoon.

Having heard Cleopas' account, Jesus says, "Oh, how foolish you are! How slow of heart to believe all that the prophets said." And then he opens the Scriptures to them, disclosing the great Biblical patterns that make sense of the "things" that they have witnessed.

Without revealing to them any new detail about himself, Jesus shows them the form, the overarching design, the meaning—and through this process they begin to "get" him: their hearts are burning within them. This is the second great evangelical lesson. The successful evangelist uses the Scriptures in order to disclose the divine patterns and, ultimately, the Pattern who is made flesh in Jesus.

Without these clarifying forms, human life is a hodgepodge, a blur of events, a string of meaningless happenings. The effective evangelist is a man of the Bible, for Scripture is the means by which we "get" Jesus Christ and, through him, our lives.

The two disciples press him to stay with them as they draw near the town of Emmaus. Jesus sits down with them, takes bread, says the blessing, breaks it, and gives it to them, and in that moment they recognize him. Though they were, through the mediation of Scripture, beginning to see, they still did not fully grasp who he was. But in the Eucharistic moment, in the breaking of the bread, their eyes are opened.

The ultimate means by which we understand Jesus Christ is not the Scriptures but the Eucharist, for the Eucharist is Christ himself, personally and actively present. The embodiment of the paschal mystery, the Eucharist is Jesus' love for the world unto death, his journey into godforsakenness in order to save the most desperate of sinners, his heart broken open in compassion. And this is why it is through the lens of the Eucharist that Jesus comes most fully and vividly into focus.

And thus we see the third great evangelical lesson. Successful evangelists are persons of the Eucharist. They are immersed in the rhythms of the Mass; they practice Eucharistic adoration; they draw the evangelized to a participation in the Body and Blood of Jesus. They know that bringing sinners to Jesus Christ is never primarily a matter of personal witness, or inspiring sermonizing, or even exposure to the patterns of Scripture. It is primarily a matter of seeing the broken heart of God through the broken bread of the Eucharist.

So prospective evangelists, do what Jesus did. Walk with sinners, open the Book, break the Bread.

Revisiting
Spiritual Warfare

In the sixth chapter of St. Mark's Gospel, we find the account of Jesus sending out the Twelve, two by two, on mission. The first thing he gave them, Mark tells us, was "authority over unclean spirits." And the first pastoral act that they performed was to "drive out many demons." When I was coming of age in the '60s and '70s, it was common, even in seminaries, to dismiss such talk as primitive superstition—or perhaps to modernize it and make it a literary device, using symbolic language evocative of the struggle with evil in the abstract. But the problem with that approach is that it just does not do justice to the Bible. The Biblical authors knew all about evil in both its personal and institutional expressions, but they also knew about a level of spiritual dysfunction that lies underneath both of those more ordinary dimensions. They knew about the world of fallen or morally compromised spirits. Jesus indeed battled sin in individual hearts as well as the sin that dwelt in institutional structures, but he also struggled with a dark power more fundamental and more dangerous than those.

What—or, better, who—is this threatening spiritual force? It is a devil, a fallen or morally compromised angel. Imagine a truly wicked person who is also very smart, very talented and very enterprising. Now raise that person to a far higher pitch of ontological perfection, and you will have some idea of what a devil is like. Very rarely, devils intervene in human affairs in vividly frightening and dramatic ways. But typically devils act more indirectly and clandestinely, through temptation, influence, and suggestion. One of the most terrifying religious paintings in the world is in the Cathedral of Orvieto in Italy. It is a depiction of the Antichrist by the great early Renaissance painter Luca Signorelli. The artist shows the devil whispering into the ear of the Antichrist, and also working his arm through the vesture of his victim in such a way that it appears to be the Antichrist's own arm, thereby beautifully symbolizing how the dark power acts precisely with us and through us.

What are his usual effects? We can answer that question quite well by examining the names that the Bible gives to this figure. He is often called *diabolos* in the Greek of the New Testament, a word derived from *dia-balein*, to throw apart, to scatter. God is a great gathering force, for by his very nature he is love; but the devil's work is to sunder, to set one against the other. Whenever communities, families, nations, churches are divided, we sniff out the diabolic. The other great New Testament name for the devil is *ho Satanas*, which means "the accuser." Perform a little experiment: gauge how often in the course of the day you accuse another person of something or find yourself accused. It's easy enough to notice how often dysfunctional families and societies finally collapse into an orgy of mutual blaming. That's satanic work.

Another great Biblical name for the devil is "the father of lies" (John 8:44) Because God is Truth, truthfulness—about oneself, about others, about the way things really are—is the key to smooth human relations. But how often we suffer because of untruth! Perhaps many years ago someone told you a lie about yourself, and you've been wounded by it ever since. Perhaps you've deliberately lied about another person and thereby ruined his character and reputation. Consider how many wars and genocides have been predicated upon pervasive misperceptions and fabrications.

Finally, in the same passage in John's Gospel, Jesus refers to the devil as "the murderer from the beginning" (John 8:44). God *is* life, and is thus the fosterer of human life. The devil—like an unhappy person who likes nothing better than to spread unhappiness around him—is the enemy of human flourishing, the killer of life. Does anyone really think that the massive slaughters that took place in the twentieth century—the piling up of tens of millions of corpses—can be adequately explained through political or psychological categories?

An extraordinarily important aspect of the good news of Christianity is that Jesus, through his death and resurrection, has won victory over these dark forces. St. Paul said that we battle not simply flesh and blood but spiritual powers and principalities (Eph 6:12). But he also reminded us that nothing—neither height nor depth nor any other *power*—could finally separate us from the love of Christ (Rom 8:38-39). Jesus has entrusted to his Church the means to apply this victory—the weapons, if you will, to win the spiritual war. These are the sacraments (especially the Eucharist and confession), the Bible, personal prayer, the rosary, etc. One of the tragedies of our time is that so many Catholics have dropped those weapons.

Allow me to focus a bit more attention on confession by switching from a military to a medical analogy. An open wound—untreated and unbandaged—will rapidly become infected by germs and bacteria. Think of a pattern of serious sin as a sort of open wound in the spiritual order. Untreated, that is to say, un-confessed, it becomes a point of entry for less than savory spiritual powers.

Jesus sent out the Twelve to battle dark spirits. He still empowers his Church to do the same. Don't be reluctant to use the weapons—and the healing balms—that he has given.

Seeing Political Corruption
with Biblical Eyes

People all over the country reeled from the 2008 revelations concerning Governor Rod Blagojevich's alleged attempt to sell a Senate seat to the highest bidder. The tapes of a foul-mouthed governor carrying on like a character from the Sopranos have been, to say the least, disquieting. But how do Biblically-minded people in particular assess this phenomenon of gross political corruption? They do so, I would argue, with a sort of clear-eyed realism. Anyone even vaguely acquainted with the Biblical world knows that the Scriptural authors are far from naïve when it comes to the abuse of power by unscrupulous politicos.

Consider just a few representative passages. In the first book of Samuel, we hear that the people of Israel petitioned the prophet Samuel to anoint for them a king "as the other nations have" (8:5). Displeased with this request, Samuel laid out for them exactly what a king would do: "he will take your sons and assign them to his chariots and horses, and they will run before his chariot... He will set them to do his plowing and his harvesting... He will use your daughters as cooks and bakers. He will take the best of your fields and give them to his officials..." (8:11-17). In short, he will abuse his power and oppress the people for his own benefit. Despite this warning, the people persist in demanding a king, and so God tells Samuel ruefully, "Grant their request and appoint a king to rule them" (8:22). What follows, over the course of many centuries, is one of the most corrupt, incompetent, and abusive lines of monarchs in human history. It's as though God were saying, "I told you about these kings."

In the second book of Samuel, we read of a particularly grievous sin of King David, one that went beyond personal evil and involved the conscious and wicked abuse of political authority (11-12). David wanted to marry Bathsheba, whom he had impregnated, but he faced the inconvenient fact that Bathsheba was already married to Uriah the Hittite, an officer in the Israelite army. Undeterred, David arranged for Uriah to be placed in the thick of the battle, where the unfortunate man was killed. Once he had Uriah out of the way, David married Bathsheba, but the Lord was deeply displeased with what David had done. God sent to the king the prophet Nathan, who confronted him bluntly with his crime and detailed for him the Lord's punishment.

In the Gospel of Matthew, we find the account of Jesus' confrontation with the devil in the desert (4:1-11). After tempting Christ with sensual pleasure ("turn these stones into bread") and with glory ("throw yourself down and the angels will hold you up"), the devil entices him with the allure of power: "all these kingdoms I will give you if you but fall down and worship me." What is most interesting about this final temptation is that the devil wouldn't be able to offer all of the kingdoms of the world to Jesus unless he, the devil, owned them. Indeed, in Luke's account, this is made explicit. Satan says, "I shall give to you all this power...for it has been handed over to me, and I may give it to whomever I wish" (4:6). I don't know a passage in any of the literature of the world that is as critical of political power as that one! All the kingdoms of the world belong to a fallen spiritual force.

Whereas many (if not most) cultures both ancient and modern tend to apotheosize their political leaders, the Bible sees right through politics and politicians. One of the most important contributions of the Scriptures to contemporary politics, at least in the West, is this deep suspicion that power tends to corrupt. The institutionalization of this suspicion in complex systems of checks and balances is a healthy outgrowth of the Biblical view.

To be sure, Scripturally minded people should not allow their suspicions to give way to a complete cynicism regarding politics. Since God is powerful, power in itself cannot be construed as something evil, and indeed the Bible frequently states that legitimate political authority participates in God's own governance of the cosmos. But given the general human tendency toward self-absorption and violence—about which the Bible is remarkably clear-eyed—one should never put one's total trust in political systems, leaders, or programs. And one should ever be aware of the fact that human legal arrangements are under the judgment and authority of God. And when a politician abuses his office and uses his power for his own aggrandizement, Biblical people should rise up and protest with all of the insistence, courage, and eloquence of Nathan in the court of David.

Wise Words from the Bishop of Rome Concerning the Clergy Sex Abuse Scandal

It is the custom of the pope to offer Christmas greetings to his official family, the bishops and Cardinals who direct the various departments of the Roman Curia. But his words at this occasion are typically much more than mere pleasantries. They usually constitute a kind of review of the previous year from the perspective of the Bishop of Rome. The Christmas statement that Benedict XVI made to his official entourage in 2010 was of particular gravity, precisely because it represents one of his most thorough and insightful assessments of the clerical sex abuse scandal.

The pope drew attention to an arresting vision experienced by the twelfth-century German mystic Hildegard of Bingen. Hildegard saw an incomparably beautiful woman stretching from earth to heaven, clothed in luminous vestments. But the woman's radiant face was covered in dust, her vesture was ripped on one side, and her shoes were blackened. Then the mystic heard a voice from heaven announcing that this was an image of the Church, beautiful but compromised. The pope appropriated this image and interpreted it in light of our present struggles, commenting, "the face of the Church is stained with dust, and this is how we have seen it. Her garment is torn—by the sins of priests. The way Hildegard saw and expressed it is the way we have experienced it this year." Pretty blunt language, that. The pope specified that the Church must pose some serious questions about its own life if it is to understand the conditions that made the sex abuse crisis possible. Strikingly, he observed, "We must ask ourselves what was wrong in our proclamation, in our whole way of living the Christian life, to allow such a thing to happen."

These are not the words of someone who is exculpating the Church or trying to brush the problem under the carpet. The pope was implying that there was something seriously awry in regard to the Church's entire manner of self-presentation, the way in which Church representatives taught Christ, and more importantly, showed him. Mind you, this has nothing to do with inadequacies in the teachings themselves (does anyone think that the Church has ever been anything but clear in regard to the immorality of sexually abusing children?); but I think the holy father was indeed critiquing a lack of focus, a loss of energy and purpose, a certain drift and uncertainty on the part of those charged with presenting the demands of the Christian life in their full integrity. The pope concluded that the Church must be willing to do penance. No excuses here, no attempts at self-justification, no passing of the buck. Just a clear and simple call for penitence and reform.

But then the pope introduced a wider horizon, a further context for analysis and interpretation. The Church, he reminded us, does not exist in isolation from trends and tendencies in society at large, and therefore, this terrible ecclesiastical problem of clerical sexual abuse should be understood in relation to certain dysfunctions within the environing culture. The pope pointed out, for example, that child pornography, a curse throughout the world, is being considered "more and more normal by society" and that "the psychological destruction of children, in which human persons are reduced to articles of merchandise, is a terrifying sign of the times."

Moreover, he related that numerous bishops who come to see him in Rome inform him of the horror of "sexual tourism," the exploitation of children, often in the undeveloped world, by predators from wealthier nations. Though stating this inevitably exposes him to the charge of not taking the issue of ecclesiastical corruption with requisite seriousness, the pope was correctly situating the clerical sex abuse crisis in the context of a far more pervasive moral crisis in society. The sexual abuse of children takes place, to state it bluntly, everywhere in our culture: in families, in schools, in hospitals, in locker rooms, and on playgrounds. The difficulty is by no means unique to the Catholic Church or to the celibate priesthood; it is, sadly enough, a human problem.

The deepest problem—and this brings Pope Benedict back to one of his favorite themes—is an ethical relativism that dictates that no act can ever be described as intrinsically evil, that is to say, wrong no matter what the context or motivation or consequences. The pope's own characterization of this attitude is pithy and clear: "anything can be good or also bad, depending upon purposes and circumstances." It is this faulty philosophy, born of our profound reluctance to have any limits set to our self-determination and freedom, which has produced the moral atmosphere in which the sexual abuse of children became such a pervasive reality.

I believe that this extraordinary statement of the pope effectively holds off two approaches that are simply non-starters, namely, an ecclesiastical defensiveness that refuses to own up to the deep and wicked dysfunction within the Church itself, and an anti-Catholicism that refuses to own up to the disturbing presence of this problem throughout our morally confused culture. If we are truly interested in solving the problem of the sexual abuse of children by the clergy, we should attend to these wise words from the Bishop of Rome.

René Girard,
Church Father

René Girard, one of the most influential Catholic philosophers in the world, died in November 2015 at the age of 91. Born in Avignon and a member of the illustrious *Académie Française*, Girard nevertheless made his academic reputation in the United States, as a professor at Indiana University, Johns Hopkins University, and Stanford University.

There are some thinkers that offer intriguing ideas and proposals, and there is a tiny handful of thinkers that manage to shake your world. Girard was in this second camp. In a series of books and articles, written across several decades, he proposed a social theory of extraordinary explanatory power. Drawing inspiration from some of the greatest literary masters of the West—Dostoevsky, Shakespeare, Proust, among others—Girard opined that desire is both mimetic and triangular. He meant that we rarely desire objects straightforwardly; rather, we desire them because others desire them: as we imitate (*mimesis*) another's desire, we establish a triangulation between self, other, and object. If this sounds too rarefied, think of the manner in which practically all advertising works: I come to want those gym shoes not because of their intrinsic value, but because the hottest NBA star wants them. Now, what mimetic desire leads to, almost inevitably, is conflict. If you want to see this dynamic in action, watch what happens when toddler A imitates the desire of toddler B for the same toy, or when dictator A mimics the desire of dictator B for the same route of access to the sea.

The tension that arises from mimetic desire is dealt with through what Girard called the scapegoating mechanism. A society, large or small, that finds itself in conflict comes together through a common act of blaming an individual or group purportedly responsible for the conflict. So, for instance, a group of people in a coffee klatch will speak in an anodyne way for a time, but in relatively short order, they will begin to gossip, and they will typically find a real feeling of fellowship in the process. What they are accomplishing, according to Girard's reading, is a discharging of the tension of their mimetic rivalry onto a third party. The same dynamic holds true among intellectuals. When I was doing my post-graduate study, I heard the decidedly Girardian remark: "the only thing that two academics can agree upon is how poor the work of a third academic is!" Hitler was one of the shrewdest manipulators of the scapegoating mechanism. He brought the deeply divided German nation of the 1930s together precisely by assigning the Jews as a scapegoat for the country's economic, political, and cultural woes. Watch a video of one of the Nuremberg rallies of the mid-30s to see this Girardian theory on vivid display.

Now, precisely because this mechanism produces a kind of peace, however ersatz and unstable, it has been revered by the great mythologies and religions of the world and interpreted as something that God or the gods smile upon. Perhaps the most ingenious aspect of Girard's theorizing is his identification of this tendency. In the founding myths of most societies we find some act of primal violence that actually establishes the order of the community, and in the rituals of those societies we discover a repeated acting out of the original scapegoating. For a literary presentation of this ritualization of society-creating violence, look no further than Shirley Jackson's masterpiece "The Lottery."

The main features of this theory were in place when Girard turned for the first time in a serious way to the Christian Scriptures. What he found astonished him and changed his life. He discovered that the Bible knew all about mimetic desire and scapegoating violence, but it also contained something altogether new, namely, the desacralizing of the process that is revered in all of the myths and religions of the world. The crucifixion of Jesus is a classic instance of the old pattern. It is utterly consistent with the Girardian theory that Caiaphas, the leading religious figure of the time, said to his colleagues, "Is it not better for you that one man should die for the people than for the whole nation to perish?" (John 11:49-50) In any other religious context, this sort of rationalization would be valorized. But in the resurrection of Jesus from the dead, this stunning truth is revealed: God is not on the side of the scapegoaters, but rather on the side of the scapegoated victim. The true God does not sanction a community created through violence; rather, he sanctions what Jesus called the Kingdom of God, a society grounded in forgiveness, love, and identification with the victim. Once Girard saw this pattern, he found it everywhere in the Gospels and in Christian literature. For a particularly clear example of the unveiling process, take a hard look at the story of the woman caught in adultery (John 8:1-11).

In the second half of the twentieth century, academics tended to characterize Christianity—if they took it seriously at all—as one more iteration of the mythic story that can be found in practically every culture. From the *Epic of Gilgamesh* to *Star Wars*, the "mono-myth," to use Joseph Campbell's formula, is told over and again. What Girard saw was that this tired theorizing has it precisely wrong. In point of fact, Christianity is the revelation (the unveiling) of what the myths want to veil; it is the deconstruction of the mono-myth, not a reiteration of it—which is exactly why so many within academia want to domesticate and defang it.

The recovery of Christianity as *revelation*, as an unmasking of what all the other religions are saying, is René Girard's permanent and unsettling contribution.

The Field Hospital
is Open

In 2013, Pope Francis offered a lengthy and wide-ranging interview to the editor of *Civiltà Cattolica*, which was subsequently published in sixteen Jesuit-sponsored journals from a variety of countries. As we've come to expect practically anytime that this pope speaks, the interview provoked a media frenzy. To judge by the headlines in the *New York Times* and on CNN, the Catholic Church was in the midst of a moral and doctrinal revolution, led by a maverick pope bent on dragging the old institution into the modern world. I might recommend that everyone take a deep breath and prayerfully (or at least thoughtfully) read what Pope Francis actually said. For what he actually said is beautiful, lyrical, spirit-filled, and, in its own distinctive way, revolutionary.

The first question to which the pope responded in this interview was simple: "Who is Jorge Mario Bergoglio (his given name)?" After a substantial pause, he said, "a sinner whom the Lord has looked upon." At the heart of the matter, at the core of the "Catholic thing," is this encounter between us sinners and the God of amazing grace. Long before we get to social teaching, to debates about birth control and abortion, to questions about homosexual activity, to disputes about liturgy, etc., we have the graced moment when sinners are accepted, even though they are unacceptable. Pope Francis aptly illustrated his observation by drawing attention to Caravaggio's masterful *Conversion of St. Matthew*, which depicts the instant when Matthew, a thoroughly self-absorbed and materialistic man, found himself looked upon by Christ's merciful gaze. Because of that look, Matthew utterly changed, becoming first a disciple, then a missionary, and finally a martyr.

I believe that this first answer given by Pope Francis provides the interpretive lens for reading the rest of the interview. He is confessing to be a sinner who has found grace and conversion, and who has thereby been transformed into a missionary. On the basis of that master insight, he is able to survey both Church and society with astonishing clarity and serenity. One of the most commented-upon remarks in the interview is the following: "This Church with which we should be thinking is the home of all, not a small chapel that can hold only a small group of selected people." What the Pope is signaling here is that the Church, as his predecessor Paul VI put it, doesn't *have* a mission; it *is* a mission, for its purpose is to cause the merciful face of Jesus to gaze upon everyone in the world. It is not an exclusive club where only the morally perfect are welcome, but, rather, a home for sinners, which means a home for everybody.

And this insight provides the right context for understanding another controversial remark from the interview: "The Church sometimes has locked itself up in small things, in small-minded rules. The most important thing is the first proclamation: Jesus Christ has saved you." The Pope is not suggesting that rules—moral, spiritual, liturgical, etc.—are unnecessary or unimportant, but he is indeed suggesting that they are secondary to the central reality of encountering the living Christ. If the Church leads with moral regulations, it will appear, especially to our postmodern culture, to be fussy, puritanical, censorious. And it will most likely awaken a defensive reaction on the part of those it wishes to reach. It ought to lead with its always-appealing central message, namely, the saving cross of Jesus, and only then should it speak of the moral and spiritual disciplines that will bring people into greater conformity with Christ. If I might proffer a perhaps trite analogy: when attempting to attract a young kid to the game of baseball, you don't begin with the rulebook; rather, you begin with the beauty and majesty and rhythm of the game—and then you trust that he will come in time to understand the nature and purpose of the rules from the inside.

One of Pope Francis's gifts as a communicator is a peculiar feel for the memorable image: "Shepherds should smell like their sheep;" and that seminarians and priests ought to be willing to "make a mess" come readily to mind. The most striking analogy in the interview is this: "I see the Church as a field hospital after battle." No doctor doing triage on a battlefield is going to be fussing about his patients' cholesterol or blood sugar levels. He is going to be treating major wounds and trying desperately to stop the bleeding. What we find today, the pope is implying, are millions of people who are, in a spiritual sense, gravely wounded. They are alienated from God, stuck in the no-man's-land of moral relativism, adrift with no sense of direction, and tempted by every form of errant desire. They require, therefore, not the finer points of moral doctrine but basic healing. Perhaps this explains why the Church's altogether valid teachings on ethics are so often met with incomprehension or hostility: far more elemental instruction is required.

I will confess to sharing some of the misgivings of commentators who have lamented that the pope's criticism of excessive legalism gave comfort to the wrong people. NARAL (National Abortion Rights Action League) published an ad that simply said, "Dear Pope Francis, Thank you. Signed, Pro-choice women everywhere," and Planned Parenthood expressed its approval of the Pope's call to Catholics not to "obsess" over the issue of abortion. I certainly understand that those who have stood on the front lines of the pro-life battles for years feel that the Pope has unfairly characterized them as fanatics.

In the end, I feel that this relatively casual interview, precisely because it is *not* a formal encyclical, will provide a route of access to the Church for many people who might otherwise not have bothered to pay attention. It might, in fact, appeal to many of the walking wounded today who are in desperate need of mercy and healing.

The Parable of
the Talents

When I was Rector at Mundelein Seminary, the attendance at Mass one particular Labor Day weekend was sparse. Many of the students had gone home while others were on a special tour of Chicago churches. The celebrant and preacher for the Sunday Mass was Fr. Robert Schoenstene, our veteran Old Testament professor. Fr. Schoenstene offered the best interpretation I've ever heard of a particularly puzzling parable of the Lord, and I wanted to make sure his reading got a wider audience.

The parable in question is the one concerning the rich man who gives talents to three of his servants and then sets out on a journey (Matt 25:14-30). Upon his return, he assesses the situation and discovers that the servant to whom he had given five talents had invested them fruitfully, and the servant to whom he had given three talents had done the same. But he finds, to his chagrin, that the slave to whom he had entrusted one talent had simply buried the wealth and had garnered neither gain nor interest. Angered, he orders that the one talent be taken from the timid servant and given to the servant who had invested most boldly. And then comes the devastating moral lesson: "For to everyone who has, more will be given and he will grow rich; but from the one who has not, even what he has will be taken away."

The standard reading of this story—on display in thousands of sermons and fervorinos—is that the talents symbolize gifts and abilities that God has given to us, which he expects us to "spend" generously or "invest" wisely. This interpretation is supported by the fairly accidental relationship that obtains between "talent" in the ancient Biblical sense of the term and "talent" in ordinary English today. Fr. Schoenstene specified that a talent in ancient times was a measure of something particularly weighty, usually silver or gold. A single talent might represent as much as 50 pounds of precious metal, and, as such, was not something that one carried around in one's pocket. We might make a comparison between a talent and a unit of gold kept at Fort Knox, or an ingot of silver preserved in a safe deposit box. What the contemporary reader will likely miss, and what the ancient Jewish reader would have caught immediately, is the connection to heaviness: a talent was weighty, and five talents was massively heavy. Heaviness would have brought to mind the heaviest weight of all, which was the *kabod* of Yahweh. That term was rendered in Greek as *doxa* and in Latin as *gloria*, both of which carry the connotation of luminosity, but the basic sense of the Hebrew word is heaviness, gravitas.

And this *kabod Yahweh* was to be found in the Jerusalem Temple, resting upon the mercy seat within the Holy of Holies. Therefore, what was heaviest (most glorious) of all was the mercy of God, which abided in infinite, inexhaustible abundance in the Holy Temple.

In light of these clarifications, we can read Jesus' parable with fresh eyes. The talents given to the three servants are not so much monetary gifts or personal capacities; they are a share in the mercy of God, a participation in the weightiness of divine love. But since mercy is always directed to the other, these "talents" are designed to be shared. In point of fact, they will increase precisely in the measure that they are given away. The problem with the timid servant who buried his talent is not that he was an ineffective venture capitalist but that he fundamentally misunderstood the nature of what he had been given. The divine mercy, received as a pure gift, is meant to be given to others as a pure gift. Buried in the ground, that is to say, hugged tightly to oneself as one's own possession, such a talent necessarily evanesces. And this is why the master's seemingly harsh words should not be read as the punishment of an angry God but as an expression of spiritual physics: divine mercy will grow in you only inasmuch as you give it to others. To "have" the *kabod Yahweh* is precisely not to have it in the ordinary sense of the term.

What comes to mind here is the most famous of all of Jesus' parables, namely, the story of the Prodigal Son (Luke 15:11-32). Using a term that also carried a monetary sense in ancient times, the younger son says, "Father give me my share of the *ousia* (substance or wealth) that is coming to me." Notice how in one sentence, he manages to mention himself three times! The father gives away his *ousia*, for that is all he knows how to do, but the foolish son squanders the money in short order. The spiritual lesson is the same: the divine *ousia* is a gift, and it can be "had" only inasmuch as it becomes a gift for others. When we try to cling to it as a possession, it disappears.

How wonderful that these ancient stories, once we unpack their spiritual significance, still sing to us today.

Pope Benedict and the
Logic of Gratuity

One of the most intriguing—and original—ideas in Pope Benedict XVI's encyclical on the social order, *Caritas in veritate*, is that the ethics of obligation and mutuality have to be supplemented by an ethic of gratuity. By an "ethic of mutuality" he means the moral logic that obtains in the marketplace whereby people, according to the terms of a contract, give in order to receive something in return. So you pay me a certain amount, and I provide certain goods and services to you. This is the essence of what the Catholic tradition calls commutative justice, the fair play among the various members of a society or economic community. By an "ethic of obligation" he means the moral logic that obtains within the political arena, whereby people are compelled by law to give to others in order to realize distributive justice, that is, a fairer allotting of the total goods of a society. For example, through taxation one is obliged to transfer some of one's wealth to the government for the sake of the common good.

Now the pope insists that these two types of giving are essential to the right ordering of any human community; we should never, he thinks, fall short of them, preferring injustice to justice. Nevertheless, they must be complemented, leavened, if you will, by a more radical type of giving, what he terms the "ethic of gratuity." According to this mode, one gives, not because he is contractually obligated or legally compelled to give, but simply because it is good so to do. This is the kind of giving that mimics most fully the divine manner of giving. The God who made the universe *ex nihilo* could never, even in principle, have done so out of contractual or legal obligation. He received nothing in return for creation, and nothing outside of his own will could ever have compelled him to create. He gave of himself and let the world be simply because it was good to do so.

Without the presence of sheerly graceful or gratuitous giving, the pope contends, even a just society will, in time, become cold and less than fully human. There is an interesting parallel here with the moral life. In traditional Catholic theology, justice is recognized as a natural virtue, that is to say, a form of excellence that can exist apart from divine grace and that can be appreciated even by unelevated human reason. But love is a theological (properly supernatural) virtue, which can come only through a participation in the divine life. The just person is morally praiseworthy, admirable, a gentleman; but the person of love is a saint. And without love, even natural justice can devolve into calculation and gamesmanship, a play of tit for tat.

So far, you might say, so abstract. But I think we can show that the pope's principle plays out very concretely in history. In 1945, Germany lay in ruins, devastated by the wicked behavior of its leaders. Many in the West felt that, in justice, a harsh peace should be imposed on the defeated nation, but Secretary of State George Marshall and President Harry Truman decided that a merciful response was called for. They implemented what came to be known as the Marshall Plan, a comprehensive effort to rebuild German society and restore the German people to dignity. Though one might cynically suggest pragmatic motives for this policy, I think Winston Churchill had it right when he called the Marshall Plan "the most unsordid act in history." A logic of strict justice would have dictated a punitive response to the nation that had caused so much misery; Truman and Marshall intuited that in the wake of the calamity of the World War, a logic of gratuity was more appropriate.

By the 1950s, African Americans had endured two hundred years of slavery, oppression, discrimination, and segregation. In strict justice, they could claim a right to defend themselves, even through violence, and to demand various forms of compensation for years of abuse. Figures such as Malcolm X and James Baldwin militated for this kind of justice. But Martin Luther King, who fully acknowledged the deep injustice that blacks had suffered, nevertheless advocated the path of non-violence and reconciliation, thereby exercising toward mainstream America a logic of gratuity. And it was precisely this approach that proved so practically transformative.

In ancient Israel, there was the custom of celebrating every fifty years a year of Jubilee, during which all debts were cancelled. The Jubilee gave hope to those who had labored under the weight of debilitating financial obligations. This wiping clean of the economic slate was, in the strict sense, a violation of justice, but it was a prime example of the logic of gratuity, and a conscious imitation of the generosity of God. Pope Saint John Paul II also called for a revival of the Biblical Jubilee in regard to third world countries who have been saddled with enormous debt toward the nations of the developed world. Under the weight of this obligation, these economies, the pope saw, couldn't develop and expand. And so he urged the wealthier societies to wipe away the debt and give the poorer peoples a clean slate. Bankers and investors in the first world balked, of course, at this violation of justice, but the pope insisted that, given the gravity of the situation, only the logic of gratuity would conduce toward an economic renewal in underdeveloped nations.

And so, Pope Benedict teaches, we must never fail to meet the demands of justice, but, at the same time, we must never remain the prisoners of mere justice. According to the Christian vision, justice must be leavened by love, and equity complemented by gratuity.

Pope Francis and
True Mercy

When I returned from a week covering Pope Francis's triumphant journey to the United States in 2015, I could confidently conclude that the news media are in love with the vicar of Christ. Time and again, commentators, pundits, anchorpersons, and editorialists opined that Pope Francis is the bomb. They approved, of course, of his gentle way with those suffering from disabilities and his proclivity to kiss babies, but their approbation was most often awakened by this Pope's "merciful" and "inclusive" approach, his willingness to reach out to those on the margins. More often than not, they characterized this tenderness as a welcome contrast to the more rigid and dogmatic style of Benedict XVI. Often, I heard words such as "revolutionary" and "game-changing" in regard to Pope Francis, and one commentator sighed that she couldn't imagine going back to the Church as it was before the current pontiff.

Well, I love Pope Francis, too, and I certainly appreciate the novelty of his approach and his deft manner of breathing life into the Church. In fact, a number of times on the air I have commented that the pope's arrival to our shores represented a new springtime after the long winter of the sex abuse scandals. But I balk at the suggestion that the new pope represents a revolution or that he is dramatically turning away from the example of his immediate predecessors. And I strenuously deny that he is nothing but a soft-hearted powder-puff, indifferent to sin.

A good deal of the confusion stems from a misinterpretation of Francis's stress on mercy. In order to clear things up, a little theologizing is in order. It is not correct to say that God's essential attribute is mercy. Rather, God's essential attribute is love, since love is what obtains among the three divine persons from all eternity. Mercy is what love looks like when it turns toward the sinner. To say that mercy belongs to the very nature of God, therefore, would be to imply that sin exists within God himself, which is absurd.

Now this is important, for many receive the message of divine mercy as tantamount to a denial of the reality of sin, as though sin no longer mattered. But just the contrary is the case. To speak of mercy is to be intensely aware of sin and its peculiar form of destructiveness. Or, to shift to one of the pope's favorite metaphors, it is to be acutely conscious that one is wounded so severely that one requires not minor treatment but the emergency and radical attention provided in a hospital on the edge of a battlefield. Recall that when Francis was asked in a famous interview to describe himself, he responded, "a sinner." Then he added, "who has been looked upon by the face of mercy." That's getting the relationship right. Remember as well that the teenage Jorge Mario Bergoglio came to a deep and life-changing relationship to Christ precisely through a particularly intense experience in the confessional. As many have indicated, Papa Francesco speaks of the devil more frequently than any of his predecessors of recent memory, and he doesn't reduce the dark power to a vague abstraction or a harmless symbol. He understands Satan to be a real and very dangerous person.

When Pope Francis speaks of those on the margins, he does indeed mean people who are economically and politically disadvantaged, but he also means people who are cut off from the divine life, spiritually poor. And just as he reaches out to the materially marginalized in order to bring them to the center, so he reaches out to those on the existential periphery *in order to bring them to a better place.* In speaking of mercy and inclusivity, he is decidedly not declaring that "I'm okay and you're okay." He is calling people to conversion. In the words of my mentor, Cardinal Francis George, "All are welcome in the Church, but on Christ's terms and not their own."

Nowhere has the confusion on this score been greater than in relation to the Pope's famous remark regarding a priest with a homosexual orientation, "Who am I to judge?" I would wager that 95% of those who took in those words understood them to mean that, as far as Pope Francis is concerned, homosexual activity is not really sinful. Nothing could be further from the truth. The Pope was responding to a hypothetical involving a priest with same-sex attraction, who had fallen in the past and who was now endeavoring to live in accord with the moral law—a sinner, in a word, who has been looked upon by the face of mercy.

So as we quite legitimately exult in the beauty of Pope Francis's unique style and theological emphasis, let us not turn him into an advocate of an "anything goes" liberalism. As St. Augustine long ago reminded us, *misericordia* (mercy) and *miseria* (misery) are two sides of the same coin.

The iPhone App and the Return to Confession

The practice of sacramental confession in the Catholic Church dropped off precipitously and practically overnight about forty years ago. Prior to the Second Vatican Council, Catholics came regularly and in great numbers to confess their sins to a priest, but then, just like that, they stopped coming. Analysts have proposed a variety of reasons for this sharp decline—a greater stress on God's love, a desire to move away from a fussy preoccupation with sexual peccadilloes, the sense that confession is not necessary for salvation, etc.—but whatever the cause or causes, the practice has certainly fallen into desuetude.

Fr. Andrew Greeley, the well-known priest-sociologist, once formulated the principle that whatever Catholics drop, someone else inevitably picks up. So, for example, we Catholics, after the Council, stopped talking about the soul, out of fear that the category would encourage dualistic thinking—and then we discovered, in the secular culture, a plethora of books on the care of the soul, including a wildly popular series on "chicken soup for the soul." Similarly, the Catholic Church became reluctant to speak of angels and devils—and then we witnessed, in the wider society, an explosion of books and films about these fascinating spiritual creatures.

Well, a very good example of the Greeley principle is the way in which the practice of sacramental confession—largely extinct in the Church—pops up in somewhat distorted form all over the extra-ecclesial world. What do we witness on the daytime talk shows—Oprah, Jerry Springer, Montel, Maury, etc.—but a series of people coming forward to confess their sins, usually of a sexual nature? And what do we see on the numerous "judgment" shows—Judge Judy, Judge Mathis, American Idol, Dr. Phil, Dancing With the Stars, etc.—but people being forced to accept a kind of punishment for their bad or inadequate behavior? What this demonstrates, I would argue, is that the need to confess our sins and to receive some sort of judgment and/or word of comfort is hard-wired into our spirits. When we don't have the opportunity to deal with our sin in the proper ecclesiastical context, we will desperately cast about for a substitute.

All of this came to mind when I read about an iPhone application called "Confession: A Roman Catholic App" which is designed not to forgive sins (you still need to see a priest for that!) but to prepare people for reconciliation. The app includes an examination of conscience, a step-by-step guide to the celebration of the sacrament, and other prayers. Official Vatican spokesman Fr. Federico Lombardi weighed in to clarify that this program is not a substitute for actual confession to a priest, but he also noted that it might be a very helpful aid, especially for those who have been away from the sacrament for a long time as well as for young people who are attuned to the digital world.

I think that, on balance, this iPhone app is a good thing, for I strongly believe that whatever helps Catholics experience the beauty and power of confession is of great value. Many Catholics of a certain age can tell you horror stories about psychological abuse in the confessional by priests who were hung up on sexual sins, or all too eager to threaten eternal damnation, or perhaps just cranky from sitting in a box for hours. And many priests (including myself) could tell you tales of people coming to confession for trivial reasons or out of obsessive-compulsive neuroses. But, as the Romans said long ago, *abusus non tollit usum*—just because something can be abused, that doesn't mean that we should get rid of it.

I can honestly say that some of the best and most spiritually rewarding moments in all my years of priesthood have been in the context of hearing confessions. And I can't tell you the number of people who have said to me over the years some version of "Father, I'm so grateful that I came to confession after all this time." Not long ago, I was discussing the issue of general absolution with a group of priests, and a number of my colleagues were suggesting that it would be a legitimate means to bring people back to the sacrament. But then one priest spoke up: "Don't all of you go to a priest and confess your sins and receive individual absolution?" We all agreed. And then he said, "And don't you all find it to be a powerful experience?" We all concurred. "Then why," he continued, "do you want something less for lay people?" It was a very good question.

So I would say to my fellow Catholics—especially to those who have been away from Confession for a long time—try this app. It can't hurt—and it might prove to be a way to encounter the Christ who came to forgive our sins.

The Revolutionary Message
of Palm Sunday

The texts that Christians typically read on Palm Sunday have become so familiar that most probably don't sense their properly revolutionary power. But no first-century Jew would have missed the excitement and danger implicit in the coded language of the accounts describing Jesus' entry into Jerusalem just a few days before his death.

In Mark's Gospel we hear that Jesus and his disciples "drew near to Jerusalem, to Bethphage and Bethany on the Mount of Olives" (11:1). A bit of trivial geographical detail, we might be tempted to conclude. But we have to remember that pious Jews of Jesus' time were immersed in the infinitely complex world of the Hebrew Scriptures and stubbornly read everything through the lens provided by those writings.

About five hundred years before Jesus' time, the prophet Ezekiel had relayed a vision of the *Shekinah* (the glory) of Yahweh leaving the temple, due to its corruption: "The glory of the Lord went out from the threshold of the house (the temple) and stopped above the cherubim. The cherubim...rose from the earth in my sight as they went out... They stopped at the entrance of the east gate of the house of the Lord; and the glory of the God of Israel was above them" (Ezek 10:18-19). This was one of the most devastating texts in the Old Testament. The temple of the Lord was seen as, in almost a literal sense, the dwelling place of God, the meeting place of heaven and earth. Thus even to imagine that the glory of the Lord had quit his temple was shocking in the extreme. However, Ezekiel also prophesied that one day the glory of God would return to the temple, and precisely from the same direction in which it had left: "Then he brought me to the gate, the gate facing east. And there, the glory of the God of Israel was coming from the east; the sound was like the sound of mighty waters; and the earth shone with his glory" (Ezek 43:1-2). Furthermore, upon the return of the Lord's glory, Ezekiel predicted, the corrupt temple would be cleansed, restored, rebuilt.

Now let's return to Jesus, who, during his public ministry, consistently spoke and acted in the very person of God and who said, in reference to himself, "you have a greater than the temple here" (Matt 12:6). As the Jews of Jesus' day saw him approaching Jerusalem from the east, they would have remembered Ezekiel's vision and would have begun to entertain the wild but thrilling idea that perhaps this Jesus was, in person, the glory of Yahweh returning to his dwelling place on earth. And, in light of this, they would have understood the bewildering acts that Jesus performed in the temple. He was, in fact, another Ezekiel, pronouncing judgment on the old temple and then announcing a magnificent rebuilding campaign: "I will tear down this place and in three days rebuild it" (John 2:19). Jesus, they came to understand, was the new and definitive temple, the meeting place of heaven and earth.

And there is even more to see in the drama of Jesus' arrival in the Holy City. As the rabbi from Nazareth entered Jerusalem on a donkey, no one could have missed the reference to a passage in the book of the prophet Zechariah: "Rejoice greatly, O daughter Zion! Shout aloud, O daughter Jerusalem! Lo, your king comes to you; triumphant and victorious is he, humble and riding on a donkey, on a colt, the foal of a donkey" (Zech 9:9). A thousand years before the time of Jesus, David had taken possession of Jerusalem, dancing before the Ark of the Covenant. David's son Solomon built the great temple in David's city in order to house the Ark, and therefore, for that brief, shining moment, Israel was ruled by righteous kings. But then Solomon himself and a whole slew of his descendants fell into corruption, and the prophets felt obligated to criticize the kings as thoroughly as they criticized the temple. The people began to long for the return of the king, for the appearance of the true David, the one who would deal with the enemies of the nation and rule as king of the world. They expected this new David, of course, to be a human figure, but something else rather surprising colored their expectation, namely, that through this human being, God would personally come to rule the nation. Here are just two passages, chosen from dozens, that express this hope: "For I am a great king, says Yahweh of hosts, and my name is reverenced among the nations" (Mal 1:14); and "I will extol you, my God and King, and bless your name forever... Your kingdom is an everlasting kingdom, and your dominion endures throughout all generations" (Ps 145). So, to draw these various strands together, we might say that the Biblical authors expected Yahweh to become king, precisely through a son of David, who would enter the Holy City not as a conquering hero, riding a stately Arabian charger, but as a humble figure, riding a young donkey. Could anyone have missed that this was exactly what they were seeing on Palm Sunday? Jesus was not only the glory of Yahweh returning to his temple; he was also the new David, indeed Yahweh himself, reclaiming his city and preparing to deal with the enemies of Israel.

He fought, of course, not in the conventional manner. Instead, he took all of the dysfunction of the world upon himself and swallowed it up in the ocean of the divine mercy and forgiveness. He thereby dealt with the enemies of the nation and emerged as the properly constituted king of the world. And this is why Pontius Pilate, placing over the cross a sign in Latin, Greek, and Hebrew announcing that this crucified Jesus is King of the Jews, became, despite himself, the first great evangelist!

And so the message, delivered in the wonderfully coded and ironic language of the Gospel writers, still resonates today: heaven and earth have come together; God is victorious; Jesus is Lord.

REASON AND FAITH

*Thoughtful Christians must battle the myth of
the eternal warfare of science and religion.
We must continually preach, as John Paul II did,
that faith and reason are complementary and
compatible paths toward the knowledge of truth.*

— BISHOP BARRON

The Indecipherable Writing
of Thomas Aquinas

I was once in Rome giving lectures at the North American College, the great seminary for Americans, Canadians, and Australians at the Vatican. One morning toward the end of my stay, I met with my good friend Fr. Paul Murray, the Irish Dominican spiritual writer, and we headed to the Vatican Library, where we met a colleague of Fr. Paul's who worked there in the manuscript section.

Fr. Murray had secured permission to view some "autographs" of St. Thomas Aquinas, that is to say, some writings in Thomas' own hand. I was approaching this appointment with enormous enthusiasm, for Thomas, the church's greatest theologian, is my hero, my patron saint, the person who, more than any other, had directed me toward the priesthood, and the scholar whose work I have been studying and writing about most of my adult life. I was not disappointed.

Fr. Paul's friend invited us to sit down at a long table and told us that she would return in a few minutes with the sample of Aquinas's writing. I was expecting, frankly, one page that we would be permitted to view, perhaps, under glass. But she returned with a dossier filled with eighty pages of text! They were vellum, which is to say, treated sheepskin, expensive enough and rather hard to come by in the Middle Ages; and they were covered in Aquinas's famously cramped, illegible script.

We were able to see these pages directly, to handle them, to hover over them, just as Aquinas must have nearly eight centuries ago.

The texts we were looking at were from the *Summa contra gentiles*, the first and lesser of Thomas's two great *Summae* or summaries of Christian doctrine, which he wrote in Paris in the late 1250s, when he was a relatively young man (35 or so). Though both Fr. Paul and I had been studying Thomas's Latin texts for years, neither one of us could make out a single word. This is because Thomas wrote in a kind of shorthand, filled with symbols, squiggles, and odd connectives. They say that only his secretary, a man named Reginald of Piperno, could read Thomas's writing fluently. And indeed, in the margins of certain pages another hand, far more legible, could be seen; it was undoubtedly that of the faithful Reginald.

The curator pointed out a wonderful detail. She showed us a particular page with a rather large hole in the middle. "You can tell," she said, "that that defect was already there in the Middle Ages." We wondered how she knew that, and she said, "Look at the writing." And, sure enough, there was the illegible handwriting suddenly taking a detour up and around the hole. On another page, we saw a fine little sketch of the head of a horse. Did Thomas draw it? Was it from a later time and another hand? There is no way to tell, but it certainly proves that the doodler's art is a venerable one.

My favorite page was one that was covered with Thomas's writing, practically top to bottom and side to side, all the margins filled in with new arguments or modifications or glosses. And at the foot of this page were the numbers 1, 2, 3, and 4, each with an uneven line stretching from it to a particular piece of text—probably four objections to which Thomas was responding. What these medieval writings communicated to me was the dense reality of Thomas Aquinas, that very particular thirteenth-century scholar, scribbling on these sheets of vellum, as he thought and wrote his way to greater clarity about the things of God. The sheer concentration and effort that this required were inscribed in the still very black ink of those pages.

I have seen many beautiful things in Rome—the Pantheon, the Dome of St. Peter's, Santa Maria in Trastevere, the Caravaggios in San Luigi dei Francesi, Raphael's "School of Athens"—but I can honestly say that those pages of Aquinas were the most striking, memorable, and, yes, beautiful things I have ever seen in the Eternal City. They reminded me of how much Thomas Aquinas has meant to me personally, but also of how much he continues to mean for the entire Church.

At a time when religious conversation far too often devolves into shouting matches and ad hominem attacks, Thomas calls us back to reasoned discourse. At a time when religious passions have run amok and have resulted in terrible acts of violence, Thomas calls us back to hard thinking about God. At a time when adherents to different religions often gaze at one another suspiciously, the Thomas who happily dialogued with pagan philosophers, Jewish rabbis, Muslim sages, and Christian heretics calls us back to an attitude of broad-minded respect. I think that the Church's turning away from Aquinas in the years following Vatican II was a dreadful mistake. We lost something of massive importance when we set aside his balance, his deep intelligence, and his sanity. Happily, there is a rather impressive Thomas Aquinas revival going on throughout the Church, as a number of gifted younger scholars (and some older ones, too) are turning back with enthusiasm to his works. May their tribe increase.

The Myth of the War between Science and Religion

For the past several years, I've been posting short commentaries on YouTube, one of the most popular websites in the world. I've covered everything from movies and music to books and cultural trends, but I've given special attention to the problem of the "new" atheism. I've posted three answers to Christopher Hitchens' terrible book *God is Not Great*, a brief presentation of some classical arguments for God's existence, and more recently, a response to Bill Maher's movie *Religulous*. As you might know, people are able to post comments in response to videos, and I've received a huge quantity of them—mostly negative—in regard to the aforementioned pieces. Setting aside the venomous and emotionally-driven comments, I've been able to discern, in the more serious ones, a number of patterns. If an apologist or evangelist were interested in composing a twenty-first century version of St. Irenaeus's classic *Against the Heresies*, he could do worse than to consult these YouTube responses.

The most glaring of these heretical patterns is what I would call scientism, the philosophical assumption that the real is reducible to what the empirical sciences can verify or describe. In reaction to my attempts to demonstrate that God must exist as the necessary ground to the radically contingent universe, respondent after respondent says some version of this: energy, or matter, or the Big Bang, is the ultimate cause of all things. When I counter that the Big Bang itself demonstrates that the universe in its totality is contingent and hence in need of a cause extraneous to itself, they think I'm just talking nonsense. The obvious success of the physical sciences—evident in the technology that surrounds us and facilitates our lives in so many ways—has convinced many of our young people (the vast majority of those who watch YouTube are young) that anything outside of the range of the empirical and measurable is simply a fantasy, the stuff of superstition and primitive belief. That there might be a dimension of reality knowable in a non-scientific but still rational manner never occurs to them. This prejudice, this blindness to literature, philosophy, metaphysics, mysticism, and religion is the scientism that I'm complaining about.

Another feature of this scientism—and it's evident everywhere on my YouTube forums—is the extremely disturbing assumption that science and religion are, by their very natures, implacable enemies. Again and again, my interlocutors resurrect the story of Galileo to prove that the Church has always sided with obscurantism and naïve Biblical literalism over and against the sciences. The Catholic philosopher Robert Sokolowski has argued that the founding myth of modernity is that enlightened thought was born out of, and in opposition to, pre-scientific religion. And this is why, Sokolowski continues, the conflict between religion and science must be perpetually rehearsed and revived, as a kind of ritual acting out of the primal story. If you want to see a particularly dramatic presentation of this, watch the movie *Inherit the Wind*.

But this myth is so much nonsense. Leaving aside the complexities of the Galileo story (and there are complexities to it), we can see that the vast majority of the founding figures of modern science—Copernicus, Newton, Kepler, Descartes, Pascal, Tycho Brahe—were devoutly religious. More to it, two of the most important physicists of the nineteenth century—Faraday and Maxwell—were extremely pious; and the formulator of the Big Bang theory was a priest! If you want a contemporary embodiment of the coming-together of science and religion, look to John Polkinghorne, Cambridge particle physicist and Anglican priest, and one of the best commentators on the non-competitive interface between scientific and religious paths to truth.

Indeed, as Polkinghorne and many others have pointed out, the modern physical sciences were, in fact, made possible by the religious milieu out of which they emerged. It is no accident that modern science first appeared precisely in Christian Europe, where a doctrine of creation held sway. To hold that the world is created is to accept simultaneously the two assumptions required for science, namely, that the universe is not divine, and that it is marked, through and through, by intelligibility. If the world or nature is considered divine (as it is in many philosophies and mysticisms), then one would never allow oneself to analyze it, dissect it, or perform experiments upon it. But a created world, by definition, is not divine. It is other than God, and in that very otherness, scientists find their freedom to act. At the same time, if the world were unintelligible, no science would get off the ground, since all science is based upon the presumption that nature can be known, that it has a form. But the world, precisely as created by a divine intelligence, is thoroughly intelligible, and hence scientists have the confidence to seek, explore, and experiment.

This is why thoughtful Christians must battle the myth of the eternal warfare of science and religion. We must continually preach, as John Paul II did, that faith and reason are complementary and compatible paths toward the knowledge of truth.

Playing at Atheism

Perhaps you've heard about a successful campaign sponsored by some atheists in Europe a few years ago to put placards on the sides of buses propagating the anti-god point of view. The signs displayed in and around London and Genoa read "The bad news is that God does not exist. The good news is that you do not need him." This was just one part of a worldwide campaign to debunk the very idea of God and to mock religion, especially Christianity. Like so much of the "new" atheism, which gathered steam after September 11th, 2001 and includes the work of Christopher Hitchens, Richard Dawkins and their army of disciples, it was a popular, flippant, and deeply unintelligent expression.

Around the midpoint of the twentieth century the existentialist movement flourished, led by such figures as Jean-Paul Sartre and Albert Camus. These philosophers argued rather vigorously against the proposition that God exists, but, to their credit, they saw the deep sadness and feeling of emptiness that result from atheism. They sensed that there exists in the human heart a longing for meaning that nothing in the world can satisfy, and hence they pronounced life without God absurd. The "ethic" of existentialism involved a willingness to accept this absurdity and to assert one's freedom in the face of it. Now, I don't think for a minute that Sartre and his colleagues were right about the non-existence of God, but at least they were clear-eyed enough to appreciate the terrible tension that obtains between the infinite longing of the human heart and the absence of the one reality that could possibly assuage it. The one thing that they were intelligent enough never to have said: *God does not exist, but not to worry, we don't need him.* Even as they denied him, they knew that God, by definition, is what the human heart desperately needs. The bus placards reveal that today's atheists, by contrast, are childish, playing at atheism rather than seeing to the bottom of it.

If we consult the Bible, we find a way past atheism. There are parts of the book of Job, many of the psalms, some of the lamentations of the prophets that could have been written by Sartre or Camus on their darkest days. But the most "existentialist" text in the Bible is the book of Qoheleth, known in older translations as the book of Ecclesiastes. Qoheleth presents himself as an old man who has seen it all, done it all, achieved it all. He has experienced deep friendship; he has explored the wisdom of the ages; he has built palaces and gardens; he has had sexual delight; he has wielded power. And all of it he pronounces to be "wind and chasing after the wind" (Eccles 1:14; 2:11), for none of it has finally satisfied him. But this doesn't lead Qoheleth to despair or to a willful embrace of absurdity. Rather, it leads him to confess his faith in God, to allow his desire to pass beyond the goods of this world to the supreme and transcendent Good. Every one of us, if we are honest, can move readily into the stance and attitude of Qoheleth. We experience an aching sense of incompleteness when we fail, suffer, and want, but even more so when we succeed, rejoice, and achieve. For, especially in those times of fulfillment, we become acutely aware of what the spiritual writer Ronald Rolheiser calls "the holy longing," the desperate need for God.

And the awareness of this need is precisely what pushes us past atheism. An animal eats enough, finds sufficient shelter, gets his requisite exercise—and he falls blissfully asleep, utterly satisfied. But the human animal attains all of those goods—and many others besides—and yet turns uneasily in his bed, still wanting more, even if he is unable to articulate clearly what that "more" is. What this proves, so our great tradition argues, is that we humans are very peculiar creatures indeed. We are hybrids and half-breeds, part animal and part angel. Our very desire for goods and truths that transcend this world proves that there is more in us than an animal nature. If we were, as the materialists and atheists argue, just extremely clever animals, we should remain as content as any dog when, with our superior skill, we attain those simple things that make a dog happy. But our very restlessness proves the reality of some alluring and transcendent Good that we call God.

And this brings me back to those buses and their atheist slogans. The claim that God's non-existence is a matter of indifference is not only offensive to believers; it's actually stupid, even on atheist grounds. And, at any rate, once we've been through the finally illuminating darkness of which Qoheleth speaks, we can see that another slogan is far more appropriate: "The bad news is: nothing in the world satisfies us; the good news: so what, God exists!"

Why the Sciences
Will Never Disprove the
Existence of God

Given the ruminations of Stephen Hawking, Richard Dawkins and Daniel Dennett, one might have thought that the absolute limit of scientistic arrogance had been reached. But think again. Sean Carroll, a theoretical physicist at the California Institute of Technology, was quoted in a 2012 news article asserting that science is on the verge of providing a complete understanding of the universe—an explication, it goes without saying, that precludes the antiquated notion of God altogether.

Before addressing the God issue specifically, let me make a simple observation. Though the sciences might be able to explain the chemical makeup of pages and ink, they will never be able to reveal the meaning of a book; and though they might make sense of the biology of the human body, they will never tell us why a human act is moral or immoral; and though they might disclose the cellular structure of oil and canvas, they will never determine why a painting is beautiful. This is not because science is insufficiently developed at the moment; it is because the scientific method cannot, even in principle, explore such matters, which belong to a qualitatively different category of being than the proper subject matter of the sciences. The claim that science could ever provide a total understanding of reality as a whole overlooks the rather glaring fact that meaning, truth, beauty, morality, purpose, etc., are all ingredients in the universe.

But, as is usually the case with scientistic speculation, Carroll's thought is designed, above all, to eliminate God as a subject of serious intellectual discourse. The first and most fundamental problem is that, like Hawking, Dawkins, and Dennett, Carroll doesn't seem to know what Biblical people mean by "God." With the advances of the modern physical sciences, he asserts, there remains less and less room for God to operate, and hence less and less need to appeal to him as an explanatory cause. This is a contemporary reiteration of Pierre-Simon Laplace's rejoinder when the Emperor Napoleon asked the famous astronomer how God fit into his mechanistic system: "I have no need of that hypothesis." But God, as the classical Catholic intellectual tradition understands him, is not one cause, however great, among many; not one more item within the universe jockeying for position with other competing causes. Rather, God is, as Thomas Aquinas characterized him, *ipsum esse*, or the sheer act of to-be itself—that power in and through which the universe in its totality exists. Once we grasp this, we see that no advance of the physical sciences could ever eliminate God or show that he is no longer required as an explaining cause, for the sciences can only explore objects and events within the finite cosmos.

To demonstrate the relationship between God and the universe more clearly, it would be worthwhile to explore the most fundamental argument for God's existence, namely, the argument from contingency. You and I are contingent (dependent) in our being in the measure that we eat and drink, breathe, and had parents; a tree is contingent inasmuch as its being is derived from seed, sun, soil, water, etc.; the solar system is contingent because it depends upon gravity and events in the wider galaxy. To account for a contingent reality, by definition we have to appeal to an extrinsic cause. But if that cause is itself contingent, we have to proceed further. This process of appealing to contingent causes in order to explain a contingent effect cannot go on indefinitely, for then the effect is never adequately explained. Hence, we must finally come to some reality that is not contingent on anything else, some ground of being whose very nature is to be. This is precisely what Catholic theology means by "God." Therefore, God is not one fussy cause within or alongside the universe; instead, he is the reason why there is a universe at all, why there is, as the famous formula has it, "something rather than nothing." To ask the sophomoric question, "Well, what caused God?" is simply to show that the poser of the question has not grasped the nettle of the argument.

Now, Carroll seems to acknowledge the probative power of this sort of argument of first instance, but he makes the common scientistic mistake of identifying the first cause with matter or energy or even the universe itself, in its endlessly fluctuating rhythms of inflation and deflation. But the problem with such explanations is this: they involve an appeal to patently contingent things or states of affairs. Energy or matter, for example, always exist in a particular modality or instantiation, which implies that they could just as well be in another modality or instantiation: here rather than there, up rather than down, this color rather than that, this speed rather than that, etc. But this in turn means that their being in one state rather than another requires an explanation or an appeal to an extrinsic cause. And the proposal of the fluctuating universe itself is just as much of a non-starter, for it involves the same problem simply writ large: how do you explain why the universe is expanding rather than contracting, at this rate rather than that, in this configuration rather than another, etc.?

Finally, a cause of the very being of a contingent universe must be sought, and this cannot be anything in the universe, nor can it be the universe considered as a totality. It must be a reality whose very essence is to be, and hence whose perfection of existence is unlimited. As I have tried to demonstrate in this very short compass, philosophy can shed light on the existence of God so construed. The one thing the sciences cannot ever do is disprove it.

Woody Allen's
Bleak Vision

Iwas chagrined, but not entirely surprised, when I read Woody Allen's 2014 ruminations on ultimate things. To state it bluntly, Woody could not be any bleaker in regard to the issue of meaning in the universe. We live, he said, in a godless and purposeless world. The earth came into existence through mere chance and one day it, along with every work of art and cultural accomplishment, will be incinerated. The universe as a whole will expand and cool until there is nothing left but the void. Every hundred years or so, he continued, a pack of human beings will be "flushed away," and another and another until humanity has been eliminated. So why does he bother making films—roughly one every year? Well, he explained, in order to distract us from the awful truth about the meaninglessness of everything, we need diversions, and this is the service that artists provide. In some ways, low-level entertainers are probably more socially useful than high-brow *artistes*, since the former manage to distract more people than the latter. After delivering himself of this sunny appraisal, he quipped, "I hope everyone has a nice afternoon!"

Woody Allen's perspective represents a limit–case of what philosopher Charles Taylor calls "the buffered self," which is to say, an identity totally cut off from any connection to the transcendent. On this reading, this world is all we've got, and any window to another more permanent mode of existence remains tightly shut. Prior to the modern period, Taylor observes, the contrary idea of the "porous self" was in the ascendency. This means a self that is, in various ways and under various circumstances, open to a dimension of existence that goes beyond ordinary experience. If you consult the philosophers of antiquity and the Middle Ages, you will find a very frank acknowledgement that what Woody Allen observed about the physical world is largely true. Plato, Aristotle, and Thomas Aquinas all knew that material objects come and go, that human beings inevitably pass away, that all of our great works of art will eventually cease to exist. But those great thinkers wouldn't have succumbed to Allen's desperate nihilism. Why? Because they also believed that there were real links to a higher world available within ordinary experience, that certain clues within the world tip us off to the truth that there is more to reality than meets the eye.

One of these routes of access to the transcendent is beauty. In Plato's *Symposium*, we can read an exquisite speech by a woman named Diotima. She describes the experience of seeing something truly beautiful—an object, a work of art, a lovely person—and she remarks that this experience carries with it a kind of aura, for it lifts the observer to a consideration of the Beautiful itself, the source of all particular beauty. If you want to see a more modern version of Diotima's speech, take a look at the evocative section of James Joyce's *Portrait of the Artist as a Young Man* wherein the narrator relates his encounter with a beautiful girl standing in the surf off the Dublin strand, and concludes with the exclamation, "Oh heavenly God." John Paul II was standing in this same tradition when, in his wonderful *Letter to Artists*, he spoke of the artist's vocation as mediating God through beauty. To characterize artistic beauty as a mere distraction from the psychological oppression of nihilism is a tragic reductionism.

A second classical avenue to transcendence is morality, more precisely, the unconditioned demand of the good. On purely nihilist grounds, it is exceptionally difficult to say why anyone should be morally upright. If there are starving children in Africa, if there are people dying of AIDS in this country, if Christians are being systematically persecuted around the world...well, who cares? Every hundred years or so, a pack of human beings is flushed away and the cold universe looks on with utter indifference. So why not just eat, drink, and be merry, and dull our sensitivities to innocent suffering and injustice as best we can? In point of fact, the press of moral obligation itself links us to the transcendent, for it places us in the presence of a properly eternal value. The violation of one person cries out to heaven for vengeance; and the performance of one truly noble moral act is a participation in the Good itself, the source of all particular goodness. Indeed, even some of those who claim to be atheists and nihilists implicitly acknowledge this truth by the very passion of their moral commitments, a very clear case in point being Christopher Hitchens. One can find a disturbing verification of Woody Allen's rejection of this principle in two of his better films, *Crimes and Misdemeanors* from the 1980's and *Match Point* from the 2000's. In both movies, men commit horrendous crimes, but after a relatively brief period of regret, they move on with their pampered lives. No judgment comes, and all returns to normal. So it goes in a flattened-out world in which the moral link to transcendence has been severed.

Perhaps this conviction is born of my affection for many of Woody Allen's films, but I'm convinced that the great auteur doesn't finally believe his own philosophy. There are simply too many hints of beauty, truth, and goodness in his movies, and despite all his protests, these speak of a reality that transcends this fleeting world.

What Faith Is and
What It Isn't

The Protestant theologian Paul Tillich once commented that "faith" is the most misunderstood word in the religious vocabulary. I'm increasingly convinced that he was right about this. The ground for my conviction is the absolutely steady reiteration on my Internet forums of gross caricatures of what serious believers mean by faith. Again and again, my agnostic, atheist, and secularist interlocutors tell me that faith is credulity, naïveté, superstition, assent to irrational nonsense, acceptance of claims for which there is no evidence, etc., etc. And they gladly draw a sharp distinction between faith so construed and modern science, which, they argue, is marked by healthy skepticism, empirical verification, a reliable and repeatable method, and the capacity for self-correction. How fortunate, they conclude, that the Western mind was able finally to wriggle free from the constraints of faith and move into the open and well-lighted space of scientific reason. And how sad that, like a ghost from another time and place, faith continues, even in the early twentieth century, to haunt the modern mind and to hinder its progress.

In 2012, at the impetus of Pope Benedict XVI, the universal Church celebrated a "Year of Faith." What do Catholics mean (and not mean) by that obviously controversial word? I will begin with an analogy. If you are coming to know a person, and you are a relatively alert type, your reason will be fully engaged in the process. You will look that person over, see how she dresses and comports herself, assess how she relates to others, Google her and find out where she went to school and how she is employed, ask mutual friends about her, etc. All of this objective investigation could take place even before you had the opportunity to meet her. When you finally make her acquaintance, you will bring to the encounter all that you have learned about her, and will undoubtedly attempt to verify at close quarters what you have already discovered on your own. But then something extraordinary will happen, something over which you have no real control, something that will, inevitably, reveal to you things that you otherwise would never know: she will speak. In doing so, she will, on her own initiative, disclose her mind, her heart, her feelings to you. Some of what she says will be in concord with what you have already found out, but much of it—especially if your relationship has deepened and your conversations are profound and intimate—will be new, wonderful, beyond anything you might have discovered on your own.

But as she speaks and as you listen, you will be faced with a choice: do you believe her or not? Again, some of what she says you might be able to verify through your own previous investigation, but as she speaks of her feelings, her intentions, her aspirations, her most abiding fears, you know that you have entered a territory beyond your capacity to control. And you have to decide: do you trust her or not? So it goes, whether we like it or not, anytime we deal with a person who speaks to us. We don't surrender our reason as we get to know another person, but we must be willing to go beyond our reason; we must be willing to believe, to trust, to have faith.

This is, I think, an extremely illuminating analogy for faith in the theological sense. For Catholics (and I would invite my Internet friends to pay very close attention here), authentic faith never involves a *sacrificium intellectus* (a sacrifice of the intellect). God wants us to understand all we can about him through reason. By analyzing the order, beauty, and contingency of the world, there is an enormous amount of information we can gather concerning God: his existence, his perfection, the fact that he is endowed with intellect and will, his governance of the universe, etc. If you doubt me on this, I invite you to take a good long look at the first part of Thomas Aquinas's *Summa theologiae*.

Now, one of the truths that reason can discover is that God is a person, and the central claim of the Bible is that this Person has not remained utterly hidden but has, indeed, spoken. As is the case with any listener to a person who speaks, the listener to the divine speech has to make a choice: do I believe him or not? The decision to accept in trust what God has spoken about himself is what the Church means by "faith." This decision is not irrational, for it rests upon and is conditioned by reason, but it presses beyond reason, for it represents the opening of one heart to another. In the presence of another human being, you could remain stubbornly in an attitude of mistrust, choosing to accept as legitimate only those data that you can garner through rational analysis; but in so doing, you would close yourself to the incomparable riches that that person might disclose to you. The strict rationalist, the unwavering advocate of the scientific method, will know certain things about the world, but he will never come to know a person.

The same dynamic obtains in regard to God, the supreme Person. The Catholic Church wants people to use reason as vigorously and energetically as possible—and this very much includes scientific reason. But then it invites them, at the limits of their striving, to listen, to trust, to have faith.

Why I Love My
Invisible Friend

O ne of the favorite taunts of the new atheists is that religious people believe in an "invisible friend." They are implying, of course, that religion is little more than a pathetic exercise in wishful thinking, a reversion to childish patterns of projection and self-protection. It is well past time, they say, for believers to grow up, leave their cherished fantasies behind, and face the real world. In offering this characterization, the new atheists are showing themselves to be disciples of the old atheists such as Feuerbach, Marx, Comte, and Freud, all of whom made more or less similar observations.

Well, I'm writing here to let atheists know that I think they're right, at least about God being an invisible friend. Where they're wrong is in supposing that surrendering to this unseen reality is dehumanizing or infantilizing. First, a word about invisibility. It is an extraordinary prejudice of post-Enlightenment Western thought that visible things, empirically verifiable objects and states of affairs, are the most obviously "real" things around. For centuries prior to the Enlightenment, some of the very brightest people that have ever lived thought precisely the opposite. Most famously, Plato felt that the empirical world is evanescent and contingent in the extreme, made up of unstable objects that pass in and out of existence; whereas the invisible world of forms and mathematical truths is permanent, reliable, and supremely beautiful. You can certainly see two apples combining with two oranges to make four things, but when you grasp the principle that two plus two equals four, you have moved out of the empirical realm and into a properly invisible order, which is more pure and absolute than anything that the senses could take in. Mind you, I'm not denigrating the material world, as Plato and his followers were too often wont to do; I'm simply trying to show that it is by no means obvious that the invisible can simply be equated with the fantastic or the unreal.

Now to God's invisibility. One of the most fundamental mistakes made by atheists both old and new is to suppose that God is a supreme being, an impressive item within or alongside the universe. As David Bentley Hart has argued, the gods of ancient mythology or the watchmaker God of eighteenth-century deism might fit such a description, but the God presented by the Bible and by classical theism has nothing to do with it. The true God is the non-contingent ground of the contingent universe, the reason there is something rather than nothing, the ultimate explanation for why the world should exist at all. Accordingly, he is not a being, but rather, as Thomas Aquinas put it, *ipsum esse subsistens*, the sheer act of to-be itself. Thomas goes so far as to say that God cannot be placed in any genus, even in that most generic of genera, namely, being. But all of this must imply God's invisibility. Whatever can be seen is, ipso facto, *a* being, *a* particular state of affairs, and hence something that can be placed in a genus, compared with other finite realities, etc. The visible is, by definition, conditioned—and God is the unconditioned. I hope it is clear that in affirming God's invisibility, I am not placing limits on him, as though he were a type of being—the invisible type—over and against visible things, a ghost floating above physical objects. The invisible God is he whose reality transcends and includes whatever perfection can be found in creatures, since he himself is the source and ground of creatureliness in all its manifestations. Anything other than an invisible God would be a conditioned thing, and hence utterly unworthy of worship.

But is this invisible God my friend? One of the most important spiritual and metaphysical observations that can be made is this: God doesn't need us. The sheerly unconditioned act of to-be itself is in possession of every possible ontological perfection, and hence requires no completion, no improvement. He *needs* nothing. And yet the universe, in all of its astonishing complexity and beauty, exists. Since God could not have made it out of self-interest, it can only follow that he made it out of love, which is to say, a desire to share his goodness. Though there is always the danger that this sort of language will be misconstrued in a sentimental way, it must be said: God continually loves the universe into existence. Thus, God's fundamental stance toward all finite things is one of friendship. Can't we hear an overtone of this in Genesis's insistence that the Creator, looking with infinite satisfaction on all he had made, found it "good, indeed very good"? If I might stay within the framework of the book of Genesis, the role of human beings within God's good creation is to be the image of God, which is to say, the viceroy of the Creator, reflecting divine goodness into the world and channeling the world's praise back to God. In a word, human beings are meant to be the friends of God *par excellence.*

Is any of this dehumanizing? It would be, if God were a supreme being and hence a rival to human flourishing. If you want the details on that problem, consult any of the Greek or Roman myths. But the unconditioned Creator, the invisible God, is not a rival to anything he has made. Rather, as St. Irenaeus put it so memorably, *Gloria Dei homo vivens* (the glory of God is a human being fully alive). So God is my invisible friend? Guilty as charged—and delightedly so.

What Makes the
Church Grow?

O n the website maintained by the episcopal conference of Germany there appeared an editorial concerning Pope Francis's
apostolic visit to Africa in 2015. As many have pointed out, the piece
was breathtaking in its arrogance and cultural condescension. The
author's take on the surprisingly rapid pace of Christianity's growth
on the "dark continent" (his words)? Well, the level of education in
Africa is so low that the people accept easy answers to complex questions. His assessment of the explosion in vocations across Africa?
Well, the poor things don't have many other avenues of social ad-
vancement; so they naturally gravitate toward the priesthood.

What made this analysis especially dispiriting is that it came
not from a secularist or professionally anti-religious source but directly from the editor of the official website of the Catholic Church
in Germany. It is no accident, of course, that the article appeared
immediately in the wake of a very pointed oration of Pope Francis to
the hierarchy of Germany, in which the holy father indicated the obvious, namely, that the once-vibrant German Catholic Church is in
severe crisis: its people leaving in droves, doctrine and moral teaching regularly ignored, vocations disappearing, etc. Thus this editorial might be construed as a not-so-subtle shot across the papal bow.

But it was born too, I think, of an instinct that is at least a couple hundred years old, that northern Europe—and Germany in particular—naturally assumes the role of teacher and intellectual leader within the Catholic Church. In the nineteenth century, so many

of the great theologians were Germans: Drey, Döllinger, Mohler, Scheeben, Franzelin, etc. And in the twentieth century, especially in the years just prior to Vatican II, the intellectual heavyweights were almost exclusively from northern Europe: Maritain, Gilson, Congar, de Lubac, Schillebeeckx, Bouyer, Rahner, von Balthasar, Ratzinger, Küng, etc. Without these monumental figures, the rich teachings of Vatican II may never have emerged.

But something of crucial importance has happened in the years since the Council. The churches that once supported and gave rise to those intellectual leaders have largely fallen into desuetude. Catholicism is withering on the vine in Holland, Belgium, France, Germany, and Austria. Meanwhile, the center of gravity for Christianity in general and Catholicism in particular has shifted dramatically to the south, especially to the African continent. In 1900, there were about 9 million Christians in all of Africa, but today there are upwards of 500 million, accounting for roughly 45% of the total population of the continent. And these numbers and percentages are likely to grow, since Africa also has one of the fastest rates of population growth in the world. So though it is perhaps still a German instinct to seize the intellectual high ground and cast a somewhat patronizing gaze at the churches of the developing world, it is easy to understand how the leaders of those churches might remain politely—or not so politely—unwilling to accept criticism from their European colleagues.

I would argue that the German editor has, in point of fact, misdiagnosed the situation rather dramatically. The Church is growing in Africa not because the people are poorly educated but because the version of Christianity on offer there is robustly supernatural. As Philip Jenkins and others have shown, African Christianity puts a powerful stress on the miraculous, on eternal life, on the active providence of God, on healing grace, and on the divinity of Jesus. If such an emphasis is naïve, then every Biblical author, every Doctor of the Church, and every major theologian until the nineteenth century was naïve. The reason a supernaturally oriented Christianity grows is that it is congruent with the purposes of the Holy Spirit, and also that it presents something that the world cannot. A commitment to social justice, service of the poor, and environmentalism is obviously praiseworthy, but such a commitment could be made by decent atheists, agnostics, or secularists. Though it follows quite clearly from a supernatural sensibility, it is not, in itself, distinctively Christian. Accordingly, when Christianity collapses into purely this-worldly preoccupations—as it has, sadly, in much of Europe—it rapidly dries up.

Something very similar obtains in regard to the priesthood. I would contend that vocations are thriving in Africa not because African young men have so few professional options but precisely because the African theology of the priesthood is unapologetically supernatural. If the priest is basically social worker, psychologist, and activist for justice, as he often is in the European context, he loses any distinctive profile; but if he is mystic, soul doctor, healer, and steward of the mysteries of God, then he will present a compelling and attractive profile indeed.

I would recommend not spending much time mulling over the resentful and wrong-headed musings of the German editor, but I would indeed recommend a thoughtful consideration of the pivotal European theologians of the Vatican II era. And I would most warmly counsel careful attention to the voices of the vibrant Church of Africa.

Does Religion Really Have a "Smart-People Problem"?

D aniel Dennett, one of the "four horsemen" of contemporary atheism, proposed in 2003 that those who espouse a naturalist, atheist worldview should call themselves "the brights," thereby distinguishing themselves rather clearly from the dim benighted masses who hold on to supernaturalist convictions. In the wake of Dennett's suggestion, many atheists have brought forward what they take to be ample evidence that the smartest people in our society do indeed subscribe to anti-theist views. By "smartest" they usually mean practitioners of the physical sciences, and thus they point to surveys that indicate that only small percentages of scientists subscribe to religious belief.

In a 2014 article published in the online journal *Salon* titled "Religion's Smart-People Problem," University of Seattle philosophy professor John Messerly reiterates this case. However, he references not simply the lack of belief among scientists but also the atheism among academic philosophers, or, as he puts it, "professional philosophers." He cites a recent survey showing that only 14% of such professors admit to theistic convictions, and he states that this unbelief among the learned elite, though not in itself a clinching argument for atheism, should at the very least give religious people pause. Well, I'm sorry Professor Messerly, but please consider me unpaused.

Since I have developed these arguments many times before in other forums, let me say just a few things in regard to the scientists. I have found that, in practically every instance, the scientists who declare their disbelief in God have no idea what serious religious people mean by the word "God." Almost without exception, they think of God as some supreme worldly nature, an item within the universe for which they have found no "evidence," a gap within the ordinary nexus of causal relations, etc. I would deny such a reality as vigorously as they do. If that's what they mean by "God," then I'm as much an atheist as they—and so was Thomas Aquinas. What reflective religious people mean when they speak of God is not something within the universe, but rather the condition for the possibility of the universe as such, the non-contingent ground of contingency. And about that reality, the sciences, strictly speaking, have nothing to say one way or another, for the consideration of such a state of affairs is beyond the limits of the scientific method. And so when statistics concerning the lack of belief among scientists are trotted out, my honest response, is "who cares?"

But what about the philosophers, 86% of whom apparently don't believe in God? Wouldn't they be conversant with the most serious and sophisticated accounts of God? Well, you might be surprised. Many academic philosophers, trained in highly specialized corners of the field, actually have little acquaintance with the finer points of philosophy of religion, and often prove ham-handed when dealing with the issue of God. Time and again we hear the breezy claim that the traditional arguments for God's existence have been "demolished" or "refuted," but when these supposed refutations are brought forward, they prove remarkably weak, I have found, often little more than the batting down of a straw man. A fine example of this is Bertrand Russell's deeply uninformed dismissal of Thomas Aquinas's demonstration of the impossibility of an infinite regress of conditioned causes.

But more to the point, the percentage of atheists in the professional philosophical caste has at least as much to do with academic politics as it does with the formulation of convincing arguments. If one wants to transform a department of philosophy from largely theist to largely atheist, all one has to do is to make sure that the chairman of the department and a small coterie of the professoriat are atheist. In rather short order, that critical mass will control hiring, firing, and granting of tenure within the department. Once atheists have come to dominate the department, only atheist faculty will be hired, and students with theistic interests will be sharply discouraged from writing dissertations defending religious points of view. In time, very few doctorates supporting theism will be produced, and a new generation, shaped by thoroughly atheist assumptions, will come of age. To see how quickly this transformation can happen, take a good look at the philosophy department at any of the leading Catholic universities: what were in the 1950's overwhelmingly theistic professoriates are today largely atheistic. Does anyone really think that this happened because lots of clever new arguments were discovered?

Another serious problem with trumpeting current statistics on the beliefs of philosophers is that such a move is based on the assumption that, in regard to philosophy, newer is better. One could make that argument in regard to the sciences, which do seem to progress in a steadily upward direction: no one studies the scientific theories of Ptolemy or Descartes today, except out of historical interest. But philosophy is a horse of a different color, more akin to poetry. Does anyone think that the philosophical views of, say, Michel Foucault are necessarily better than those of Plato, Aristotle, Kant, or Hegel, just because Foucault is more contemporary? It would be like saying that the verse of Robert Frost is necessarily superior to that of Dante or of Shakespeare, just because Frost wrote in the twentieth century. I, for one, think that philosophy, so marked today by nihilism and postmodern relativism, is passing through a particularly corrupt period. Why should we think, therefore, that the denizens of philosophy department lounges today are necessarily more correct than Alfred North Whitehead, Edmund Husserl, Ludwig Wittgenstein, Jacques Maritain, Emmanuel Levinas, and Jean-Luc Marion, all of whom were well-acquainted with modern science and rigorously trained in philosophy—and affirmed the existence of God?

I despise the arrogance of Dennett and his atheist followers who would blithely wrap themselves in the mantle of "brightness"; but I also despise the use of statistics to prove any point about philosophical or religious matters. I would much prefer that we return to argument.

America Needs You,
Thomas Aquinas

I will admit that when I went to Toulouse France, to film my ten-part documentary on Catholicism, it was for fairly personal reasons. In the Dominican church of the Jacobins, in a golden casket situated under a side altar, are the remains of my hero, St. Thomas Aquinas. I spent a good amount of time in silent prayer in front of Thomas's coffin, thanking him for giving direction to my life. When I was a fourteen-year-old freshman at Fenwick High School outside Chicago, I was privileged to hear from a young Dominican priest the arguments for God's existence that Thomas Aquinas had formulated in the thirteenth century. I don't entirely know why, but hearing those rational demonstrations lit a fire in me that has yet to go out. They gave me a sense of the reality of God and thereby awakened in me a desire to serve God, to order my life radically toward him. I'm a priest because of God's grace, but that grace came to me through the mediation of Thomas Aquinas.

As I prayed before the tomb of Aquinas, I found myself ruminating on the importance for our own time of the one whom the Church calls its "common doctor." What can this thirteenth-century Dominican master teach us? First, Thomas Aquinas saw with utter clarity that since all truth comes from God, there can never be any real conflict between the data of the sciences and the facts of revelation. In his own time, there were advocates of the so-called "double truth theory," which held that the "truths" of philosophy and science were in one category and the "truths" of the faith in another. On this interpretation, one could hold mutually exclusive positions as long as one remained cognizant that the opposing views were in separate departments of the mind.

Well, Thomas saw this as so much nonsense and said so. Apparent conflicts between science and religion (to use our terms) are born of either bad science or bad religion, and they should compel the puzzled thinker to dig deeper and think harder. Following Augustine, Thomas said that if an interpretation of the Bible runs counter to clearly established findings of the sciences, we should move to a more mystical and symbolic reading of the Scriptural passage. How important this is today when forms of fundamentalism have given rise to a terrible rationalist counter-reaction. Biblical literalism—a modernism, alien to the patristic and medieval minds—produces a variety of views repugnant to physics, evolutionary biology, cosmology, etc. And this has led to the sequestration of some religious types and some scientific types into separate and mutually hostile camps. Thomas Aquinas would see how foolish and counter-productive this is for both science and religion. The faith, he claimed, should always go out to meet the culture with confidence, and the culture should see its own deepest aspirations realized in the faith.

Secondly, Thomas knew that the Creator God of the Bible is the only finally satisfying explanation for the existence of the contingent things of the world. He was deeply impressed by the actual existence of those things that do not contain within themselves the reason for their being. Clouds, trees, plants, animals, human beings, buildings, planets, and stars certainly exist, but they don't have to exist. This means, he saw, that their being is not self-explanatory, that it depends on some primordial reality which does exist through the power of its own essence. This "necessary" being is what Thomas called "God." He was moved by the correspondence between this philosophical sense of God and the self-designation that God gives in Exodus 3:14: "I am who I am." How significant this is in our time when "new" atheists have raised their voices to dismiss belief in God as a holdover from a pre-scientific time. Thomas would remind the Christopher Hitchens and Richard Dawkins of the world that no scientific advance could ever, even in principle, eliminate the properly metaphysical question to which God is the only satisfying answer. God is not a superstitious projection of human need; rather, God is the reason why there is something rather than nothing.

Thirdly, Thomas Aquinas was a deep humanist, precisely because he was a Christian. He saw that since God became human in Christ, the destiny of the human being is divinization, participation in the inner life of God. No other religion or philosophy or social theory has ever held out so exalted a sense of human dignity and purpose. And this is why, Aquinas intuited, there is something inviolable about the human person. How indispensably important that teaching is in our era of stem-cell research, euthanasia, legalized abortion, and preemptive war, practices that turn persons into means.

Thomas's bones lie in that golden casket in Toulouse, but his mind and his spirit, thank God, still inform the counter-cultural voice of the Church.

Revisiting the Argument
from Motion

One of the unintended but happy consequences of the emergence of the new atheism is a renewed interest in the classical arguments for God's existence. Eager to defend the faith that is so vigorously attacked today, Catholic apologists and evangelists have been recovering these rational demonstrations of the truth of God; and the atheists, just as eager to defend their position, have entered into the fray. In the process, these ancient arguments, long thought by many to be obsolete, have found a new relevance and have been brought to greater clarity through the give and take of both critics and advocates.

Thomas Aquinas famously laid out five arguments for the existence of God, but he characterized one of them as "the first and more manifest way." This is the proof from motion, which can be presented simply and schematically as follows. Things move. Since nothing moves itself, everything that is moved must be moved by another. If that which causes the motion is itself being moved, then it must be moved by another. This process cannot go on to infinity. Therefore, there must exist a first unmoved mover, which all people call God.

In order to avoid misunderstanding (and it's fair to say that this argument has been misunderstood for centuries), several observations are in order. When Aquinas speaks of motion, he means change of any kind, not simply change of location. Growth in wisdom, fluctuation in temperature, birth, death—these are all examples of motion, or, in his more technical language, the transition from potency to actuality. Once we grasp what Aquinas means by motion, it is relatively easy to understand why he insists that nothing can move or change itself. Whatever is in motion must be in potency, while that which causes change must be in actuality, just as the one learning French doesn't yet possess the language and the one teaching it does. Now since the same thing cannot be potential and actual at the same time in the same respect, nothing can be, simultaneously, both mover and moved. No one, strictly speaking, teaches himself French.

But let us suppose that the cause which is putting something in motion is itself being put in motion; then by the same principle, its change must be prompted by another. But this chain of moved movers cannot be indefinite, since the suppression of a first element would imply the suppression of every subsequent mover, and eventually of the motion that is evident to our senses. In regard to the negation of this sort of infinite causal series, the twentieth-century philosopher Bertrand Russell had a particularly unhelpful observation. Russell opined that Thomas Aquinas couldn't imagine such a series, because medievals hadn't yet come to terms with the idea of infinite series. Nothing could be further from the truth. Aquinas had absolutely no problem imagining infinite series, since he speculated about them all the time. What he denied is the possibility of an infinite causal series in which each element in the chain is, here and now, dependent upon the influence of a higher cause. Think of a pen that is is here and now being moved by a hand, which is here and now being moved by muscles, which are here and now being moved by nerves, which are here and now being stimulated by the brain, which is here and now being sustained by blood and oxygen, etc. If we suppress the first element in this sort of chain, the entire causal nexus would collapse and the motion under immediate consideration would not be adequately explained. Therefore it follows that there exists a prime mover, that is to say, an unactualized source of actualization, an unenergized energizer, an ultimate source of all of the change in the cosmos.

Now there are many atheists and agnostics who acknowledge that this demonstration is logically airtight but who quarrel with the association that Aquinas makes, almost casually, at the very end: "and this all people call God." There might indeed, they say, be a prime mover or uncaused principle, but this first element in the causal chain might be matter or energy or some such physical element. Many point to the famous law of the conservation of energy and conclude that the fundamental stuff of the universe just undergoes continual change of form throughout time.

In order to answer this objection, we have to examine the nature of the unmoved mover a bit more carefully. That which is truly the uncaused or unmoved source of energy must be fully actualized (*actus purus* in Aquinas's pithy Latin), which means that it is not capable of further realization. But energy or matter is that which is capable of undergoing practically infinite change. Energy or matter is endlessly malleable, and hence is about as far from *actus purus* as can be imagined. A rather simple thought experiment shows that such primal physical elements cannot be the unmoved mover. Neither matter nor energy exists as such but always in a particular form or configuration. In regard to either, one can always ask: what color is it, at what velocity does it move, under what conditions does it exist? A given piece of matter is one color, but it could be any other color; energy is at one quantum level, but it could be at any other. Therefore, we are compelled to inquire about the cause that made it to exist this way rather than that. We can appeal, of course, to some other material cause, but then we are compelled to ask the same question about that cause, and having recourse indefinitely to similarly material movers won't get us anywhere closer to an ultimate explanation. The philosophical dictum that sums up this state of affairs is that "act precedes potency." The first cause of change cannot itself be subject to change.

The unmoved mover is that which exists in a state of pure realization, that which cannot be improved in its being, that which simply is, that which is utterly in act. Do you see now why Thomas Aquinas equated it with God?

Revisiting the Arguement
from Desire

One of the classical demonstrations of God's existence is the so-called argument from desire. It can be stated in a very succinct manner as follows. Every innate or natural desire corresponds to some objective state of affairs that fulfills it. Now, we all have an innate or natural desire for ultimate fulfillment, ultimate joy, which nothing in this world can possibly satisfy. Therefore there must exist objectively a supernatural condition that grounds perfect fulfillment and happiness, which people generally refer to as "God."

I have found in my work as an apologist and evangelist that this demonstration, even more than the cosmological arguments, tends to be dismissed out of hand by skeptics. They observe, mockingly, that wishing something doesn't make it so, and they are eager to specify that remark with examples: I may want to have a billion dollars, but the wish doesn't make the money appear; I wish I could fly, but my desire doesn't prove that I have wings, etc. This rather cavalier rejection of a venerable demonstration is a consequence, I believe, of the pervasive influence of Ludwig Feuerbach and Sigmund Freud, both of whom opined that religion amounts to a pathetic project of wish-fulfillment. Since we want perfect justice and wisdom so badly, and since the world cannot possibly provide those goods, we invent a fantasy world in which they obtain. Both Feuerbach and Freud accordingly felt that it was high time the human race shake off these infantile illusions and come to grips with reality as it is. In Feuerbach's famous phrase: "The no to God is the yes to man."

The same idea is contained implicitly in the aphorism of Feuerbach's best-known disciple, Karl Marx: "Religion is the opiate of the masses."

In the wake of this criticism, can the argument from desire still stand? I think it can, but we have to probe a bit behind its deceptively simple surface if we are to grasp its cogency. The first premise of the demonstration hinges on a distinction between natural or innate desires and desires of a more artificial or contrived variety. Examples of the first type include the desire for food, for sex, for companionship, for beauty, and for knowledge; while examples of second type include the longing for a fashionable suit of clothes, for a fast car, for Shangri-La, or to fly through the air like a bird. Precisely because desires of the second category are externally motivated or psychologically contrived, they don't prove anything regarding the objective existence of their objects: some of them exist and some of them don't. But desires of the first type do indeed correspond to, and infallibly indicate, the existence of the states of affairs that will fulfill them: hunger points to the objective existence of food, thirst to the objective existence of drink, sexual longing to the objective existence of the sexual act, etc. And this is much more than a set of correspondences that simply happen to be the case; the correlation is born of the real participation of the desire in its object. The phenomenon of hunger is unthinkable apart from food, since the stomach is built for food; the phenomenon of sexual desire is unthinkable apart from the reality of sex, since the dynamics of that desire are ordered toward the sexual act. By its very structure, the mind already participates in truth.

So what kind of desire is the desire for perfect fulfillment? Since it cannot be met by any value within the world, it must be a longing for truth, goodness, beauty, and being in their properly unconditioned form. But the unconditioned, by definition, must transcend any limit that we might set to it. It cannot, therefore, be *merely* subjective, for such a characterization would render it not truly unconditioned. And this gives the lie to any attempt—Feuerbachian, Freudian, Marxist, or otherwise—to write off the object of this desire as a wish-fulfilling fantasy, as a projection of subjectivity. In a word, the longing for God participates in God, much as hunger participates in food. And thus, precisely in the measure that the desire under consideration is an innate and natural desire, it does indeed prove the existence of its proper object.

One of the best proponents of this argument in the last century was C.S. Lewis. In point of fact, Lewis made it the cornerstone of his religious philosophy and the still-point around which much of his fiction turned. What particularly intrigued Lewis was the sweetly awful quality of this desire for something that can never find its fulfillment in any worldly reality, a desire that, at the same time, frustrates and fascinates us. This unique ache of the soul he called "joy." In the *Narnia* stories, Aslan the lion stands for the object of this desire for the unconditioned. When the good mare Hwin confronts the lion for the first time, she says, "Please, you are so beautiful. You may eat me if you like. I would sooner be eaten by you than fed by anyone else." To understand the meaning of that utterance is to grasp the point of the argument from desire.

Einstein and God

It's been revealed that, toward the end of his life, Albert Einstein wrote a letter in which he dismissed belief in God as superstitious and characterized the stories in the Bible as childish. During a time when atheists have emerged rather aggressively in the popular culture, it was, to say the least, discouraging to hear that the most brilliant scientist of the twentieth century seemed to be antipathetic to religion. It appeared as though Einstein would have agreed with people such as Christopher Hitchens and Sam Harris and Richard Dawkins that religious belief belongs to the childhood of the human race.

It just so happens that the revelation of this letter coincided with my reading of Walter Isaacson's wonderful biography of Einstein, a book that presents a far more complex picture of the great scientist's attitude toward religion than his late-career musing would suggest. In 1930, Einstein composed a kind of creed entitled "What I Believe," at the conclusion of which he wrote: "To sense that behind everything that can be experienced there is something that our minds cannot grasp, whose beauty and sublimity reaches us only indirectly: this is religiousness. In this sense... I am a devoutly religious man." In response to a young girl who had asked him whether he believed in God, he wrote: "Everyone who is seriously involved in the pursuit of science becomes convinced that a spirit is manifest in the laws of the Universe—a Spirit vastly superior to that of man." And during a talk at Union Theological Seminary in New York on the relationship between religion and science, Einstein declared: "The situation may be expressed by an image: science without religion is lame, religion without science is blind."

These reflections of Einstein—and he made many more like them throughout his career—bring the German physicist close to the position of a rather influential German theologian. In his 1968 book *Introduction to Christianity*, Joseph Ratzinger, who later became Pope Benedict XVI, offered this simple but penetrating argument for God's existence: the universal intelligibility of nature, which is the presupposition of all science, can only be explained through recourse to an infinite and creative mind that has thought the world into being. No scientist, Ratzinger said, could even begin to work unless and until he assumed that the aspect of nature he was investigating was knowable, intelligible, marked by form. But this fundamentally mystical assumption rests upon the conviction that whatever he comes to know through his scientific work is simply an act of re-thinking, re-cognizing, what a far greater mind has already conceived. Ratzinger's elegant proof demonstrates that, at bottom, religion and science ought never to be enemies, since both involve an intuition of God's existence and intelligence. In fact, many have argued that it is no accident that the modern physical sciences emerged precisely out of the universities of the Christian West, where the idea of creation through the divine Word was clearly taught. Unhappily, in far too many tellings of the history of ideas, modernity is seen as emerging out of, and in stark opposition to, repressive, obscurantist, and superstitious Christianity. (How many authors, up to the present day, rehash the struggles of Galileo to make just this point.) As a result, Christianity—especially in its Catholic expression—is often presented as a kind of foil to science, when in fact there is a deep congruity between the disciplines that search for objective truth and the religion that says, "in the beginning was the Word" (John 1:1).

What sense, then, can we make of Einstein's recently discovered letter? Given the many other things he said about belief, perhaps it's best to say that he was reacting against primitive and superstitious forms of religion, just as St. Paul was when he said that we must put away childish things when we've come of age spiritually. And what of his dismissal of the Bible? Here I think we have to make a distinction. A person can be a genius in one field of endeavor and remain naïve, even inept, in another. Few would dispute that Einstein was the greatest theoretical physicist of the last century, but this is no guarantee that he had even an adequate appreciation for Sacred Scripture. The "infantile" stories of the Bible have been the object of sophisticated interpretation for two and half millennia. Masters such as Origen, Philo, Chrysostom, Augustine, Aquinas, and Newman have uncovered the complexity and multivalence of the Bible's symbolism and have delighted in showing the literary artistry that lies below its sometimes deceptively simple surface.

So I think we can conclude that religious people can, to a large extent, claim Einstein as an ally, though in regard to Scripture interpretation, we can find far better guides than he.

Pope Benedict and
How to Read the Bible

The first volume of Pope Benedict's masterful study *Jesus of Nazareth* dealt with the public life and preaching of Jesus, while the second installment concentrates on the events of the Lord's passion, death, and resurrection. Like the first volume, the second is introduced by a short but penetrating introduction wherein the pope makes some remarks about the method he has chosen to employ. What I found particularly fascinating was how Joseph Ratzinger developed a motif that has preoccupied him for the past thirty years, namely, how Biblical scholarship has to move beyond an exclusive use of the historical-critical method.

The roots of this method stretch back to the seventeenth and eighteenth centuries, to the work of Baruch Spinoza, Hermann Samuel Reimarus, and D.F. Strauss. The approach was adapted and developed largely in Protestant circles in the nineteenth and early twentieth centuries by such figures as Julius Wellhausen, Albert Schweitzer, Rudolf Bultmann, and Gerhard von Rad. Upon the publication of Pius XII's encyclical *Divino afflante Spiritu* in 1943, Catholic scholars were given permission to use the historical-critical method in the analysis of the Bible, and a whole generation of gifted Catholic historical critics subsequently emerged: Joseph Fitzmeyer, Roland Murphy, Raymond E. Brown, John Meier, and many others.

At the risk of oversimplifying a rather complex and multivalent method, I would say that historical criticism seeks primarily to discover the intentions of the human authors of the Bible as they addressed their original audiences. It endeavors to know, for instance, what the author of the book of the prophet Isaiah wanted to communicate to those for whom he was originally writing his text. It wants to understand what, say, an Israelite community in fifth-century-B.C. Palestine expected, hoped for, or was able to hear; or it seeks to grasp, for example, the theological intentions of Matthew or John as they composed their Gospels. Accordingly, historical criticism is extremely sensitive to the cultural, political, and religious setting in which a given Biblical author operated, as well as to the particular literary forms that he chose to utilize.

Now, it would be foolish to deny the value of the historical-critical method. When employed by responsible and faithful scholars, it has yielded tremendous fruit. One of its principal advantages is that it grounds our interpretations of the Bible in the rich soil of history. The Hebrew and Christian Scriptures are not predominantly mythological in form. By this I mean that they do not trade in timeless, ahistorical truths; rather, they convey how God has interacted with very real people across many centuries. With this in mind, the historical-critical method has allowed us to see through some of the distorting layers of interpretation that have been imposed on the Bible throughout the tradition and to return to the bracing truth of the texts themselves as they were originally meant to be read. Again and again, in both his pre-papal and papal writings, Joseph Ratzinger affirmed the permanent value of this approach to the Scriptures.

However, he also remarked upon the shadowy side of this method, and consequently cautioned against a one-sided use of it. The first problem he noticed is that the method, precisely in the measure that it concentrates so exclusively on the intention of the human author, can easily overlook the intention and activity of the divine author of Scripture. To be sure, Catholic Biblical theology does not have a naïve appreciation of God's authorship of the Bible, as though

God simply dictated his words to robotic human instruments. Nevertheless, it holds to God's inspiration of the whole of the Bible and hence defends the claim that God, in a very real sense, is the principal author of the Biblical books. What follows from this claim is that the Scriptures as a whole have coherence and are marked by discernible patterns and trajectories—all traceable to the intention of a supernatural agent. A significant limitation of the historical-critical method is that its hyper-focus on human authorship tends to leave us with a jumble of (at best) vaguely related texts, each with its own distinctive finality and meaning. We have, in a word, what Isaiah meant, and what the author of the book of Job meant, and what Mark and Paul meant—but not what God means across the whole of the Bible.

A second and related limitation is that the historical-critical method, precisely by looking so intently at the meaning of the Biblical texts in their time, tends to leave them locked in history, and hence unable to speak across the ages to us. We might uncover fascinating truths about what the Psalms meant for their original audience, but unless we discover what, through God's spirit, they mean for us now, they are denigrated to the status of ancient poems.

And this is why Pope Benedict wants to recover what he calls a "theological hermeneutic" that can be used along with the historical-critical method of interpretation. This theological approach is similar to the method that the Church Fathers used in interpreting Scripture. It takes with utmost seriousness the inner coherency of the Bible, born of its divine authorship, and it assumes that God's Word is given ever-new illumination through the theological, dogmatic, and spiritual traditions of the Church. In point of fact, Pope Benedict proposed his three-volume study of Jesus as the fruit of both the historical-critical and the theological methods of reading, and hence as a model for future scholarship of the Bible. Benedict's books are filled with important insights about Jesus, but I have a suspicion that the most lasting contribution he made through this project was a reshaping of the way we read the Bible itself.

Preaching the
Strange Word

About fifteen years ago, I prepared an elective class at Mundelein Seminary which I entitled "The Christology of the Poets
and Preachers." In this course, I endeavored to explore the Catholic tradition's non-technical, more lyrical manner of presenting the
significance of Jesus. I studied the literary works of Dante, Gerard
Manley Hopkins, and G.K. Chesterton, and I also investigated in detail the sermons of many of the greatest masters: Origen, Augustine,
Chrysostom, Bernard, Aquinas, Newman, and Knox, among others.
What struck me with particular power, and caused me, I confess, to
rethink things rather thoroughly was this: none of these figures—
from the late second century to the twentieth century, whose sermons we specially revere and hold up for imitation—preached the
way I was taught to preach.

I came of age and went through my theological and pastoral
formation in the years immediately following the Second Vatican
Council. The watchwords of the time were "relevance" and "experience." Practically every teacher and Church leader of the time insisted that our theological language had become increasingly irrelevant
to modern people, and that we had to find, accordingly, a way to
relate the Bible to lived human experience. In line with instincts that
go back at least to early-nineteenth-century Protestantism, we felt
obliged to engage in a great "translation project," transposing the
obscure and puzzling world of the Scriptures into the language and
conceptuality of our time. The consequences of this shift for preach-

ing were obvious. Sermons should be filled with references to the actual lived experiences of the congregation; they should be marked by stories and cultural references; and they should use a good deal of humor. Now don't get me wrong: the emphases of the postconciliar period were not entirely misplaced, and the sermons that came out of that time were not entirely bad. But they were indeed egregious when seen in the context of the great tradition. It's simply the case that none of the master preachers that Catholicism reverences actually preached in that way.

How *did* they preach? They took their listeners/readers on a careful tour of the densely-textured world of the Bible. The Scriptures, they knew, open up an entirely new acting area, filled with distinctive characters who do and say anomalous and surprising things. And they understood that through all of the twists and turns of the Biblical story, the strangest and most unnerving character of all comes into view: the God of Israel. To *get* these figures and to grasp the nettle of the great story, one has to enter into the jungle of the Bible with patience and under the direction of an experienced and canny explorer. And this was precisely the role of the preacher: to be a mystagogue, a knowing guide through the tangled forest of the Scriptures.

I might propose an analogy with some well-known literary texts. Umberto Eco's novel *The Name of the Rose* is a wonderful amalgam of detective story, bildungsroman, and metaphysical exploration; and it commences with a lengthy description of life in a fourteenth-century Benedictine monastery. To those who questioned why this lengthy propaedeutic was required, Eco said, "my reader must go through a sort of monastic novitiate if he is to understand the story I'm trying to tell." J.R.R. Tolkien's masterpiece *The Lord of the Rings*, which is a rollicking adventure story and an evocation of the Catholic faith, begins with about 75 pages describing the birthday party of Bilbo Baggins. When Tolkien was challenged on this score, he responded in a manner very similar to Eco: his reader, he explained, had to learn the languages, characters, weather, topography, and history of his imaginative world; otherwise they would never get what Tolkien was trying to communicate. Though he never said so explicitly, we could deduce the same principle from Melville's lengthy (even tiresome) detailing of the arcana of whaling in the middle of *Moby Dick*. We might sum this up as follows: entering the world of a text is required if one is to understand the thematics of a text.

So a good preacher unfolds the patterns of meaning within the Biblical universe—precisely so as to draw our world into that world. The fundamental problem with much of the preaching after Vatican II is that it got this principle backward. It tended to make the Bible accessible to our consciousness, and so tamed it and domesticated it, often turning it into a faint echo of what could be heard in any other religious text or even within the culture itself. But if what the preacher is offering can be found, often in more compelling form, elsewhere, people will leave the Church in droves.

The Methodist theologian Stanley Hauerwas relates a story of his time as Gifford Lecturer in Scotland. He had been invited to preach at the Cathedral of Edinburgh and discovered a practice that went back to the Reformation period: a sexton of the cathedral literally locked Hauerwas into the pulpit and told him that he wouldn't let him out until he had preached the Gospel! Now I don't entirely subscribe to the sixteenth-century Protestant idea of what the Gospel is, but I love the instinct behind that discipline. We shouldn't allow preachers to run away from the density, complexity, and sheer weirdness of the Bible. We should lock them into their pulpits until they display the world of the Scriptures!

The Genesis
Problem

I'm continually amazed how often the "problem" of Genesis comes up in my work of evangelization and apologetics. What I mean is the way people struggle with the seemingly bad science that is on display in the opening chapters of the first book of the Bible. How can anyone believe that God made the visible universe in six days, that all the species were created at the same time, that light existed before the sun and moon, etc., etc.? How can believers possibly square the naïve cosmology of Genesis with the textured and sophisticated theories of Newton, Darwin, Einstein, and Hawking?

One of the most important principles of Catholic Biblical interpretation is that the reader of the Scriptural texts must be sensitive to the genre or literary type of the text with which he is dealing. Just as it would be counter-intuitive to read *Moby Dick* as history or "The Waste Land" as social science, so it is silly to interpret, say, "The Song of Songs" as journalism or the Gospel of Matthew as a spy novel. In the same way, it is deeply problematic to read the opening chapters of Genesis as a scientific treatise. If I can borrow an insight from Fr. George Coyne, a Jesuit priest and astrophysicist, no Biblical text can possibly be scientific in nature, since science, as we understand it, first emerged some fourteen centuries after the composition of the last Biblical book. The author of Genesis simply wasn't doing what Newton, Darwin, Einstein, and Hawking were doing; he wasn't attempting to explain the origins of things in the characteristically modern manner, which is to say, on the basis of empirical observation, testing of hypotheses, marshalling of evidence, and experimentation. Therefore, to maintain that the opening chapters of Genesis are "bad science" is a bit like saying that *The Iliad* is bad history or *The Chicago Tribune* is not very compelling poetry.

So what precisely was that ancient author trying to communicate? Once we get past the "bad science" confusion, the opening of the Bible gives itself to us in all of its theological and spiritual power. Let me explore just a few dimensions of this lyrical and evocative text. We hear that Yahweh brought forth the whole of created reality through great acts of speech: "'Let there be light,' and there was light; 'Let the dry land appear' and so it was." In almost every mythological cosmology in the ancient world, God or the gods establish order through some act of violence. They conquer rival powers or they impose their will on some recalcitrant matter. (How fascinating, by the way, that we still largely subscribe to this manner of explanation, convinced that order can be maintained only through violence or the threat of violence). But there is none of this in the Biblical account. God doesn't subdue some rival or express his will through violence. Rather, through a sheerly generous and peaceful act of speech, he gives rise to the whole of the universe. This means that the most fundamental truth of things—the metaphysics that governs reality at the deepest level—is peaceful and nonviolent. Can you see how congruent this is with Jesus' great teachings on nonviolence and enemy love in the Sermon on the Mount? The Lord is instructing his followers how to live in accord with the elemental grain of the universe.

Secondly, we are meant to notice the elements of creation that are explicitly mentioned in this account: the heavens, the stars, the sun, the moon, the earth itself, the sea, the wide variety of animals that roam the earth. Each one of these was proposed by various cultures in the ancient world as objects of worship. Many of the peoples that surrounded Israel held the sky, the stars, the sun, the moon, the earth, and various animals to be gods. By insisting that these were, in fact, created by the true God, the author of Genesis was not-so-subtly dethroning false claimants to divinity and disallowing all forms of idolatry. Mind you, the author of Genesis never tires of reminding us that everything that God made is good (thus holding off all forms of dualism, Manichaeism, and Gnosticism), but none of these good things is the ultimate good.

A third feature that we should notice is the position and role of Adam, the primal human, in the context of God's creation. He is given the responsibility of naming the animals, "all the birds of heaven and all the wild beasts" (Gen 2:20). The Church fathers read this as follows: naming God's creatures in accord with the intelligibility placed in them by the Creator, Adam is the first scientist and philosopher, for he is, quite literally, "cataloguing" the world he sees around him. (*kata logon* means "according to the word"). From the beginning, the author is telling us, God accords to his rational creatures the privilege of participating, through their own acts of intelligence, in God's intelligent ordering of the world. This is why, too, Adam is told not to dominate the world but to "cultivate and care for it" (Gen 2:16), perpetuating thereby the nonviolence of the creative act.

These are, obviously, just a handful of insights among the dozens that can be culled from this great text. My hope is that those who are tripped up by the beginning of the book of Genesis can make a small but essential interpretive adjustment and see these writings as they were meant to be seen: not as primitive science, but as exquisite theology.

Mother Nature Is
One Unreliable Lady

Conservation International has sponsored a series of videos that have become YouTube sensations, garnering millions of views. They feature famous actors—Harrison Ford, Kevin Spacey, Robert Redford, and others—voicing different aspects of the natural world, from the ocean to the rain forest to redwood trees. The most striking is the one that presents Mother Nature herself, given voice by Julia Roberts.

They all have more or less the same message, namely, that nature finally doesn't give a fig for human beings; that it is far greater than we, and will outlast us. Here are some highlights from the Mother's speech: "I've been here for over four and a half billion years, 22,500 times longer than you; I don't really need people, but people need me." And "I have fed species greater than you; and I have starved species greater than you." And "my oceans, my soil, my flowing streams, my forests—they all can take you or leave you."

I must confess that when I first came across these videos I thought, "just more tree-hugging extremism," but the more I watched and considered them, the more I became convinced that they are fundamentally right and actually serve to make a point of not inconsiderable theological significance. That nature in all of its beauty and splendor doesn't finally care about human beings came home to me dramatically many years ago. I was standing in the surf just off the coast of North Carolina, gazing out to sea and remarking how beautiful the vista was. For just a moment, I turned around to face the shore, and a large wave came up suddenly and knocked me off my feet and, for a few alarming seconds, actually pinned me to the ocean floor. In a moment, it was over and I got back on my feet, but I was shaken. The sea, which just seconds before had beguiled me with its serenity and beauty, had turned on a dime and almost killed me.

The ancients knew this truth, and they expressed it in their mythology. The gods and goddesses of Greece, Rome, and Babylon were basically personifications of the natural necessities: water, the sky, the mountain, the fertile earth, etc. Like the natural elements they symbolized, these divine figures were fickle in the extreme. One minute, Poseidon smiles on you, and the next minute he sinks your ship; now Zeus is pleased with you, now he sends a thunderbolt to destroy you; Demeter can be a gentle mother, and Demeter can be an avenging enemy. And indeed, so it goes with the ocean, with the weather, and with the soil. But this is precisely why the worship of these natural necessities is always such a dicey business, for the best one can hope for is to mollify these finally indifferent divinities to some degree through worship and sacrifice.

Biblical religion represents something altogether new, a fact signaled in the opening verses of the book of Genesis, where it is emphatically stated that God *creates* earth, sky, stars, and planets, the animals that move upon the earth and the fishes that inhabit the ocean depths. All of these natural elements were, at one time or another, worshipped as divine. So even as he celebrates them, the author of Genesis is effectively dethroning them, desacralizing them. Nature is wonderful indeed, he is telling us; but it is not God. And the consistent Biblical message is that this Creator God is not like the arbitrary and capricious gods of the ancient world; rather, he is reliable, rock-like in his steadfast love, more dedicated to human beings than a mother is to her child. The entire Scriptural revelation comes to a climax with the claim, in the fourth chapter of John's first letter, that God simply *is* love. St. Augustine celebrated this Biblical departure from the ancient worship of nature in a lyrical and visionary passage in his *Confessions*. He imagines the natural elements coming before him, one by one. Each says to him, "Look higher," and then, in a great chorus, they gesture toward God and then shout together, "He *made* us!"

As classical Christianity came to be questioned by some of the intellectual elite in the early modern period, the ancient worship of nature made an unhappy comeback. One thinks of Baruch Spinoza's blithe equation *Deus sive natura* (God or nature) and then of the many forms of pantheism that it spawned, from Schleiermacher's "infinite" to Emerson's "Oversoul" to George Lucas's "Force." In fact, the return to the classical sense of divinity is on particularly clear display in the "dark" and "light" sides of the Force that play such a vital role in the *Star Wars* narrative. Though it can be used for good or ill, the Force is finally as indifferent to human beings as is Mother Nature.

And this is why the Julia Roberts video functions as an effective antidote against all forms of nature worship. It vividly reminds us that when we make Mother Nature our ultimate concern, we are turning to an exceptionally cruel and unreliable lady. Though I don't think this was her intention, Ms. Roberts is urging us to "look higher."

Laudato Si' and
Romano Guardini

In 1986, after serving in a variety of capacities in the Jesuit province of Argentina, Jorge Mario Bergoglio commenced doctoral studies in Germany. The focus of his research was the great twentieth-century theologian and cultural critic Romano Guardini, who had been a key influence on, Karl Rahner, Henri de Lubac, and Joseph Ratzinger, among many others. As things turned out, Bergoglio never finished his doctoral degree (he probably started too late in life), but his immersion in the writings of Guardini decisively shaped his thinking. Most of the commentary on Pope Francis's encyclical *Laudato Si'* has focused on the issue of global warming and the pope's alignment with this or that political perspective, but this is to miss the forest for one very particular tree. As I read through the document, I saw, on practically every page, the influence of Romano Guardini and his distinctive take on modernity.

To get a handle on Guardini's worldview, one should start with a series of essays that he wrote in the 1920s, gathered into book form as *Letters from Lake Como*. Like many Germans (despite his very Italian name, Guardini was culturally German), he loved to vacation in Italy, and he took particular delight in the lake region around Milan. He was enchanted, of course, by the physical beauty of the area, but what intrigued him above all was the manner in which human beings, through their architecture and craftsmanship, interacted non-invasively and respectfully with nature. When he first came to the region, he noticed, for example, how the homes along Lake Como imitated the lines and rhythms of the landscape and how the boats that plied the lake did so in response to the swelling and falling of the waves. But by the 1920's, he had begun to notice a change. The homes being built were not only larger, but more "aggressive," indifferent to the surrounding environment, no longer accommodating themselves to the natural setting. And the motor-driven boats on the lake were no longer moving in rhythm with the waves, but rather cutting through them carelessly.

In these unhappy changes, Guardini noted the emergence of a distinctively modern sensibility. He meant that the attitudes first articulated by Francis Bacon in the sixteenth century and René Descartes in the seventeenth were coming to dominate the mentality of twentieth-century men and women. Consciously departing from Aristotle, who had declared knowledge is a modality of contemplation, Bacon opined that knowledge is power, more precisely, power to control the natural environment. This is why he infamously insisted that the scientist's task is to put nature "on the rack" so that she might give up her secrets. Just a few decades later, Descartes told the intellectuals of Europe to stop fussing over theological matters and philosophical abstractions and to get about the business of "mastering" nature. To be sure, this shift in consciousness gave rise to the modern sciences and their attendant technologies, but it also, Guardini worried, led to a deep alienation between humanity and nature. The typical modern subject became aggressive and self-absorbed, the natural world simply something for him to manipulate for his own purposes.

If you want to see an English version of Guardini's perspective, I would recommend a careful reading of C.S. Lewis, J.R.R. Tolkien, and their Inklings colleagues on the relation between capitalist, technocratic humanity and an increasingly attacked nature. If you want vivid images for this, turn to the pages in *The Lord of the Rings* dealing with the battle between Saruman and the Ents or to the section of *The Lion, the Witch, and the Wardrobe* detailing the permanent winter into which Narnia had fallen.

It is only against this Guardinian background that we can properly read the pope's encyclical. Whatever his views on global warming, they are situated within the far greater context of a theology of nature that stands athwart the typically modern point of view. That the earth has become "piled with filth"; that pollution adversely affects the health of millions of the poor; that we live in a "throwaway" culture; that the unborn are treated with indifference; that huge populations have little access to clean drinking water; that thousands of animal species are permitted to fall into extinction; and, yes, even that we live in housing that bears no organic relation to the natural environment—all of it flows from the alienated Cartesian subject going about his work of mastering nature. In the spirit of the author of the book of Genesis, the Biblical prophets, Irenaeus, Thomas Aquinas, Francis of Assisi—indeed of any great pre-modern figure—Pope Francis wants to recover a properly cosmological sensibility, whereby the human being and her projects are in vibrant, integrated relation with the world that surrounds her.

What strikes the Pope as self-evident is that the nature we have attempted to dominate for the past several centuries has now turned on us, like Frankenstein's monster. As he put it in a recent press conference, "God always forgives; human beings sometimes forgive; but when nature is mistreated, she never forgives." These lessons, which he learned many years ago from Romano Guardini, are still worthy of careful attention today.

The Hundredth Anniversary
of Thomas Merton's Birth

I write these words on the one hundredth anniversary of the birth of Thomas Merton, one of the greatest spiritual writers of the twentieth century and a man who had a decisive influence on me and my vocation to the priesthood. I first encountered Merton's writing in a peculiar way. My brother and I were both working at a bookstore in the Chicago suburbs. One afternoon, he tossed to me a tattered paperback with a torn cover that the manager had decided to discard. My brother said, "You might like this; it's written by a Trappist monk." I replied, with the blithe confidence of a sixteen-year-old, "I don't want to read a book by some Buddhist." With exquisite sensitivity, he responded, "Trappists are Catholics, you idiot."

The book in question was *The Seven Storey Mountain*, Thomas Merton's passionate, articulate, smart, and deeply moving account of his journey from worldling to Trappist monk. Though much of the philosophy and theology was, at that time, over my head, I became completely caught up in the drama and romance of Merton's story, which is essentially the tale of how a man fell in love with God. The book is extraordinarily well written, funny, adventurous, and spiritually wise. In one of the blurbs written for the first edition, Fulton Sheen referred to it as a contemporary version of St. Augustine's *Confessions*, and it was fulsomely praised by both Evelyn Waugh and Graham Greene. Moreover, it contributed massively to the startling influx of young men into monasteries and religious communities across the United States in the postwar era.

I was so thrilled by my first encounter with Merton that I dove headlong into his body of writing. *The Sign of Jonas*, a journal that Merton kept in the years leading up to his priestly ordination, became a particular favorite. That work concludes with an essay called "Firewatch: July 4, 1952," which Jacques Maritain called the greatest piece of spiritual writing in the twentieth century. In this powerful meditation, Merton uses the mundane monastic task of walking through the monastery checking for fires as a metaphor for a Dantesque examination of the soul. *The Sign of Jonas* is marked by Merton's playful and ironic sense of humor, but it also gives evidence of the enormous range of his reading and intellectual interests. To devour that book as a nineteen-year-old, as I did, was to receive an unparalleled cultural education. For many people of my generation, Merton opened the door to the wealth of the Catholic spiritual tradition: I first learned about John of the Cross, Meister Eckhart, Teresa of Avila, Bernard of Clairvaux, Odo of Cluny, the Victorines, Origen, Thérèse of Lisieux, and Hans Urs von Balthasar from him.

Perhaps the central theme of all of Merton's writings is contemplation. What he stressed over and again in regard to this crucial practice is that it is not the exclusive preserve of spiritual athletes, but rather something that belongs to all the baptized and that stands at the heart of Christian life. For contemplation is, in his language, "to find the place in you where you are here and now being created by God." It is to consciously discover a new center in God and hence at the same time to discover the point of connection to everyone and everything else in the cosmos. Following the French spiritual masters, Merton called this *le point vierge*, the virginal point, or, to put it in the language of the fourth Gospel, "water bubbling up in you to eternal life" (4:14). In his famous epiphanic experience at the corner of 4th and Walnut in downtown Louisville, Merton felt, through *le point vierge*, a connection to the ordinary passersby so powerful that it compelled him to exclaim, "There is no way of telling people that they are all walking around shining like the sun."

Sadly, for many younger Catholics today, Merton, if he is known at all, is viewed with a certain suspicion, and this for two reasons. First, when he was a man of fifty-one, he fell in love with a young nurse who cared for him after back surgery. Though it is almost certain that this was exclusively an affair of the heart, it was certainly, to say the very least, unseemly for a middle-aged monk and priest to have been so infatuated with a much younger woman. On the other hand, Merton worked through this confusing period and returned to his vowed monastic life. And the journal that he kept during that year, *Learning to Love*, is so spiritually alert and illuminating that I often recommend it to brother priests who are wrestling with the promise of celibacy. To dismiss Merton out of hand because of this admittedly inappropriate relationship strikes me as disproportionate.

The second reason that some younger Catholics are wary of Merton is his interest, in the last roughly ten years of his life, in Eastern religions, especially Buddhism. They see this as an indication of a religious relativism or a vague syncretism. Nothing could be further from the truth. Merton was indeed fascinated by the Eastern religions and felt that Christians could benefit from a greater understanding of their theory and practice, but he never for a moment felt that all religions were the same or that Christians should move to some space "beyond" Christianity. In order to verify this, all one has to do is read the prefaces to his major books on Zen and Buddhism. About ten years ago, I had the privilege of giving a retreat to the monks at Merton's monastery of Gethsemani in Kentucky. Just after the retreat ended, Merton's secretary, Br. Patrick Hart, took me out in a jeep to see the hermitage that Merton occupied for the last few years of his life. While we were sitting on the front porch of the small house, he looked at me intently and asked, "Could you tell anyone that's interested that Thomas Merton died a monk of Gethsemani Abbey and a priest of the Catholic Church?" He was as bothered as I am by the silly suggestion that Merton, at the end of his life, was on the verge of leaving the priesthood or abandoning the Catholic faith.

Thomas Merton was not perfect, and he might not have been a saint. But he was indeed a master of the spiritual life, and his life and work had a profound effect on me and an army of others around the world. I offer this birthday tribute as a small token of gratitude.

The Pope, the Congress, and a Trappist Monk

I had the extraordinary privilege of following Pope Francis' pilgrimage to the United States at very close quarters. I had this access both as a bishop and as a commentator for NBC News. It was thrilling indeed to witness just how rapturously the American people received the pope, and how affected the holy father was by this reception. Many images stay vividly in my mind: the pope kissing the forehead of the ten-year-old boy with cerebral palsy, the rabbi and the imam praying together with him at the September 11th memorial, a little boy from a New York Catholic school showing the pope how to maneuver his way around a Smart Board. But what stays most powerfully with me is the pope speaking to a joint meeting of the United States Congress in Washington, D.C.

My first assignment for NBC on this trip was the *Today Show*'s coverage of the pope's arrival on the south lawn of the White House. As I sat on the platform with Matt Lauer and Maria Shriver, I looked across at the stately obelisk of the Washington Monument, and I remembered an extraordinary event from the mid-nineteenth century. Along with many other world leaders, Pope Pius IX had sent a block for the construction of the monument to the Father of our country, but an angry mob of anti-Catholic bigots took that piece of marble and threw it into the Potomac. This, of course, was not an isolated or purely egregious act of vandalism; rather, it partook of a widespread and deeply-rooted hatred of Catholicism that lasted in this country in fairly virulent form up to the election of John F. Kennedy in 1960. That the pope of Rome would be graciously received at the White House and welcomed to speak before the entire Congress of the United States would have struck most Americans for much of our history as simply unthinkable. And this is why (and I'll confess it openly) my eyes filled with tears as I saw the pope standing at the rostrum in the House of Representatives, the cheers of the gathered lawmakers washing over him.

And as I listened to the pope's words that day, I was even more astonished. As is his wont, Francis didn't trade in abstractions. Instead, he focused his remarks on four outstanding figures from American history—Abraham Lincoln, Martin Luther King, Jr., Dorothy Day, and Thomas Merton—each of whom spoke of some dimension of authentic freedom. Anyone familiar with my work over the years would know that all four of these people are heroes of mine. I have a photo of Lincoln over the desk in my office; I have written extensively on King and have done a number of videos on his life and legacy; Dorothy Day is featured prominently in my documentary *Catholicism* (see Episode 2); and Thomas Merton is, quite simply, one of the major reasons that I entered the priesthood, and a photo of him is in eyeshot as I type these words.

I would love to explore the pope's analysis of each of these giants, but given the limited scope of this article, I will focus on the one I consider the most important, namely, Merton. What Merton signaled for the pope was openness to dialogue with other religions, to be sure, but also, and more significantly, contemplative openness to the reality of God, to a dimension that goes beyond the empirical world and the achievements of the individual ego. This is of supreme importance, for when a sense of God evanesces—as it has done increasingly in our secularized Western world—all we have left for understanding human affairs are psychological and political categories. Armed only with these, we fall into the customary patterns of left and right, liberal and conservative, open to change and suspicious of change, etc. This is part of what makes Catholic social teaching so confounding to the pundits and politicos. How can the Catholic Church simultaneously advocate against abortion and assisted suicide but for immigration reform and attention to the poor? How can it stand against the abuse of the environment and for the free market, against the death penalty and for the family? With God out of the picture, it is indeed hard to make sense of such an array of opinions, but with God at the heart of things, the various positions of the Church fall into harmony, much like the medallions in a rose window. If God exists, then every individual person that he has created is a subject of rights, freedom, and dignity. If God exists, then no one is expendable and everyone is equally worthy of respect. It is none other than the contemplative attitude exemplified by Thomas Merton that reveals this deep consistency.

How wonderful and strange that a pope would be addressing Congress at all, but how surpassingly wonderful and strange it was that he should use the occasion to hold up before the lawmakers of the most powerful nation on earth the example of a Trappist monk who gave his life to the contemplation of God.

Ross Douthat and the
Catholic Academy

Many years ago, a local Chicago sportscaster named Howard Sudberry recounted a curious controversy surrounding a major league baseball game. Late in the contest, the team that would eventually win was up by ten runs. A player for that squad hit a single and then stole second base. The catcher of the trailing team whined after the game that this base-stealer was rubbing it in, essentially being unsportsmanlike. Well, Sudberry was having none of it. He looked into the camera and spoke, as it were, to the catcher himself: "Then throw him out!" He was implying that the base-stealer had done absolutely nothing opposed to the rules of baseball and that, if the catcher didn't like it, he should try to beat him fair and square within the context of those same rules.

This incident came to mind when I read about a similarly curious controversy, this one within the groves of academia. The *New York Times* columnist Ross Douthat has been opining quite a bit about the Synod on the Family in Rome, suggesting, among other things, that clear factions among the bishops have emerged, that Pope Francis favors a more liberal resolution of the key questions, and that heretical viewpoints are afoot in Rome. In response to Douthat's ruminations, a letter, signed by some of the leading lights of the Catholic academy, was sent to the editors of the *Times*. The professors and pundits complained that Douthat was proposing a politicized reading of Church affairs and that he was, at the end of the day, unqualified to speak on such complex matters, presumably because he doesn't have a graduate degree in theology. Their prim closing remark—"This is not what we expect of the *New York Times*"—was an unmistakable insinuation that views such as Douthat's simply should not be allowed into the arena of public conversation.

Are all of Ross Douthat's opinions on the Synod debatable? Of course. Do I subscribe to everything he has said in this regard? No. But is he playing outside the rules of legitimate public discourse in such an egregious way that he ought to be censored? Absolutely not! Anyone even casually familiar with Douthat knows that he is exceptionally smart, articulate, careful in his expression, and a committed Catholic. So he has argued that divisions at least analogous to political factions have emerged at the synod. From the Council of Jerusalem in the first century through Vatican II in the twentieth, the Church has been marked by conflict, rivalry, and faction. If you doubt me in regard to the first, take a good look at chapters eleven through fifteen of the Acts of the Apostles; and if you're skeptical in regard to the second, peruse any two pages of Yves Congar's tome *My Journal of the Council*. And while you're at it, read John Henry Newman's history of the Council of Nicea in the fourth century, or any treatment of the sixteenth-century Council of Trent. When has the life of the Church *not* been susceptible to a political reading?

And the suggestion that, because he doesn't have a credential from the academy, Douthat isn't qualified to enter into the discussion? Please. If a doctorate in theology were a bottom-line prerequisite, we would declare the following people unqualified to express an opinion on matters religious: Thomas Merton, Flannery O'Connor, Graham Greene, Evelyn Waugh, C.S. Lewis, William F. Buckley, W.H. Auden, or, to bring things more up to date, Fr. James Martin, George Weigel, and E.J. Dionne. In point of fact, it is often the case that those outside of the official academy often have the freshest and most insightful perspectives, precisely because they aren't sequestered in the echo-chamber of politically correct faculty lounge discourse.

This letter to the *Times* is indicative of a much wider problem in our intellectual culture, namely, the tendency to avoid real argument and to censor what makes us, for whatever reason, uncomfortable. On many of our university campuses this incarnates itself as a demand for "safe spaces," where students won't feel threatened by certain forms of speech or writing. For the first time in my life, I agreed with Richard Dawkins, who declared on Twitter around this time, "A university is not a 'safe space'. If you need a safe space, leave, go home, [and] hug your teddy...until [you are] ready for university."

So, in the spirit of Howard Sudberry, I would say to those who signed the letter against Ross Douthat, "Make an argument against him; prove him wrong; marshal your evidence; have a debate with him; take him on. But don't attempt to censor him." I understand that the signatories disagree with him, but he's playing by the rules.

John Henry Newman at the Synod on the Family

The controversies surrounding the recent Extraordinary Synod on the Family have often put me in mind of John Henry Cardinal Newman, possibly the greatest Catholic churchman of the nineteenth century. Newman wrote eloquently on an extraordinary range of topics, including university education, the interplay between faith and reason, the nature of papal authority, and the subtle manner in which we come to assent in matters of religion. But the arguments around this synod compel us to look at Newman's work regarding the evolution of doctrine.

When he was at mid-career and in the process of converting from Anglicanism to Roman Catholicism, Newman penned a masterpiece entitled *On the Development of Christian Doctrine*. In line with the evolutionary theories that were just emerging at that time—Hegel's work was dominant in most European universities and Darwin's *On the Origin of Species* would appear just a few years later—Newman argued that Christian doctrines are not given once for all and simply passed down unchanged from generation to generation. Rather, like seeds that unfold into plants or rivers that deepen and broaden over time, they develop, their various aspects and implications emerging in the course of lively rumination. It is assuredly not the case, for example, that the doctrine of the Trinity was delivered fully-grown into the minds of the first disciples of Jesus and then passed on like a football across the ages. On the contrary, it took hundreds of years for the seed of that teaching to grow into the mighty tree of Augustine's formulations in *De Trinitate* or Aquinas's complex treatise in the first part of the *Summa theologiae*. Moreover, Newman felt that even those definitive theological achievements in turn develop and unfold as they are mused over, turned around, questioned, and argued about. He concludes: "a real idea is equivalent to the sum total of its possible aspects." And those aspects appear only in the course of time and through the play of the lively minds that consider them. It is precisely in this context that Newman penned the most famous line of *On the Development of Christian Doctrine*: "In a higher world it is otherwise; but here below, to live is to change and to be perfect is to have changed often." Ideas change because they are living things.

I realize that many, upon considering this view, will get nervous—as did many in Newman's day. Does this mean that doctrine is up for grabs? Should we keep our dogmatic statements, as one cynical wag once put it, in loose-leaf binders? To get some clarity on this point, I would recommend that we delve a little further into Newman's great book and examine the criteria that he laid out to determine the difference between a legitimate development (which makes the doctrine in question more fully itself) and a corruption (which undermines the doctrine). Newman presents seven in total, but I should like to examine just three.

The first is what he calls "preservation of type." A valid development preserves the essential form and structure of what came before. If that type is undermined, we are dealing with a corruption. Mind you, type can be maintained even through enormous superficial changes, as, to use Newman's own example, "a butterfly is a development of the caterpillar but not in any sense its image." And, by the same token, superficialities can remain largely unchanged even as the type utterly morphs, as happened, say, in the transition from the Roman Republic to the Roman Empire.

A second criterion is what Newman refers to as "conservative action upon its past." An evolution that simply reverses or contradicts what came before it is necessarily a corruption and not a development. In Newman's own words, an authentic development "is an addition that illustrates, not obscures; corroborates, not corrects, the body of thought from which it proceeds." In accord with this idea, Christianity could be seen as the development of Judaism, since it preserves the essential teachings and practices of that faith, even as it moves beyond them. Cardinal George Pell alluded to this principle when he said, during the synod debates, "the Church does not do backflips on doctrine." So, for example, if a proposal were put forth at the Extraordinary Synod that clearly contradicted the teaching of John Paul II in *Familiaris consortio* or Paul VI in *Humanae vitae*, it would certainly reflect a corruption.

A third criterion that Newman puts forward is what he calls "the power of assimilation." Just as a healthy organism takes in what it can from its environment, even as it resists what it must, so a sane and lively idea can take to itself what is best in the intellectual atmosphere, even as it throws off what is noxious. Both total accommodation to the culture and total resistance to it are usually signs of intellectual sickness.

Now how does all of this apply to the synod? Well, let's consider the proposal made by Cardinal Walter Kasper regarding Communion for the divorced and remarried. Is it an authentic development or a corruption of Catholic moral teaching and practice? Might I suggest that all of the disputants in that argument take a step back and assess the matter using Cardinal Newman's criteria? Would Newman be opposed in principle to change in this regard? Not necessarily, for he knew that to live is to change. Would he therefore enthusiastically embrace what Cardinal Kasper has proposed? Not necessarily, for it might represent a corruption. As the conversation continues to unfold, I think all sides would benefit from a careful reading of *On the Development of Christian Doctrine.*

A Lion of the American Church: Thoughts on the Passing of Cardinal George

Cardinal Francis George, who died in April 2015 at the age of 78, was obviously a man of enormous accomplishment and influence. He was a Cardinal of the Roman Church, a past president of the United States Conference of Catholic Bishops, the Archbishop of one of the largest and most complicated archdioceses in the world, and the intellectual leader of the American Church. A number of American bishops have told me that when Cardinal George spoke at the Bishops' meetings, the entire room would fall silent and *everyone* would listen.

But to understand this great man, I think we have to go back in imagination to when he was a kid from St. Pascal's parish on the northwest side of Chicago, who liked to ride his bike and run around with his friends, and who was an accomplished pianist and painter as well. At the age of thirteen, that young man was stricken with polio, a disease that nearly killed him and left him severely disabled. Running, bike riding, painting, and piano playing were forever behind him. I'm sure he was tempted to give up and withdraw into himself, but young Francis George, despite his handicap, pushed ahead with single-minded determination. The deepest longing of his heart was to become a priest, and this led him to apply to Quigley Seminary. Convinced that this boy with crutches and a brace couldn't make the difficult commute every day or keep up with the demands of the school, the officials at Quigley turned him away. Undeterred, he applied to join the Oblates of Mary Immaculate, a missionary congregation. Recognizing his enormous promise and inner strength, they took him in.

I bring us back to this moment of the cardinal's life, for it sheds light on two essential features of his personality. First, he was a man who never gave up. I had the privilege of living with Cardinal George for six years, and thus I was able to see his life close-up. He had an absolutely punishing schedule, which had him going morning, noon, and night practically every day of the week: administrative meetings, private conversations, banquets, liturgies, social functions, public speeches, etc. Never once, in all the years I lived with him, did I ever hear Cardinal George complain about what he was obliged to do. He simply went ahead, not grimly but with a sense of purpose. When he first spoke to the priests of the archdiocese as our Archbishop, he said, "Never feel sorry for yourself!" That piece of advice came, you could tell, from the gut.

Second, his identity as an Oblate of Mary Immaculate deeply marked him as a man of mission. The OMIs are a missionary congregation, whose work takes them all over the world, from Africa and Asia to Latin America, the Yukon, and Alaska—not to mention Texas and Belleville, Illinois. When he was a novice and young OMI seminarian in Belleville, Francis George heard the stories of missioners from the far reaches of the globe, and he imbibed their adventurous spirit. As the vicar general of his order, he undertook travels to dozens of countries on six continents, visiting with thousands of OMI evangelist priests. I was continually amazed at his detailed knowledge of the politics, culture, and history of almost any country or region you could name. It was born of lots of direct experience.

This missionary consciousness is precisely what informed the intellectual and pastoral project that was closest to his heart, namely, the evangelization of contemporary culture. In this, he showed himself a disciple of his great mentor Karol Wojtyla, Pope John Paul II. What Cardinal George brought rather uniquely to the table in this regard was a particularly clear grasp of the philosophical underpinnings of the Western, and especially the American, cultural matrix. Cardinal George often signaled his impatience with the term "countercultural" in regard to the Church's attitude vis-à-vis the ambient culture. His concern was that this can suggest a simple animosity, whereas the successful evangelist must love the culture he is endeavoring to address. But he saw a deeper problem as well, namely that, strictly speaking, it is impossible to be thoroughly countercultural, since such an attitude would set one, finally, against oneself. It would be a bit like a fish adamantly insisting that he swims athwart the ocean. Therefore, the one who would proclaim the Gospel in the contemporary American setting must appreciate that the American culture is sown liberally with *semina verbi* (seeds of the Word).

The first of these, in Cardinal George's judgment, is the modern sense of freedom and its accompanying rights. Following the prompts of Immanuel Kant, modern political theorists have held that all human beings possess a dignity which dictates that they should never be treated merely as a means but always as an end. It is interesting to note that the young Karol Wojtyla, in his early work in philosophical ethics, put a great premium on this second form of the Kantian categorical imperative. What Cardinal George helped us see is that, at its best, this modern stress is grounded in a fundamentally theological understanding of the human person as a creature of God. Were the human being simply an accidental product of the evolutionary process, then he would not enjoy the irreducible dignity that is assumed by Kant. Indeed, Kant's contemporary Thomas Jefferson rather clearly indicated that his understanding of human rights was conditioned by the Christian theological heritage when he specified that those rights are granted not by the state but by the Creator.

The Kantian-Jeffersonian philosophical anthropology must be distinguished, Cardinal George insisted, from that of Thomas Hobbes. On the Hobbesian reading, rights are grounded not so much in divine intentionality but in the unavoidability of desire. Hobbes opined—and John Locke essentially followed him—that we have a right to those things that we cannot *not* desire. For Hobbes this meant the sustenance of biological life and the avoidance of violent death, whereas for Locke it was somewhat broadened to include life, liberty, and property. The problem is that Hobbes's interpretation is thoroughly non-theological and his consequent understanding of the purpose of government is non-teleological, purely protective rather than directive. Government exists not for the achievement of the common good but for the mutual protection of the citizens. That the Hobbesian strain found its way into the American political imagination is clear from Jefferson's refusal to characterize the nature of happiness, even as he insisted on the universal right to pursue it. In a word, therefore, the Church can and must affirm, at least in its basic form, the Kantian understanding of freedom and rights, even as it can and must stand against the purely secularist Hobbesian notion.

Cardinal George knew that the prime spokesperson for this deft act of affirmation and negation was Pope John Paul II, who emerged, in the late twentieth century, as the most articulate and vociferous defender of human rights on the world stage. The cardinal drew attention to a speech that the pope made in Philadelphia in 1979. John Paul sang the praises of our Declaration of Independence, with its stress on God-given rights, but he filled in the theological background by referencing the Genesis account of our creation in the image and likeness of God. Pressing well past any sort of Hobbesian secularism and utilitarianism, the pope insisted that

Jefferson's ideal should inspire Americans to build a society that is marked by its care for the weakest and most vulnerable, especially the aged and the unborn.

The second major feature of modernity that Cardinal George identified is an extreme valorization of the physical sciences, in his own words, "the imposing of scientific method as *the* point of contact between human beings and the world and society into which they are born." The founders of modernity appreciated the sciences not only for their descriptive and predictive powers, but also for their liberating potential. Bacon, Descartes, Leibniz, Newton, Kant, and many others held that the mastery over nature provided by burgeoning physics, chemistry, medicine, etc. would free the human race from its age-old captivity to sickness and the strictures of time and space. But what this led to—and I see it practically every day in my evangelical work—was the development of a "scientism" which, as a matter of ideological conviction, excludes non-scientific or extra-scientific ways of knowing, including and especially religious ways. The scientistic attitude has also obscured the undeniably theological foundations for the scientific enterprise, namely, the assumptions that the world is not God (and hence can be analyzed) and that the world is stamped, in every detail, by intelligibility. Both of these assumptions are predicated upon the doctrine of creation, which the founders of modern science took in, along with their astronomy, mathematics, and physics, at Church-sponsored universities. In the measure that the sciences flow from and rest upon the properly theological presumptions that the non-divine universe is well-ordered and intelligible, Catholic theology can involve itself in a very fruitful dialogue with them; but in the measure that scientism comes to hold sway, the Church must resist.

One of Cardinal George's most memorable remarks is that liberal Catholicism is an exhausted project. It is important that we parse his words here carefully. By "liberal Catholicism" he means an approach to the Catholic faith that takes seriously the positive achievements of the modern culture. In this sense, Lacordaire, Lord Acton, Lamennais, von Döllinger, and Newman were all liberal Catholics—and their successors would include de Lubac, Rahner, Guardini, Ratzinger, and Congar. One of the permanent achievements of the liberal Catholic project, in Cardinal George's judgment, was "restoring to the center of the Church's consciousness the Gospel's assertion that Christ has set us free, but also for the insight and analysis that enabled the Church herself to break free of the conservative social structures in which she had become imprisoned." In this same vein, Hans Urs von Balthasar had called in the 1950s for a "razing of the bastions" behind which the Church had been crouching, in order to let out the life that she had preserved. And this is very much in line with Vatican II's limited accommodation to modernity in service of the evangelical mission. Liberal Catholicism also took into account the second great achievement of modernity, stressing that certain doctrinal formulations and Biblical interpretations had to be reassessed in light of the findings of modern science. One thinks in this context of the vociferous interventions, made by a number of bishops on the Council floor at Vatican II, concerning certain naïvely literalistic readings of the Old Testament.

All of this assimilation of the best of the modern represents the permanent achievement of Catholic liberalism, and this is why Cardinal George never argued that liberalism is simply a failed or useless project. He said it was an *exhausted* project, parasitical on a substance that no longer exists. What are the signs of this exhaustion? The cardinal explained that the liberal project has gone off the rails inasmuch as it "seems to interpret the Council as a mandate to change whatever in the Church clashes with modern society," as though, in the words of a notorious slogan from the 1960s, "the world sets the agenda for the Church." If the Church only provides vaguely religious motivation for the mission and work of secular society, then the Church has lost its soul, devolving into a cheerleader for modernity. The other principal sign of the exhaustion of the liberal project is its hyper-stress on freedom as self-assertion and self-definition. In Cardinal George's words: "the cultural fault line lies in a willingness to sacrifice even the Gospel truth in order to safeguard personal freedom construed as choice." We might suggest that another shadow side of Catholic liberalism is a tendency to accept the scientistic vision of reality as so normative that the properly supernatural is called into question. We see this both in a reduction of religion to ethics and the building of the kingdom on earth, as well as in extreme forms of historical-critical Biblical interpretation that rule out the supernatural as a matter of principle.

What is too often overlooked—especially in liberal circles— is that Cardinal George was just as impatient with certain forms of conservative Catholicism. Correctly perceiving that authentic Catholicism clashes with key elements of modern culture, some conservatives instinctively reached back to earlier cultural instantiations of Catholicism and absolutized them. They failed thereby to realize that robust Catholicism is, in Cardinal George's words, "radical in its critique of any society," be it second-century Rome, eighteenth-century France, or 1950s America. What he proposed, finally, was neither liberal nor conservative Catholicism, but "simply Catholicism," by which he meant the faith in its fullness, mediated through the successors of the Apostles.

At the heart of this Catholicism in full is relationality. Cardinal George often pointed out that Catholic ontology is inescapably relational, since it is grounded in the Creator God who is, himself, a communion of subsistent relations. More to it, the Creator, having made the universe *ex nihilo*, does not stand over and against his creatures in a standard "being-to-being" rapport; rather, his creative act here and now constitutes the to-be of creatures, so that every finite thing *is* a relation to God. Aquinas expressed this when he said that creation is "a kind of relation to the Creator, with freshness of being." This metaphysics of relationality stands in sharp distinction to the typically modern and nominalist ontology of individual things, which gave rise to the Hobbesian and Lockean political philosophy sketched above, whereby social relations are not natural but rather artificial and contractual. Since grace rests upon and elevates nature, we should not be surprised that the Church is marked by an even more radical relationality. Through the power of Christ, who is the Incarnation of the subsistent relation of the Trinity, creation is given the opportunity of participating in the divine life. This participation, made possible through grace, is far more intense than the relationships that ordinarily obtain between God and creatures and among creatures themselves, and Catholic ecclesiology expresses that intensity through a whole set of images: bride, body, mother, temple, etc.

In Cardinal George's striking language: "the Church is aware of herself as vital, and so calls herself a body. The Church is aware of herself as personal, and so calls herself a bride who surrenders to Christ. The Church is aware of herself as a subject, as an active, abiding presence that mediates a believer's experience, and so calls herself mother. The Church is aware of herself as integrated, and so describes herself as a temple of the Holy Spirit." Notice please the words being used here: vital, personal, present, surrendering, mother, integrated. They all speak of participation, interconnection, relationship, what Cardinal George called *esse per* (being through). This is the living organism of the Church, which relates in a complex way to the culture, assimilating and elevating what it can and resisting what it must. This is simply Catholicism.

Cardinal George was a spiritual father to me. In his determination, his pastoral devotion, his deep intelligence, his kindness of heart, he mediated the Holy Spirit. For this I will always be personally grateful to him. I believe that the entire Church, too, owes him a debt of gratitude for reminding us who we are and what our mission is.

Priests, Prophets, Kings

A classic characterization of Jesus is that he is priest, prophet, and king. As priest, he sanctifies, that is to say, he reestablishes the lost link between divinity and humanity; as prophet, he speaks and embodies the divine truth; and as king, he leads us on the right path, giving guidance to the human project. You might say that, as priest he is the life; as prophet he is the truth; and as king he is the way.

Not only is this *munus triplex* (triple office) a rich way to characterize the Lord; it is also a very good way to designate who the baptized are supposed to be. According to Catholic theology, baptism is much more than merely a symbolic sign of belonging to the Church. It is the means by which a person is incorporated into Christ, becoming a member of his mystical body. Baptism, accordingly, makes the baptized an *alter Christus*, "another Christ." This is precisely why, for example, every candidate for baptism is anointed with oil, just as, in the Old Testament, priests, prophets, and kings were anointed upon assumption of their offices.

So what does this look like in practice? How does it show itself in the lives of ordinary believers? Let us look at priesthood first. A priest fosters holiness, precisely in the measure that he or she serves as a bridge between God and human beings. In ancient Roman times, the priest was described as a pontifex, bridge-builder, and this remains a valid designation in the Christian context. The reconciliation of divinity and humanity produces in human beings a wholeness or integration, a coming together of the often warring elements within the self. The same dynamic obtains on a grander scale as well: when cities, societies, and cultures rediscover a link to God, they find an inner peace. And therefore baptized priests are meant, first, to embody the harmony that God wants between himself and those made in his image and likeness. They affect this through their own intense devotion to prayer, the sacraments, and the Mass. In their cultivation of a real friendship with the living Christ, they act out their priestly identity and purpose. Then they are sent out into families, communities, places of work, the political and cultural arenas, etc. in order to carry the integration they have found like a holy contagion. If baptized priests stop praying, stop going to Mass, stop frequenting the sacraments, they will become, in short order, like salt that has lost its savor.

What does it mean for the average baptized person to be a prophet? A person is a prophet in the measure that he or she bears the truth of God. G.K. Chesterton said that in an upside-down world such as ours, the prophet is the one who stands on his head so that he might see things aright. This is why, of course, prophets have always appeared more than a little insane. In fact, the Hebrew word for prophet, *nabi*, has the overtone of "madman." Well, of course: in a world that has lost its bearings, those who speak the divine truth will, perforce, appear unhinged. How does one cultivate this salutary madness? Baptized prophets should exercise their brains by studying philosophy, theology, spirituality, Church history, and the lives of the saints. And they can't be satisfied with reading superficial tracts designed for children. Augustine, Origen, Bernard, Aquinas, Ignatius, Newman, Chesterton, and Ratzinger beckon. If those classic authors are a bit intimidating, Fulton Sheen, C.S. Lewis, Peter Kreeft, George Weigel, and Robert Spitzer provide more accessible but still meaty fare. Having been illumined, these prophets are then sent out into their worlds as beacons of light. God knows that in our increasingly secularized society, such illumination is desperately needed, but if baptized prophets stop studying and stop speaking, they are like lamps over which a bushel basket has been placed.

Finally, what does it mean for the ordinary Catholic to be a king? In the theological sense, a king is someone who orders the charisms within a community so as to direct that community toward God. In this way, he is like the general of an army or the conductor of an orchestra: he coordinates the efforts and talents of a conglomeration of people in order to help them achieve a common purpose. Thus, a Catholic parent directs her children toward the accomplishment of their God-given missions, educating them, shaping them interiorly, molding their behavior, disciplining their desires, etc. A Catholic politician appreciates the moral dimension of his work, and legislates, cajoles, and directs accordingly. A Catholic private equity investor saves a company that provides indispensable jobs in a declining neighborhood, etc. How does one grow in the capacity to exercise kingly leadership? One can do so by overcoming the cultural prejudice in favor of a privatized religion. Most of the avatars of secularism would accept religion as a personal preoccupation, something along the lines of a hobby. But such an attenuated spirituality has nothing to do with a robustly Biblical sense of religion. On the Catholic reading, religious people—the baptized—come forth boldly and publicly and are more than willing to govern, to be kings, out of religious conviction. If you are looking for examples of what I'm describing here, look no further than William Lloyd Garrison, Fulton Sheen, Martin Luther King, or Dorothy Day. Baptized kings who refuse to reign are like a hilltop city covered in clouds.

The key to the renewal of our society is a recovery of the deepest meaning of baptism, to become priestly, prophetic, and kingly people.

MATTER AND SPIRIT

*Many Christians today remain haunted by the
Platonic view that matter and spirit are opponents
and that the purpose of life is finally to affect a
prison-break, releasing the soul from the body.
This might have been Plato's philosophy, but it has
precious little to do with the Bible. The hope of
ancient Israel was not a jail-break, not an escape
from this world, but precisely the unification of
heaven and earth in a great marriage.*

– BISHOP BARRON

St. John's Christmas Sermon

I would like to reflect, however inadequately, on one of the most magnificent passages in the Scriptures, indeed one of the gems of the Western literary tradition: the prologue to the Gospel of John (1:1-18). In many ways, the essential meaning of Christmas is contained in these elegantly crafted lines.

John commences: "In the beginning was the Word..." No first-century Jew would have missed the significance of that opening phrase, for the first word of the Hebrew Scriptures, *bereshit*, means "beginning." The evangelist is signaling that the story he will unfold is the tale of a new creation, a new beginning. The Word, he tells us, was not only with God from the beginning, but indeed was God. Whenever we use words, we express something of ourselves. For example, as I type these words, I'm telling you what I know about the prologue to the Johannine Gospel; when you speak to a friend, you're telling him or her how you feel or what you're afraid of; when an umpire shouts out a call, he's communicating how he has assessed a play, etc. But God, the sheer act of being itself, the perfect Creator of the universe, is able to utterly speak himself in one great Word, a Word that does not simply contain an aspect of his being but rather the whole of his being. This is why we say that the Word is "God from God, Light from Light, True God from True God;" and this is why St. John says that the Word was God.

Then we hear that through this Word "all things came to be." The *Logos* of God would necessarily contain the fullness of rationality and order, for he is nothing other than the mind of God. Hence when the Father made the universe, he "consulted" the Son, in the way that an artist might consult a preliminary draft or an architect a diagram. The Word is the prototype in which all forms of reasonable structure are implicitly present. And this is precisely why the universe is not dumbly there but intelligibly there, why it is marked, in every nook and cranny, by reasonability. As I have argued elsewhere, this mystical theology of creation through the Word is one of the conditions for the possibility of the physical sciences, for every scientist must assume the intelligibility of what she investigates.

Next, we are told of a "man sent by God" whose name was John. The Baptist came, St. John tells us, "as a witness to speak for the light," for he was not himself the light. From time immemorial, God has sent messengers, spokespersons. Think of all of the prophets and patriarchs of Israel, indeed of every sage, philosopher, artist, or poet who has communicated something of God's truth and beauty. All of these could be characterized as witnesses to the light. The point is that the one to whom the Baptist bears witness is someone qualitatively different, not one more bearer of the Word, however impressive, but the Word himself. What is being held off here is the tendency—as prevalent today as in the ancient world—to domesticate Jesus and turn him into one more in a long line of prophets and seers.

"He was in the world that had its being through him, and the world did not know him." In that pithily crafted line, we sense the whole tragedy of sin. Human beings were made by and for the Logos, and therefore they find their joy in a sort of sympathetic attunement to the Logos. Sin is the disharmony that comes when we fall out of alignment with God's reasonable purpose. But then comes the incomparably good news: "But to those who did accept him he gave power to become children of God." It is a basic principle of nature that nothing at a lower level of being can rise to a higher level unless it is drawn upward. A chemical can become part of a more complex structure only if it is assimilated by a plant; a plant can become an ingredient in a sentient nature only if it is devoured by an animal; an animal can participate in rationality only if it is taken in by a human being. By this same principle, a human being can become something higher not through his own efforts but only when a superior reality assimilates him. The Church fathers consistently taught that God became human so that humans might become God, which is to say, participants in the divine nature. In a word, we can become children of God precisely because God reached down to us and became a son of man.

The entire prologue comes to its climax with the magnificent phrase, "the Word was made flesh and lived among us." The gnostic temptation has tugged at the Church, on and off, for nearly the past two thousand years. This is the suggestion, common to all forms of puritanism, that the spiritual is attained through a negation of the material. But authentic Christianity, inspired by this stunning claim of St. John, has consistently held off gnosticism, for it knows that the Word of God took to himself a human nature and thereby elevated all of matter and made it a sacrament of the divine presence.

The Greek phrase behind "lived among us" is literally translated as "tabernacled among us" or "pitched his tent among us." No Jew of John's time would have missed the wonderful connection implied between Jesus and the temple. According to the book of Exodus, the Ark of the Covenant—the embodiment of Yahweh's presence—was originally housed in a tent or tabernacle. The evangelist is telling us that now, in the flesh of Jesus, Yahweh has established his definitive tabernacle among us.

All of this sublime theology is John the Evangelist's great Christmas sermon. I would invite you to return to it often in prayer and meditation.

Why You Need
Spiritual Food

Every third summer, the Catholic lectionary provides a series of readings for Sunday Mass from the sixth chapter of the Gospel of John. This is the magnificently crafted chapter in which the evangelist's Eucharistic theology is most fully presented. It is a curiosity of John's Gospel that the Last Supper scene includes no "institution narrative," which is to say, the account of what Jesus did with the bread and cup the night before he died. But, as many scholars have indicated, the Eucharist is a theme that runs right through the entirety of this Gospel, which finds its richest expression in the famous chapter six.

I won't focus in this essay on the great issue of the real presence—"My flesh is real food and my blood real drink"—but rather on the more general matter of spiritual nourishment. In early 2015 I spent a week in the hospital recovering from surgery, and for about three days I was not permitted to eat any solid food. What amazed me was how rapidly my body shrank. The muscles of my arms and legs began to quickly—and rather alarmingly—atrophy, and it proved difficult even to cross the room and sit up in a chair. Almost twenty years ago, a good friend and I undertook a bicycle trip from Paris to Rome, covering about seventy miles a day. We really pushed ourselves to the limit. One day, somewhere in the south of France, after about five hours of pedaling, I hit the wall. Though I had heard of this phenomenon, I had never experienced it before. When you hit the wall, you don't gradually slow down or calmly realize that you have to take a rest; you just stop, your body simply unable to go on.

May I suggest that these examples are very exact analogies to spiritual health and spiritual nourishment? Without food, the body quickly collapses; without spiritual food, the soul atrophies. It really is as simple as that. Though materialists of all stripes want to deny it, there is a dimension of the human person that goes beyond the merely physical, a dynamism that connects him or her with God. Classically, this link to the eternal is called the soul. (We oughtn't construe this, by the way, in the Cartesian manner, as though the soul is imprisoned by the body. Rather, we ought to follow Thomas Aquinas, who said, "the soul is in the body, not as contained by it, but containing it.")

What the soul requires for nourishment is the divine life, what the spiritual masters call "grace." It is of this sustenance that Jesus speaks in John 6: "Do not work for food that perishes but for the food that endures for eternal life." Most people are at least inchoately aware of the soul and its hunger, but they feed it with insufficient food: wealth, pleasure, power, honor. All of these are good in themselves, but none of them is designed to satisfy the longing of the soul. And this is precisely why some of the wealthiest, most famous, most accomplished people in our society are dying of spiritual starvation.

So where and how do we find the divine life? First, I would suggest, through prayer. The soul wants to pray every day, to speak to God and to listen to him. So we should spend time before the Blessed Sacrament, pray the rosary, do the Stations of the Cross, read the Bible in a meditative spirit, confess our sins, and, above all, go to Mass. A second way in which we encounter grace is through serious spiritual reading. One of the principal marks of an engaged Catholic is the faithful reading of spiritual and theological books. Most of us fill our minds with junk; but the mind, the soul, wants to be filled with the lofty things of God. Why have so many Catholic bookstores faded away? Because Catholics have stopped taking spiritual reading seriously. A third way to feed the soul is to practice the corporal and spiritual works of mercy. If you are spiritually hungry, feed the physically hungry, give drink to the thirsty, counsel the doubtful, visit the sick and imprisoned, pray for the living and the dead. You'll find that the more you empty yourself in love, the more satisfied your soul will feel.

Finally, and most importantly, you can receive the Eucharist regularly. In his discourse on the Eucharist in John 6, Jesus says, "I am the bread of life; whoever comes to me will never hunger, and whoever believes in me will never thirst." The divine life is found, *par excellence*, in the transfigured bread and wine of the Eucharist. Aquinas said that the other sacraments contain the *virtus Christi* (the power of Christ) but that the Eucharist contains *ipse Christus* (Christ himself). What the soul is hungry for, finally, is the person of Jesus, the body and blood of Christ. Without feeding regularly on that food, the soul will atrophy.

Why are so many Catholics feeling lost today? Well, 75% of them stay away from the Mass and the Eucharist on a regular basis. This is not rocket science: if you want to be healthy spiritually, you've got to eat!

Bruce Jenner, the "Shadow Council," and St. Irenaeus

Two news items from 2015 put me in mind of St. Irenaeus and the battle he waged, nineteen centuries ago, against the Gnostic heresy. The first was the emergence of Bruce Jenner as a "woman" named Caitlyn, and the second was a "shadow council" that took place in Rome and apparently called for the victory of a "theology of love" over John Paul II's theology of the body.

I realize this requires a bit of unpacking. Let me begin with Irenaeus. Toward the end of the second century, Irenaeus, the bishop of Lyons, wrote a text called *Adversus haereses* (Against the Heresies), and the principle heresy that he identified therein was Gnosticism. Gnosticism was, and is, a multi-headed beast, but one of its major tenets is that matter is a fallen, inferior form of being, produced by a low-level deity. The soul is trapped in matter, and the whole point of the spiritual life is to acquire the *gnosis* (knowledge) requisite to facilitate an escape of the soul from the body. On the Gnostic interpretation, the Yahweh of the Old Testament, who foolishly pronounced the material world good, is none other than the compromised god described in Gnostic cosmology, and Jesus is the prophet who came with the saving knowledge of how to rise above the material realm. What Irenaeus intuited—and his intuition represented one of the decisive moments in the history of the Church—is that this point of view is directly repugnant to Biblical Christianity, which insists emphatically upon the goodness of matter. Scan through Irenaeus' voluminous writings, and you will find the word "body" over and over again. Creation, Incarnation, Resurrection; the theology of the Church, sacraments, redemption, the Eucharist, etc.; these all involve, he argued, bodiliness, materiality. For Irenaeus, redemption is decidedly not tantamount to the escape of the soul from the body; rather, it is the salvation and perfection of the body.

Now you might think that this is all a bit of ancient intellectual history, but think again. As I hinted above, the Gnostic heresy has proven remarkably durable, reasserting itself across the centuries. Its most distinctive mark is the denigration of matter and the tendency to set the spirit and the body in an antagonistic relationship. This is why many thinkers have identified the anthropology of René Descartes, which has radically influenced modern and contemporary attitudes, as neo-Gnostic. Descartes famously drove a wedge between spirit and matter, or in his language, between the *res cogitans* (thinking thing) and the *res extensa* (thing extended in space). In line with Gnostic intuitions, Descartes felt that the former belongs to a higher and more privileged dimension and that the latter is legitimately the object of manipulation and re-organization. Hence he says that the purpose of philosophy and science is to master nature, rather than to contemplate it. One would have to be blind not to notice how massively impactful that observation has proven to be. Echoes of Descartes's dualism can be heard in the writings of Kant, Hegel, and many of the master philosophers of modernity, and they can also be discerned in the speech and attitudes of millions of ordinary people today.

All of which brings me back to Bruce Jenner and to the "shadow council" in Rome. In justifying the transformation that he has undergone, Jenner consistently says something along these lines: "Deep down, I always knew that I was a woman, but I felt trapped in the body of a man. Therefore, I have the right to change my body to bring it in line with my true identity." Notice how the mind or the will—the inner self—is casually identified as the "real me" whereas the body is presented as an antagonist which can and should be manipulated by the authentic self. The soul and the body are in a master/slave relationship, the former legitimately dominating and remaking the latter. This schema is, to a tee, Gnostic—and just as repugnant to Biblical religion as it was nineteen hundred years ago. For Biblical people, the body can never be construed as a prison for the soul, nor as an object for the soul's manipulation. Moreover, the mind or will is not the "true self" standing over and against the body; rather, the body, with its distinctive form, intelligibility, and finality, is an essential constituent of the true self. Until we realize that the lionization of Caitlyn Jenner amounts to an embracing of Gnosticism, we haven't grasped the nettle of the issue.

And that brings us to the "shadow council" that took place in Rome. I want to be careful here, for I'm relying on a few reports concerning what was intended to be a private gathering of Church leaders and intellectuals. I certainly want to give all of the participants the benefit of the doubt, and I remain sincerely eager to hear their own accounting of what was discussed. But what particularly bothered me—in fact, it caused every single anti-Gnostic sensor in me to vibrate—was the claim that the secret council was calling for a "theology of love" that would supplant the theology of the body proposed by John Paul II. For Biblical people, human love is never a disembodied reality. Furthermore, love—which is an act of the will—does not hover above the body, but rather expresses itself through the body and according to the intelligibility of the body. To set the two in opposition, or to maintain that an inner act is somehow more important or comprehensive than the body, is to walk the Gnostic road—which is just as dangerous a path today as it was in the time of St. Irenaeus.

A Case for Celibacy
by Priests

Many people today have questioned the Catholic Church's discipline of priestly celibacy. Why does the Church continue to defend a practice that seems so unnatural and so unnecessary?

There is a very bad argument for celibacy, which has appeared throughout the tradition and which is, even today, defended by some. It goes something like this: Married life is spiritually suspect; priests, as religious leaders, should be spiritual athletes above reproach; therefore, priests shouldn't be married

This approach to the question is, in my judgment, not just stupid but dangerous, for it rests on presumptions that are repugnant to solid Christian doctrine. The Biblical teaching on creation implies the essential integrity of the world and everything in it.

Genesis tells us that God found each thing he had made good and that he found the ensemble of creatures very good. Catholic theology, at its best, has always been resolutely anti-dualist—and this means that matter, the body, marriage, and sexual activity are never, in themselves, to be despised.

But there is more to the doctrine of creation than an affirmation of the goodness of the world. To say that the finite realm in its entirety is created is to imply that nothing in the universe is God. All aspects of created reality reflect God and bear traces of the divine goodness—just as every detail of a building gives evidence of the mind of the architect—but no creature and no collection of creatures is divine, just as no part of a structure is the architect.

This distinction between God and the world is the ground for the anti-idolatry principle that is reiterated from the beginning to the end of the Bible: Do not turn something less than God into God.

Isaiah the prophet put it thus: "As high as the heavens are above the earth, so high are my thoughts above your thoughts and my ways above your ways, says the Lord" (cf. Isa 55:8-9) And it is at the heart of the First Commandment: "I am the Lord your God; you shall have no other gods besides me" (Exod 20:2-3; Deut 5:6-7). The Bible thus holds off all the attempts of human beings to divinize or render ultimate some worldly reality. The doctrine of creation, in a word, involves both a great "yes" and a great "no" to the universe.

Now there is a behavioral concomitant to the anti-idolatry principle, and it is called detachment. Detachment is the refusal to make anything less than God the organizing principle or center of one's life.

Anthony de Mello looked at it from the other side, and said that "an attachment is anything in this world—including your own life—that you are convinced you cannot live without." Even as we reverence everything that God has made, we must let go of everything that God has made, precisely for the sake of God.

This is why, as G.K. Chesterton noted, there is a tension to the Christian life. In accord with its affirmation of the world, the Church loves color, pageantry, music and rich decoration (as in the liturgy and papal ceremonials), even as, in accord with its detachment from the world, it loves the poverty of St. Francis and the simplicity of Mother Teresa.

The same tension governs its attitude toward sex and family. Again, in Chesterton's language, the Church is "fiercely for having children" (through marriage) even as it remains "fiercely against having them" (in religious celibacy).

Everything in this world—including sex and intimate friendship—is good, but impermanently so; all finite reality is beautiful, but its beauty, if I can put it in explicitly Catholic terms, is sacramental, not ultimate.

In the Biblical narratives, when God wanted to make a certain truth vividly known to his people, he would, from time to time, choose a prophet and command him to act out that truth, to embody it concretely.

For example, he told Hosea to marry the unfaithful Gomer in order to sacramentalize God's fidelity to wavering Israel. Thus, the truth of the non-ultimacy of sex, family, and worldly relationships can and should be proclaimed through words, but it will be believed only when people can see it.

This is why, the Church is convinced, God chooses certain people to be celibate. Their mission is to witness to a transcendent form of love, the way that we will love in heaven. In God's realm, we will experience a communion (bodily as well as spiritual) compared to which even the most intense forms of communion here below pale into insignificance, and celibates make this truth viscerally real for us now. Though one can present practical reasons for it, I believe that celibacy only finally makes sense in this eschatological context.

For years, the Rev. Andrew Greeley argued—quite rightly, in my view—that the priest is fascinating, and that a large part of this fascination comes from celibacy. The compelling quality of the priest is not a matter of superficial celebrity or charm. It is something much stranger, deeper, more mystical. It is the fascination for another world.

Why Jesus and Religion
Are Like Two Peas in a Pod

Every once in a while, a video unexpectedly becomes an internet sensation, garnering attention all over the place and spreading like wildfire through the virtual world. In 2012, a phenomenon of this type emerged in the form of a slickly produced video of a twenty-something-year-old man in a leather jacket half rapping, half speaking a poem about Jesus and religion—more specifically, how the former came to abolish the latter. Incredibly, this five-minute video (without much musical or visual enhancement) featuring a single person offering a not-very-sophisticated argument quickly garnered tens of millions of views!

What the young man in the video is presenting is a simplistic and radical form of evangelicalism, whose intellectual roots are in the thought of Martin Luther. Luther famously held that justification (or salvation) takes place through grace alone accepted in faith, and not from good works of any kind. To rely on liturgy or sacraments or moral effort for salvation, Luther thought, amounted to a pathetic "works righteousness," which he sharply contrasted to the "alien righteousness" that comes not from us but from Christ. This basic theological perspective led Luther (at least in some texts) to demonize many elements of ecclesial life as distractions from the grace offered through Jesus, and this is why we find even to this day in many evangelical Protestant churches a muting of the liturgical, the sacramental, the institutional, etc. These things constitute the "religion" that many evangelicals are against. And what the young man in the video learned from his evangelical teachers is that Jesus himself stood against these same "religious" distractions in his own day—which is why the Lord criticized the Pharisees for their fussy legalism and why he promised to tear down the temple in Jerusalem.

Now, Luther's theological theory had enormous implications culturally and politically as well. The freedom that Luther declared from Church law and institution soon morphed, in the minds of many, into a call for freedom from what were taken to be repressive political laws, traditions, and institutions. One of Luther's earliest and most provocative texts was titled *The Freedom of a Christian*, and it is no accident whatsoever that "freedom" has become the most powerful and explosive word in the modern political lexicon. Indeed, our own country, which proudly bears the title "the land of the free," was born in a great act of revolutionary anti-institutionalism—which goes a long way toward explaining why this young man's video is getting such great play in America.

Well, what does a Catholic make of all of this? Not much, as it turns out. In his theology of justification by grace alone, Luther conveniently overlooked a plethora of Biblical texts, including many from St. Paul, whom he claimed as his principal inspiration. In the parable of the sheep and the goats from Matthew 25, it is clear that salvation is dependent not primarily on faith but on the quality of our love, especially toward those who are weakest and poorest. The same Paul who spoke of justification through faith also said, "If I have faith enough to move the mountains, but have not love, I am nothing" (1 Cor 13:2) And the same Paul who experienced the risen Jesus in an intensely personal moment of conversion also spoke eloquently and often of becoming a member of Jesus' "mystical body," which is the Church. In short, the Bible drives a wedge neither between faith and love nor between individual salvation and ecclesial belonging. Further, the same Jesus who railed against the hypocritical legalism of the Pharisees also said, "I have come not to abolish the law but to fulfill it" (Matt 5:17). And the same Jesus who threatened to tear down the Temple in Jerusalem also promised "in three days to rebuild it" (John 2:19). The point is this: Jesus certainly criticized—even bitterly so—the corruptions in the institutional religion of his time, but he by no means called for its wholesale dismantling. He was, in point of fact, a loyal, observant, law-abiding Jew. What he affected was a transfiguration of the best of that classical Israelite religion—temple, law, priesthood, sacrifice, covenant—into the institutions, sacraments, practices, and structures of his Mystical Body, the Church.

If the young rapper in the video is against the corruptions of institutional religion up and down the ages, then he's got an ally in me. Finding them is like shooting fish in a barrel, and criticizing them is as easy as being against rotten eggs. But if he is advocating an individualist spirituality that ignores the thousands of ties that bind believers to one another through sacrament, practice, and institutional belonging, and if he's calling for a theology that divorces Jesus from his Body, the Church, then he's got an opponent in me. Lots of New Age devotees today want spirituality without religion, and lots of evangelicals want Jesus without religion. Both end up with abstractions. But the one thing Jesus is not is an abstraction. Rather, he is a spiritual power who makes himself available precisely in the dense institutional particularity of his Mystical Body across space and time. Jesus didn't come to abolish religion, he came to fulfill it.

What Easter Means

In first-century Judaism, there were many views concerning what happened to people after they died. Following a very venerable tradition, some said that death was the end, that the dead simply returned to the dust of the earth from which they came. Others maintained that the righteous dead would rise at the close of the age. Still others thought that the souls of the just went to live with God after the demise of their bodies. There were even some who believed in a kind of reincarnation.

What is particularly fascinating about the accounts of Jesus' resurrection is that none of these familiar frameworks of understanding is invoked. The first witnesses maintain that the same Jesus who had been brutally and unmistakably put to death and buried was, through the power of God, alive again. He was not vaguely "with God," nor had his soul escaped from his body; nor had he risen in a purely symbolic or metaphorical sense. He, Yeshua from Nazareth, the friend whom they knew, was alive again. What was expected for all the righteous dead at the end of time had happened, in time, to this one particular man, to this Jesus. It was the very novelty of the event that gave such energy and verve to the first Christian proclamation. On practically every page of the New Testament, we find a grab-you-by-the-lapels quality, for the early Christians were not trading in bland spiritual abstractions or moral bromides. They were trying to tell the whole world that something so new and astounding had happened, that nothing would ever again be the same.

Over the past couple of centuries, many thinkers, both inside and outside of the Christian churches, have endeavored to reduce the Resurrection message to the level of myth or symbol. Easter, they argued, was one more iteration of the "springtime saga" that can be found, in one form or another, in most cultures, namely, that life triumphs over death in the "resurrection" of nature after the bleak months of winter. Or it was a symbolic way of saying that the cause of Jesus lives on in his followers. But, as C.S. Lewis keenly observed, those who think the Resurrection story is a myth haven't read many myths. Mythic literature deals in ahistorical archetypes, and thus it tends to speak of things that happened "once upon a time" or "in a galaxy far, far away." But the Gospels don't use that sort of language. In describing the Resurrection, they mention particular places like Judea and Jerusalem, and they specify that the event took place when Pontius Pilate was the Roman governor of the region, and they name distinct individuals—Peter, John, Thomas, etc.—who encountered Jesus after he rose from the dead. Moreover, no one dies defending mythic claims. The myths of Greece, Rome, and Egypt are powerful and illuminating indeed, but there are no martyrs to Zeus or Dionysus or Osiris. But practically all of the first heralds of the Resurrection went to their deaths defending the truth of their message.

Yet assuming the resurrection is true, what does it *mean*? It means, first, that the customary manner in which we understand the relationship between order and violence—from the *Epic of Gilgamesh* to "Game of Thrones"—has to be rethought. On the standard realpolitik reading of things, order comes about through the violent imposition of strength. And if that order is lost or compromised, it must be restored through answering violence. In Jesus' time, the great principle of order was the Empire of Rome, which maintained its hold through the exertions of its massive army and through the imposition of harsh punishment on those who opposed its purposes. The most terrible and fearsome of these punishments was, of course, the cross, a particularly brutal mode of torture that was purposely carried out in public so as to have the greatest deterrent effect. It was on one of these Roman crosses that Jesus of Nazareth was put to death, having been betrayed and abandoned by his friends and condemned by a corrupt tribunal of collaborators.

When the risen Jesus presented himself alive to his disciples, they were afraid. Their fear might not have been simply a function of their seeing something uncanny; it might have been grounded in the assumption that he was back for vengeance. However, after showing his wounds, the risen Jesus said to his friends *Shalom*, peace. The teacher who had urged his followers to turn the other cheek and to meet violence with forgiveness exemplified his own teaching in the most vivid way possible. And what he showed thereby was that that the divine manner of establishing order has nothing to do with violence, retribution, or eye-for-an-eye retaliation. Instead, it has to do with a love that swallows up hate, with forgiveness that triumphs over aggression. It is this great resurrection principle which, explicitly or implicitly, undergirded the liberating work of Martin Luther King in America, of Gandhi in India, of Bishop Desmond Tutu in South Africa, and of John Paul II in Poland. Those great practitioners of nonviolent resistance were able to stand athwart the received wisdom only because they had some sense that in opting for the way of love they were going with the deepest grain of reality, operating in concert with the purposes of God.

Secondly, the Resurrection means that God has not given up on his creation. According to the well-known account in the book of Genesis, God made the whole array of finite things—sun, moon, planets, stars, animals, plants, things that creep and crawl on the earth—and found it all good, even very good. There is not a hint of dualism or Manichaeism in the Biblical vision, no setting of the spiritual over and against the material. All that God has made reflects some aspect of his goodness, and all created things together constitute a beautiful and tightly-woven tapestry. As the Old Testament lays out the story, human sin made a wreck of God's creation, turning the garden into a desert. But the faithful God kept sending rescue operation after rescue operation: Noah's Ark, the prophets, the Law, the temple, the people Israel itself. Finally, he sent his only Son, the perfect icon or incarnation of his love. In raising that Son from the dead, God definitively saved and ratified his creation—very much including the material dimension of it (which is why it matters that Jesus was raised bodily from death). Over and again, we have said no to what God has made, but God stubbornly says yes. Inspired by this divine yes, we always have a reason to hope.

The Startlingly Good News
of the Resurrection

In 2015, just a few weeks before the most significant Christian holy day of the year, British Prime Minister David Cameron, speaking on an evangelical radio program, articulated what, for him, is the meaning of Easter. He explained that the central message of Easter is "kindness, compassion, hard work, and responsibility." Now, I'm for all of those virtues, but so, I would venture to guess, is any decent person from any background, religious or non-religious. Buddhists, Muslims, Hindus, Jews, fair-minded agnostics and atheists would all subscribe to that rather abstract and harmless description of the significance of Easter. I suppose that, in a sense, we shouldn't blame the prime minister for his anodyne characterization, for the Christian churches in general, but especially the Anglican church, have not exactly distinguished themselves for the crispness and energy of their doctrinal formulations. But if that's all Easter is about, then the jig is up.

In point of fact, the message of Easter, properly understood, has always been and still is an explosion, an earthquake, a revolution. For the Easter faith—on clear display from the earliest days of the Christian movement—is that Jesus of Nazareth, a first-century Jew from the northern reaches of the Promised Land, who had been brutally put to death by the Roman authorities, is alive again through the power of the Holy Spirit. And not alive, I hasten to add, in some vague or metaphorical sense. That the Resurrection is a literary device, or a symbol that Jesus' cause goes on, is a fantasy born in the faculty lounges of Western universities over the past couple of centuries. The still-startling claim of the first witnesses is that Jesus rose bodily from death, presenting himself to his disciples to be seen, even handled. It is a contemporary prejudice that ancient people were naïve, easily duped, willing to believe any far-fetched tale, but this is simply not the case. They knew about visions, dreams, hallucinations, and even claims to ghostly hauntings. In fact, on St. Luke's telling, when the risen Lord appeared to his disciples in the Upper Room, their initial reaction was that they were seeing a specter. But Jesus himself moved quickly to allay such suspicions: "Look at my hands and my feet, that it is I myself. Touch me and see, because a ghost does not have flesh and bones as you can see I have" (Luke 24:39). While they were still, in Luke's words, "incredulous for joy" (24:41), the risen Jesus asked if there was anything to eat, and then consumed baked fish in their presence. This has nothing to do with fantasies, abstractions, or velleities, but rather with resurrection at every level.

Once we've come to some clarity about the Resurrection claim itself, we can begin to see why it still matters so massively. Let us look at the *kerygmatic* sermon that St. Peter preached in the Jerusalem Temple in the days immediately following Pentecost. Though it flies in the face of our expectations regarding preaching, there is nothing namby-pamby or ingratiating about what Peter tells the crowds. "The God of Abraham, the God of Isaac, and the God of Jacob...has glorified his servant Jesus, whom you handed over and denied in Pilate's presence... You denied the Holy and Righteous One and asked that a murderer be released to you. The author of life you put to death" (Acts 3:13-15). The Resurrection is being presented here as an affirmation of Jesus, to be sure, but also as a judgment on those who stood opposed to Jesus. St. Peter holds it up as the surest possible sign that God stands athwart the injustice, stupidity, and cruelty of the world and its leaders. If the Resurrection is only a bland symbol or a projection of our desires, then tyrants have nothing to fear from it. But if it is a fact of history, an act of the living God in space and time, then sinners have real cause to repent. It is absolutely no accident that the most brutal tyrants of the twentieth century moved quickly to eliminate those who would articulate, in no uncertain terms, the good news of the Resurrection. And it is, by the same token, no accident that some of the last century's most effective activists on behalf of justice—Bishop Tutu, Dr. Martin Luther King, Dorothy Day, and John Paul II—were ardent believers in the Resurrection of Jesus.

A second great implication of the Resurrection is that heaven and earth are coming together. As I've argued often before, many Christians today remain haunted by the Platonic view that matter and spirit are opponents and that the purpose of life is finally to affect a prison break, releasing the soul from the body. This might have been Plato's philosophy, but it has precious little to do with the Bible. The hope of ancient Israel was not a jailbreak, not an escape from this world, but precisely the unification of heaven and earth in a great marriage. Recall a central line from the prayer that Jesus bequeathed to his Church: "Thy kingdom come, thy will be done *on earth as it is in heaven.*" The bodily Resurrection of Jesus—the "first fruits of those who have fallen asleep" (1 Cor 15:20)—is the powerful sign that the two orders are in fact coming together. A body, which can be touched and which can consume baked fish—has found its way into the realm of heaven, or, to turn things around, heaven has reached down and transfigured a body, lifting it up into a higher pitch of perfection. Were the Resurrection but a clever myth, the two dimensions would be as separate as ever.

Do not accept a watered-down, easy-to-believe ersatz-of-the-Resurrection faith. Let it be what it was always meant to be: dynamite.

Why the Ascension of the Lord Matters

The feast of the Ascension of the Lord, which the Church cele-brates at the end of the Easter season, is, I admit, hard to explain to a lot of contemporary people. Jesus passed, in bodily form, from this world to heaven? Wouldn't his body still be in some identifiable place within the solar system or the galaxy? I'm sure that the tradi-tional formulation of the doctrine strikes many today as hopelessly pre-scientific and mythological. And even if we were to admit the possibility of such a transition happening in regard to Jesus, how would this in any way affect us spiritually?

The key to understanding both the meaning and signifi-cance of this feast is a recovery of the Jewish sense of heaven and earth. In regard to "heaven" and "earth," most of us are, whether we know it or not, Greek in our thought patterns. By this I mean that we tend to set up—in the manner of the ancient Greek philosophers—a rather sharp dichotomy between the material and the spiritual, be-tween the realm of appearance and the realm of true reality, between the fleeting earth and the permanent heaven. And if we're spiritu-ally minded, we tend to think of salvation as an escape from this world—this vale of tears—to a disembodied state called "heaven." The problem is that these convictions have far more to do with Plato than with the Bible.

Biblical cosmology is not fundamentally dualistic. It speaks indeed of "heaven" and "earth," but it sees these two realms as in-teracting and interpenetrating fields of force. Heaven, the arena of

God and the angels, touches upon and calls out to earth, the arena of humans, animals, plants, and planets. On the Biblical reading, salvation, therefore, is a matter of the meeting of heaven and earth, so that God might reign as thoroughly here below as he does on high. Jesus' great prayer, which is constantly on the lips of Christians, is distinctively Jewish in inspiration: "Thy kingdom come, thy will be done, on earth as it is in heaven." Notice please that this is decidedly not a prayer that we might escape from the earth, but rather that earth and heaven might come together. The Lord's prayer recapitulates and raises to a new level what the prophet Isaiah anticipated: "the knowledge of the Lord will fill the earth, as the water covers the sea" (11:9).

The first Christians saw the Resurrection of Jesus from the dead as the commencement of the process by which earth and heaven were being reconciled. They appreciated the risen Christ as the heavenly ruler of the nations, the one who would bring the justice of heaven to this world. And this is precisely why people like Peter, Paul, Thomas, Andrew, and John went to the ends of the earth to proclaim this new state of affairs: "Jesus is Lord!" What began in the Lord's resurrection is now ready to burst forth and flood the world through the work of the disciples. Accordingly, just before ascending to heaven, Jesus said, "You will receive power when the Holy Spirit comes upon you, and you will be my witnesses in Jerusalem, throughout Judea and Samaria, and to the ends of the earth" (Acts 1:8). It is fascinating to note how the Ascension and Pentecost are linked: in the Ascension, something of earth moves into the heavenly sphere, and at Pentecost, something of heaven—the Holy Spirit—invades the earth. The two events constitute, in short, a foretaste of the great reconciliation for which the entire Jewish religion had been yearning for centuries.

The Church, guided by the Holy Spirit down through the ages, is meant to be the privileged place where this coming-together happens. In good preaching, in great Christian art, in the architecture of our churches and cathedrals, in the corporal and spiritual works of mercy, in the lives of the saints, and perhaps especially in the liturgy, earth and heaven meet. Think of the moment at Mass, just before the singing of the Sanctus, when the priest invokes the angels (the realm of heaven) and encourages us: "May our voices, we pray, join with theirs in one chorus of exultant praise." What he is suggesting is that earth might, with Christ, ascend to heaven and that heaven, in the person of the Holy Spirit, might descend to earth—and that the two dimensions might sing together in harmony.

What I hope has become clear in the course of this discussion is that the Ascension of Jesus has nothing to do with a literal journey into the stratosphere, for that would involve simply a transfer to another position within "the world." The Ascension is Jesus' journey not to another place but to another dimension. But this dimension to which he has gone is not alien to us. It is instead a source of inspiration, power, and direction. And this is why the angels (denizens of heaven) who appear to the disciples just after Jesus' departure say, "Men of Galilee, why are you standing there looking at the sky?" (Acts 1:11). What they are hinting at, none too subtly, is this: under the influence of Jesus' spirit, get to work! Do all that you can to foster the marriage of heaven and earth! Get on with the mission of the church!

FREEDOM AND
DISCIPLINE

The view of liberty which has shaped our culture is
what we might call the freedom of indifference.
On this reading, freedom is the capacity to say "yes"
or "no" simply on the basis of one's own inclinations
and according to one's own decision. Here, personal
choice is paramount. We can clearly see this
privileging of choice in the contemporary economic,
political, and cultural arenas. But there is a
more classical understanding of liberty, which might
be characterized as the freedom for excellence.
On this reading, freedom is the disciplining of desire
so as to make the achievement of the good, first
possible, then effortless.

– BISHOP BARRON

What Is Our
Fundamental Problem?

Every few years at the beginning of Lent, we hear from Genesis 3, which deals with the creation of human beings and their subsequent fall from friendship with God. Like a baseball coach who compels even his veterans to re-learn the basics of the game every spring, the Church invites us, during the spring training of Lent, to re-visit the spiritual fundamentals. And they are on no clearer display than in this great archetypal story.

We hear that "The Lord God formed man out of the clay of the ground and blew into his nostrils the breath of life." The God of the Bible never despises matter, for he created it, and everything that he made is good. Our bodies are indeed made from the earth, from the lowly stuff of atoms, molecules, and minerals. It is of singular importance to realize that sin is not a function of matter, not the consequence of our embodied nature. God exults in our physicality, and so should we. But we are more than mere matter, for God blew into us a life akin to his own and ordered to him: minds that seek absolute Truth, wills that desire Goodness itself, and souls that will not rest until they come into the presence of the fullness of Beauty. The tragedy of the secularist ideology is that it denies this properly spiritual dimension of human existence, reducing everything in us to matter alone and construing the deepest aspirations of the heart as psychological quirks or wish-fulfilling delusions. Thomas Aquinas said that the human being is a sort of microcosm, for he contains within himself both the physical and the spiritual. To know and honor both dimensions of our humanity is the path of joyful integration; to overstress one or the other is, concomitantly, a principal source of mischief.

The book of Genesis tells us that God placed his human creatures in the midst of a garden and gave them free rein to eat of practically all of the trees found there. Unlike the gods of classical mythology, the God of the Bible is not in a rivalrous relationship to human beings. On the contrary, his glory is that we be fully alive, for he made us solely for the purpose of sharing his joy with us. This is why the Church fathers consistently interpreted the trees in the garden as evocative of philosophy, science, politics, art, stimulating conversation, friendship, sexuality—all the things that make human life rich and full. This is also why puritanical fussiness about pleasures both intellectual and sensual is simply not Biblical.

The original couple was told to refrain from eating the fruit of only one tree—and thereupon hangs a rather important tale. The tree in question is identified as the tree of "the knowledge of good and evil" (Gen 2:17), which is to say, a form of knowing that is the unique prerogative of God. Since God is himself the unconditioned good, he alone is the criterion of what is morally right and wrong. According to the semiotics of this story, therefore, the eating of the fruit of the forbidden tree is the act of arrogating to oneself what belongs in a privileged way to God. It is to make the human will itself the criterion of good and evil, and from this subtle move, on the Biblical reading, misery has followed as surely as night follows the day.

Notice how wickedly and cunningly the serpent tempted Eve: "God knows well that the moment you eat of it your eyes will be opened and you will be like gods who know what is good and what is evil." The basic sin, the original sin, is precisely this self-deification, this apotheosizing of the will. Lest you think all of this is just abstract theological musing, remember the 1992 Supreme Court decision in the matter of *Casey v. Planned Parenthood*. Writing for the majority in that case, Justice Kennedy opined that "at the heart of liberty is the right to define one's own concept of existence, of meaning, of the universe, of the mystery of human life." Frankly, I can't imagine a more perfect description of what it means to grasp at the tree of the knowledge of good and evil. If Justice Kennedy is right, individual freedom completely trumps objective value and becomes the indisputable criterion of right and wrong. And if the book of Genesis is right, such a move is the elemental dysfunction, the primordial mistake, the original calamity.

Of course, the Supreme Court simply gave formal expression to what is generally, though unthematically, accepted throughout much of contemporary Western culture. How many people—especially young people—today would casually hold that the determination of ethical rectitude is largely if not exclusively the prerogative of the individual? That's the fruit of eating of the tree of the knowledge of good and evil. Just after the fall, the first humans realized that they were naked and sought to cover themselves. I would interpret this not so much as shame but as deep and preoccupying self-consciousness. When we acknowledge that goodness and value lie outside of ourselves, in the objective order, we look outward, forgetting the self; but when we are convinced that our own freedom is the source of value, we tend to turn inward, protectively and fearfully.

What is fundamentally the problem, spiritually speaking? Why, deep down, are so many of us so unhappy? There is no better guide to answering these questions than chapter 3 of the book of Genesis.

Dietrich Von Hildebrand
and Our Relativistic Age

Postmodern relativism and deconstruction have produced, at the popular level, what I have termed the "Meh culture," that is to say, a culture dominated by the "whatever" attitude, a bland, detached indifferentism to the good and the true. How often have you heard someone say, "that's perhaps true for you but not for me," or "who are you to be imposing your values on me?" or, in the immortal words of the Dude in *The Big Lebowski*, "well, that's just, like, your opinion, man." Is it not a commonplace today that the only moral absolute that remains is the obligation to tolerate all points of view? What this subjectivism has conduced toward is a society lacking in energy and focus, one that cannot rouse itself to corporate action on behalf of some universal good. John Henry Newman said that well-defined banks are precisely what give verve and direction to a river. Once those banks are knocked down, the river will spread out, in short order, into a large, lazy lake. Applying the analogy, he argued that objective truths, clearly understood, are what give energy to a culture, and that when those truths are compromised in the name of freedom or toleration, said culture rapidly loses its purpose and cohesiveness. It is as though people today are floating on individual air mattresses on Newman's lazy lake, disconnected from one another, each locked in the isolation of his or her subjective judgments.

The great twentieth-century philosopher Dietrich von Hildebrand was one of the most articulate and incisive critics of the kind of relativism that has come to hold sway in our time. Following the prompts of both Plato and St. Augustine, Hildebrand delighted in showing the self-defeating incoherence of the position: if he is to be consistent, the relativist must hold that the claim of universal relativism is itself relative and hence not binding on anyone beside himself. Hildebrand taught that the philosophy of relativism flowed from the failure to honor the fundamental distinction between the arena of the merely subjectively satisfying and the arena of real values. There are many things and experiences that we seek because they please us or satisfy some basic need. One might find a cigarette appealing or a slice of pizza tasty or a political party useful, but in all these cases, one is bending the thing in question to his subjectivity. But there are other goods (Hildebrand's "values") that by their splendor, excellence, and intrinsic worth, draw the person out of himself, bending his subjectivity to them, drawing him toward self-transcendence.

In the presence of Beethoven's Ninth Symphony or Chartres Cathedral or Plato's *Republic* or the daily work of the Missionaries of Charity in Calcutta, one is compelled to acknowledge the preciousness of a reality that goes beyond the needs or expectations of one's ego. To characterize such things as merely subjectively satisfying, as though appreciating them were simply a matter of individual taste, would be simply ludicrous. The whole point of the moral life for Hildebrand is to cultivate the appropriate response to these objective values, to channel one's energies according to their demands. A crucial consequence of cultivating the proper response to values is that real community increases and intensifies. Whereas the merely subjectively satisfying correlates to the individual and his particular preferences, the objectively valuable correlates to the entire society of those drawn out of themselves and into a shared devotion.

One might be tempted to think, "so far, so abstract." But a new book titled *My Battle Against Hitler*, edited by two of the most devoted Hildebrandians on the scene today, John Crosby and his son John Henry Crosby, vividly demonstrates how Hildebrand himself lived out the principles of his moral philosophy in the face of the most vicious ideology of the last century. In the 1920s, as the National Socialist movement was gaining ground, Hildebrand, a professor of moral philosophy at the University of Munich, commenced to speak out against Hitler and his cronies. He saw Nazism—marked by anti-Semitism, crude nationalism, cruelty, and indifference to human dignity—as a repudiation of an entire range of objective values. Though it put his career and eventually his very life at risk, Hildebrand became an impassioned opponent of this political movement, which had begun to attract the support even of leading intellectuals. When Hitler came to power in 1933, Hildebrand was compelled to leave his beloved Munich and take up residence in Vienna. From 1933 to 1938, he continued to vocally oppose Hitler, founding and editing an anti-Nazi journal that so infuriated Hitler that the Führer referred to Hildebrand as his "number one enemy." When the German annexation of Austria took place, Hildebrand was aggressively sought by the Gestapo and narrowly escaped with his life, eventually settling in New York, where he became professor of philosophy at Fordham University.

A key concomitant of the assertion of objective value is the claim that objective disvalues exist as well. And just as we should cultivate a response of love and appreciation to value, we should cultivate a response of hatred and opposition to wickedness. Hildebrand saw that indifference to evil is as destructive as indifference to good. In our relativistic age, when we are confronted with a whole range of disvalues in our society, Hildebrand's is a voice we need to heed.

Pope Benedict XVI
Among the Germans

It was with a particular fascination that I followed the speeches that Pope Benedict XVI (Joseph Ratzinger) delivered in his native Germany in 2011. We can certainly hear Herr Doktor Professor Ratzinger in the distinctively academic rhetoric of the addresses, but we also hear the voice of a pastor, uttering a *cri de coeur* to his wandering flock. In his first speech on the tarmac in Berlin, upon being welcomed by the officials of the German government, Benedict XVI specified that his main purpose was not to foster diplomatic relations between the German nation and the Vatican City State—as welcome as that would be—but rather to speak of God.

This might appear a commonplace—a pope talking about God—but Benedict uttered those words in what is generally acknowledged to be the most secularized area on the planet, a cultural region marked by a sort of forgetfulness of God, a setting aside of ultimate reality, a complacent resting in the goods and joys of the empirically verifiable world. Sociologists have suggested that the European culture of the late twentieth and early twenty-first centuries is the very first one ever to have embraced a predominantly secularist ideology—and nowhere is this secularism more apparent and more deeply rooted than in northern Germany. There are many reasons for this—anger at the Church, disagreement over particular moral positions that the Church has taken, a newly aggressive atheism, etc.—but I believe the principle cause is a spiritual crisis prompted by the two terrible wars of the last century, fought largely on European soil and resulting in the deaths of tens of millions. Something in the European soul—especially the German soul—just broke in the twentieth century, and the damage has not yet been repaired. And so the vicar of Christ has indeed come to his homeland as a kind of missionary.

It is especially instructive to read the pope's address before the German Reichstag under this missionary rubric. Benedict reminded the lawmakers and political leaders of Germany that the Catholic Church never derived a concrete program of law from the data of revelation, as did many other religions, most notably Islam (think of Sharia law). Instead, Catholicism relied on philosophical principles articulated by ancient Greek philosophy, and on the practical wisdom inherent in the Roman legal custom. This allowed for a richly independent flourishing of political traditions and practices within the Christian cultural ambit. Though popes, emperors, and kings certainly clashed over the course of the centuries, the Catholic tradition, at its best, never pushed toward theocracy; rather, it recognized the legitimate authority of the state and the freedom legislators needed to do their practical work. In a word, the pope was saying to the German lawmakers, you should have no fear that the Church would seek to intervene in your work in a fussy, imperious manner.

However, he also reminded his hearers that all law rests finally upon certain fundamental moral principles that are not themselves the proper subject of debate and deliberation. The positive law—the concrete statutes formulated by cities and states—nests within the natural moral law, which in turn nests within the eternal law of God. When that set of relationships is ignored, positive law degenerates into pure subjectivism and relativism—and finally into an expression of the will of the most powerful within the society.

To concretize this point, he argued that the human rights so revered by the political theorists of the eighteenth century, and so respected by the secularist political establishment of the West to-day, are the moral absolutes upon which all legislative deliberation is properly founded. And he pressed the case: those rights are them-selves grounded in the existence of God, for it is only a Creator who can guarantee the equality and dignity of each individual. A healthy democracy, accordingly, must operate within this moral and spiri-tual framework, or it will devolve in short order into something at the very least dysfunctional, or, at worst, tyrannical. Speaking in the very building that Adolf Hitler's followers set on fire in order to ad-vance the Nazi program, Pope Benedict was not reluctant to invoke the example of Hitler in order to demonstrate what happens when the state sets the moral dimension aside and arrogates to itself the prerogatives of God.

The day after his address to the Reichstag, Pope Benedict journeyed to Erfurt, the little town where Martin Luther attended university and was later ordained to the priesthood. There, in the an-cient Augustinian monastery where Luther came of age spiritually, the pope addressed an ecumenical gathering. He spoke of Luther's enormous passion for God and his desire to know how he stood in regard to God. It was this burning preoccupation that conduced to-ward the development of the reformer's theology of justification by grace through faith. To be sure, Pope Benedict is not altogether com-fortable with the manner in which Luther articulated the dynamics of salvation—the pope is Catholic, after all—but he wanted to draw attention to Luther's deep and abiding interest in God and the things of God. The last thing one would ever be tempted to say about the founder of the Reformation is that he had forgotten God—and this in itself makes him, Pope Benedict thinks, an important object of meditation for the secularized Europe of the early twenty-first cen-tury.

The Death of God and the Loss of Human Dignity

I am sure that many of my readers have seen the appalling hidden-camera videos of two Planned Parenthood physicians bantering cheerfully with interlocutors posing as prospective buyers of the body parts of aborted infants. While they slurp wine in elegant restaurants, the good doctors—both women—blandly talk about what price they would expect for providing valuable inner organs, and how the skillful abortionists of Planned Parenthood know just how to murder babies so as not to damage the goods. One of the doctors specified that the abortion providers employ "less crunchy" methods when they know that the organs of a baby are going to be harvested for sale. Mind you, the "crunchiness" she's talking about is a reference to the skull-crushing and dismemberment by knife and suction typically employed in abortions. For me, the most bone-chilling moment was when one of the kindly physicians, informed that the price she was asking was too low, leered and said, "Oh good, because I'd like a Lamborghini."

Now, it is easy enough to remark and lament the moral coarseness of these women, the particularly repulsive way that they combine violence and greed. But I would like to explore a deeper issue that these videos bring to light, namely, the forgetfulness of the dignity of the human being that is on ever clearer display in our Western culture. One has only to consider the over 58 million abortions that have taken place, under full protection of the law, in our country since *Roe v. Wade* in 1973, or the ever more insistent push toward permitting euthanasia, even of children, in some European countries, or the wanton killings going on nightly in the streets of our major cities. The figures in my hometown of Chicago typically surpass those recorded in the battle grounds of the Middle East.

What makes this sort of startling violence against human beings possible, I would submit, is the attenuation of our sense of God's existence. In the classical Western perspective, the dignity of the human person is a consequence and function of his or her status as a creature of God. Precisely because the human being is made in the image and likeness of the Creator and destined, finally, for eternal life on high with God, he is a subject of inalienable rights. I use Jefferson's language from the Declaration of Independence on purpose here, for the great founding father knew that the absolute nature of the rights he was describing follows from their derivation from God: "they are endowed by their *Creator* with certain unalienable rights…" When God is removed from the picture, human rights evanesce rather rapidly, which can be seen with clarity in both ancient and modern times. For Cicero, Aristotle, and Plato, a cultural elite enjoyed rights, privileges, and dignity, while the vast majority of people were legitimately relegated to inferior status, some even to the condition of slavery. In the totalitarianisms of the last century—marked in every case by an aggressive dismissal of God—untold millions of human beings were treated as little more than vermin.

I realize that many philosophers and social theorists have tried to ground a sense of human dignity in something other than God, but these attempts have all proven fruitless. For instance, if human worth is a function of a person's intelligence or creativity or imagination, or her capacity to enter into friendship, then why not say that this worth disappears the moment those powers are underdeveloped, weakened, or eliminated altogether? Or if respect for human dignity is related to the strength of one's feelings for another person, then who is to say that that dignity vanishes once one's sentiments change or dry up? My suspicion is that if we interrogated people on the street and asked them why human beings should be respected, some version of this argument from sentimentality would emerge. But again, the problem is that feelings are so ephemeral, shifting and changing like the wind. If you doubt me, read some of the accounts of the officers and soldiers in the Nazi death camps, who, after years of killing, lost all feeling for those they were murdering, seeing them as little more than rats or insects.

For the past two hundred years, atheists have been loudly asserting that the dismissal of God will lead to human liberation. I would strenuously argue precisely the contrary. Once the human being is untethered from God, he becomes, in very short order, an object among objects, and hence susceptible to the grossest manipulation by the powerful and the self-interested. In the measure that people still speak of the irreducible dignity of the individual, they are, whether they know it or not, standing upon Biblical foundations. When those foundations are shaken—as they increasingly are today—a culture of death will follow just as surely as night follows day. If there is no God, then human beings are dispensable—so why not trade the organs of infants for a nice Lamborghini?

Your Life Does Not
Belong to You

It was recently revealed in a study that, for the first time in its history, Harvard University, which had been founded for religious purposes and named for a minister of the Gospel, has admitted a freshman class in which atheists and agnostics outnumber professed Christians and Jews. Around the same time, the House and the Senate of California passed a provision that allows for physician-assisted suicide in the Golden State. Though it might seem strange to suggest as much, I believe that the makeup of the Harvard freshman class and the passing of the suicide law are really related.

I suppose we shouldn't be too surprised that nonbelievers have come to outnumber believers among the rising cohort of the American aristocracy. For the whole of their lives, these young people have been immersed in the corrosive acids of relativism, scientism, and materialism. Though they have benefitted from every advantage that money can afford, they have been largely denied what the human heart most longs for: contact with the transcendent, with the good, the true, and the beautiful in their properly unconditioned form. But as Paul Tillich, echoing the Hebrew prophets, reminded us, we are built for worship, and therefore, in the absence of God, we will make some other value our ultimate concern. Wealth, power, pleasure, and honor have all played the role of false gods over the course of the human drama, but, today especially, freedom has emerged as the ultimate good, as the object of worship. And what this looks like on the ground is that our lives come to belong utterly to us, that we become great projects of self-creation and self-determination.

As the Bible tells it, the human project went off the rails at the moment when Adam arrogated to himself the prerogative of determining the meaning of his life, when he, in the agelessly beautiful poetry of the book of Genesis, ate of the tree of the knowledge of good and evil. Read the chapters that immediately follow the account of the fall, and you will discover the consequences of this deified freedom: jealousy, hatred, fratricide, imperialism, and the war of all against all. The rest of the Biblical narrative can be interpreted as God's attempt to convince human beings that their lives, in point of fact, do not belong to them. He did this by choosing a people whom he would form after his own mind and heart, teaching them how to think, how to behave, and, above all, how to worship. This holy people Israel—a word that means, marvelously, "the one who wrestles with God"—would then, by the splendor of their way of life, attract the rest of the world. On the Christian reading, this project reached its climax in the person of Jesus Christ, a first-century Israelite from the town of Nazareth, who was also the Incarnation of the living God. The coming-together of divinity and humanity, the meeting of infinite and finite freedom, Jesus embodies what God intended for us from the beginning.

And this is precisely why Paul, one of Jesus' first missionaries, announced him as *Kyrios* (Lord) to all the nations, and why he characterized himself as *doulos Christou Iesou* (a slave of Christ Jesus). Paul exulted in the fact that his life did not belong to him, but rather to Christ. In his letter to the Ephesians, he wrote, "there is a power already at work in you that can do infinitely more than you can ask or imagine" (3:20). He was referring to the Holy Spirit, who orders our freedom and who opens up possibilities utterly beyond our capacities. To follow the promptings of this Spirit is, for Paul and for all the Biblical authors, the source of life, joy, and true creativity.

All of which brings me back to Harvard and legalized suicide. The denial of God—or the blithe bracketing of the question of God—is not a harmless parlor game. Rather, it carries with it the gravest implications. If there is no God, then our lives do indeed belong to us, and we can do with them what we want. If there is no God, our lives have no ultimate meaning or transcendent purpose, and they become simply artifacts of our own designing. Accordingly, when they become too painful or too shallow or just too boring, we ought to have the prerogative to end them. We can argue the legality and even the morality of assisted suicide until the cows come home, but the real issue that has to be engaged is that of God's existence.

The incoming freshman class at Harvard is a disturbing omen indeed, for the more our society drifts into atheism, the more human life is under threat. The less we are willing even to wrestle with God, the more dehumanized we become.

Why Goodness
Depends on God

One of the commonest observations made by opponents of religion is that we don't need God in order to have a coherent and integral morality. Atheists and agnostics are extremely sensitive to the charge that the rejection of God will conduce automatically to moral chaos. Consequently, they argue that a robust sense of ethics can be grounded in the consensus of the human community over time, in the intuitions and sensibilities of decent people, etc.

What I would like to do is lay out, in very brief compass, the Catholic understanding of the relationship between morality and the existence of God and to show, thereby, why it is indispensably important for a society that wishes to maintain its moral integrity to maintain a vibrant belief in God.

Why do we do the things that we do? What motivates us ethically? Right now, I am typing words on my keyboard. Why am I doing that? Well, I want to finish my article. Why do I want to do that? I want to communicate the truth as I see it to an audience who might benefit from it. Why would I want that? Well, I'm convinced that the truth is good in itself. Do you see what we've uncovered by this simple exercise? By searching out the motivation for the act of typing words, we have come to a basic or fundamental good, a value that is worthwhile for its own sake. My acts of typing, writing, and communicating are subordinate, finally, to the intrinsic value of the truth. Take another example. Just before composing that last sentence, I took a swig of water from a plastic bottle on my desk. Why did I do that? Well, I was thirsty and wanted to slake my thirst. But why did I want to do that? Hydrating my system is healthy. Why is health important? Because it sustains my life. Why is life worth pursuing? Well, because life is good in itself. Once more, this analysis of desire has revealed a basic or irreducible good. Catholic moral philosophy recognizes, besides truth and life, other basic values, including friendship, justice, and beauty, and it sees them as the structuring elements of the moral life.

When Pope Benedict XVI complained about a "dictatorship of relativism," and when Catholic philosophers worry over the triumph of the subjective in our culture, they are expressing their concerns that these irreducible values have been forgotten or occluded. In her great meditations on the sovereignty of the good, the Irish philosopher Iris Murdoch strenuously insists that the authentic good legitimately imposes itself on the human will and is not a creation of that will. At the limit, contemporary subjectivism apotheosizes the will so that it becomes the source of value, but this puffing up of our freedom is actually ruinous, for it prevents the appropriation of the objective values that will truly benefit us.

This "basic goods" theory also grounds the keen Catholic sense that there are certain acts that are intrinsically evil, that is, wrong no matter the circumstances of the act or the motivations of the agent. Slavery, the sexual abuse of children, adultery, racism, murder, etc. are intrinsically evil precisely because they involve direct attacks on basic goods. The moment we unmoor a moral system from these objective values, no act can be designated as intrinsically evil, and from that state of affairs moral chaos follows.

So far we have determined the objectivity of the ethical enterprise, but how does God figure into the system? Couldn't an honest secularist hold to objective moral goods but not hold to God's existence? Let's return to our analysis of the will in action. As we saw, the will is motivated, even in its simplest moves, by some sense, perhaps inchoate, of a moral value: truth, life, beauty, justice, etc. But having achieved some worldly good—say, that of writing this article, or slaking a thirst, or educating a child—the will is only incompletely satisfied. In point of fact, the achievement of some finite good tends to spur the will to want more of that good. Every scientist or philosopher knows that the answering of one question tends to open a hundred new ones; every social activist knows that righting one wrong awakens a desire to right a hundred more. Indeed, no achievement of truth, justice, life, or beauty in this world can satisfy the will, for the will is ordered to each of those goods in its properly unconditioned form. As Bernard Lonergan said, "the mind wants to know everything about everything." And as St. Augustine said, "Lord, you have made us for yourself; therefore our heart is restless until it rests in thee." You've noticed that I've slipped God somewhat slyly into the discussion! But I haven't done so illegitimately, for in the Catholic philosophical tradition, "God" is the name that we give to absolute or unconditioned goodness, justice, truth, and life.

Now we can see the relationship between God and the basic goods that ground the moral life: the latter are reflections of and participations in the former. As C.S. Lewis points out in *Mere Christianity*, the moral absolutes are, therefore, signposts of God. And this is precisely why the negation of God leads by a short route to the negation of moral absolutes and finally to a crass subjectivism. Removing God is tantamount to removing the ground for the basic goods, and once the basic goods have been eliminated, all that is left is the self-legislating and self-creating will. Thus, we should be wary indeed when atheists and agnostics blithely suggest that morality can endure apart from God. Much truer is Dostoyevsky's observation that once God is removed, anything is permissible.

The Tiny
Whispering Sound

I have long loved the cycle of stories in the first book of Kings that deal with the prophet Elijah (17-19, 21). In fact, I've often told people who are just getting interested in the Scriptures to commence with the fascinating, adventurous, and often comical stories concerning this prophet. His name tells us all we need to know about him. "Elijah" is the Anglicization of the Hebrew *Eliyahu*, which means, "Yahweh is God." People can be named from what they worship, what they hold to be of highest value. Thus, someone who values her work above all is a "company woman," and someone who prizes his family above all is a "family man;" someone who seeks pleasure as his highest good is a "good-time Charlie," etc. Elijah is a Yahweh man, for he worships the God of Israel. Once we know this, we know all we need to know about how he thinks and how he acts and reacts. Because he is a Yahweh man, he stands athwart the idolatry of King Ahab; because he is a Yahweh man, he is forced to flee the persecution of Queen Jezebel; because he is a Yahweh man, he seeks refuge on Horeb, the mountain of God.

While sojourning on Horeb, he hears that the Lord will be passing by. A mighty wind, an earthquake, and a devouring fire ensue, but the Lord, he knows, is not in those events. Then he hears "a tiny whispering sound" (19:12), and he knows that the true God is about to speak. What is this barely noticeable sound which Elijah finds infinitely compelling? It is, I submit, the voice of the conscience, that instinct of the heart by which we determine the difference between right and wrong. John Henry Newman referred to the conscience as "the aboriginal vicar of Christ in the soul." Newman held, of course, that the pope is the legitimate vicar of Christ on earth, and yet he thought that the conscience is a more fundamental, a more elemental, a more interior representative of Christ. Now I realize that, as post-Freudians, we are all too willing to write off the conscience as the internalized voice of our fathers, as the inherited prejudices of our society, or as the bitter fruit of all of our irrational repressions and hang-ups. Nevertheless, try as we might to dismiss it, the conscience quietly but firmly reasserts its authority, rewarding us when we do something morally praiseworthy and punishing us rather sharply when we do something immoral.

A comparison might enable us to see the distinctive profile of the conscience more clearly. When I compose an article, I usually have a sense, born of many years of experience, of whether the piece is relatively good or relatively weak. My writer's sensibility, accordingly, either "rewards" me or "punishes" me for my effort. Much the same could be said of a golfer's inner sense that tells him whether he has swung smoothly or awkwardly. Now, if I have written a less than stellar article, I might feel disappointed and regretful, and I might feel the obligation to get back to work and improve what I've composed. But my writer's sense never makes me feel ashamed of what I've written. But the conscience, which accuses me of immoral behavior, produces precisely this sense of shame, the kind of feeling I have when I have hurt someone that I love. Concomitantly, when I perform an act of great generosity, forgiveness, or compassion, my conscience produces in me a feeling of satisfaction akin to that which I have when I have pleased someone that I love.

This is because the conscience is much more than a sensibility or a criterion of judgment; it is indeed the representative in us of Someone that we love. And this is why, Newman concluded, we refer quite rightly to the voice of the conscience, though we wouldn't be tempted to refer to our aesthetic or athletic sensibilities as voices. It is the voice of Someone who is himself the final criterion of right and wrong, and who is capable of probing the human heart in its deepest interiority and finding us wherever we are: "Lord, you search me and you know me; you know my resting and my rising. You discern my purpose from afar. Before ever a word is on my lips, you know it, Lord, through and through" (Ps 139:1-4). In our culture, we have all been strictly trained to notice and deplore neurotic guilt, but we are often slow to appreciate the appropriate guilt that is the fruit of a robustly functioning conscience. The sense of moral desolation should not be automatically covered up, denied, or medicated, for it can be tantamount to a keenly felt experience of God.

Elijah could hear the tiny whispering sound of God's voice, even amidst the clamor of so many competing sounds, precisely because he was a man of Yahweh. His heart and mind and feelings were attuned, above all, to God. As has always been the case, people today (especially young people) hear myriad voices promising joy, peace, success, fulfillment. Sex, pleasure, ambition, political power, wealth—they all have avatars who shout in the public arena. But the only voice that matters is the tiny whispering sound of the conscience, and you will hear it clearly if you become another Elijah, another man or woman of God.

St. Irenaeus and the God
Who Doesn't Need Us

Back in 2009, I participated in the annual meeting of the Academy of Catholic Theology in Washington, D.C., a group of about fifty theologians dedicated to thinking according to the mind of the Church. Our general topic was the Trinity, and I had been invited to give one of the papers. I chose to focus on the work of St. Irenaeus, one of the earliest and most important of the fathers of the Church. Irenaeus was born around 125 in the town of Smyrna in Asia Minor. As a young man he became a disciple of Polycarp, who, in turn, had been a student of John the Evangelist. Later in life, Irenaeus journeyed to Rome and eventually to Lyons, where he was made bishop after the martyrdom of the previous leader. Irenaeus died around the year 200, most likely as a martyr, though the exact details of his death are lost to history.

His theological masterpiece is called *Adversus haereses* (Against the Heresies), but it is much more than a refutation of the major objections to Christian faith in his time. It is one of the most impressive expressions of Christian doctrine in the history of the Church, easily ranking with the *De Trinitate* of St. Augustine and the *Summa theologiae* of St. Thomas Aquinas. In my Washington paper, I argued that the master idea in Irenaeus's theology is that God has no need of anything outside of himself. I realize that this seems, at first blush, rather discouraging, but if we follow Irenaeus' lead, we see how, spiritually speaking, it opens up a whole new world. Irenaeus knew all about the pagan gods and goddesses who stood in desperate need of human praise and sacrifice, and he saw that a chief consequence of this theology is that people lived in fear. Since the gods needed us, they were wont to manipulate us to satisfy their desires, and if they were not sufficiently honored, they could (and would) lash out. But the God of the Bible, who is utterly perfect in himself, has no need of anything at all. Even in his great act of making the universe, he doesn't require any preexisting material with which to work; rather (and Irenaeus was the first major Christian theologian to see this), he creates the universe *ex nihilo* (from nothing). And precisely because he doesn't need the world, he makes the world in a sheerly generous act of love. Love, as I never tire of repeating, is not primarily a feeling or a sentiment, but instead an act of the will. It is to will the good of the other as other. Well, the God who has no self-interest at all can only love.

From this intuition, the whole theology of Irenaeus flows. God creates the cosmos in an explosion of generosity, giving rise to myriad plants, animals, planets, stars, angels, and human beings, all designed to reflect some aspect of his own splendor. Irenaeus loves to ring the changes on the metaphor of God as artist. Each element of creation is like a color applied to the canvas or a stone in the mosaic, or a note in an overarching harmony. If we can't appreciate the consonance of the many features of God's universe, it is only because our minds are too small to take in the Master's design. And his entire purpose in creating this symphonic order is to allow other realities to participate in his perfection.

At the summit of God's physical creation stands the human being, loved into existence as all things are, but invited to participate even more fully in God's perfection by loving his Creator in return. The most oft-cited quote from Irenaeus is from the fourth book of the *Adversus haereses*, and it runs as follows: "the glory of God is a human being fully alive." Do you see how this is precisely correlative to the assertion that God needs nothing? The glory of the pagan gods and goddesses was not a human being fully alive, but rather a human being in submission, a human being doing what he's been commanded to do. But the true God doesn't play such manipulative games. He finds his joy in willing, in the fullest measure, our good.

One of the most beautiful and intriguing of Irenaeus' ideas is that God functions as a sort of benevolent teacher, gradually educating the human race in the ways of love. He imagined Adam and Eve not so much as adults, endowed with every spiritual and intellectual perfection, but more as children or teenagers, inevitably awkward in their expressions of freedom. The long history of salvation is, therefore, God's patient attempt to train his human creatures to be his friends. All of the covenants, laws, commandments, and rituals of both ancient Israel and the Church should be seen in this light: not arbitrary impositions, but the structure that the Father God gives to order his children toward full flourishing.

There is much that we can learn from this ancient master of the Christian faith, especially concerning the good news of the God who doesn't need us!

The Glory of God Is a
Human Being "Fully Alive"

The evangelical bottom line is the cry, "Jesus Christ is risen from the dead." Tightly linked to that declaration is the conviction that Jesus is who he said he was, that Jesus' own claims to act and speak in the very person of God are justified. And from the divinity of Jesus there follows the radical humanism of Christianity.

It is this third evangelical principle that I should like to explore, however briefly, in this article. The Church Fathers consistently summed up the meaning of the Incarnation by using the formula "God became human, that humans might become God." God's entry into our humanity, even to the point of personal union, amounts, they saw, to the greatest possible affirmation and elevation of the human. St. Irenaeus, the great second-century theologian, expressed the essence of Christianity with the pithy adage "the glory of God is a human being fully alive!"

Now I realize that much of this is counter-intuitive. For many, Catholic Christianity is anti-humanist, a system characterized by an array of laws controlling self-expression, especially in the area of sexuality. According to the standard modern telling of the story, human progress is tantamount to an increase of personal freedom, and the enemy of this progress (if the darker sub-text of the narrative is allowed to emerge) is fussy, moralizing Christianity. How did we get from St. Irenaeus's exuberant Christian humanism to the modern suspicion of Christianity as the chief opponent of human progress? Much depends on how we construe freedom.

The view of liberty that has shaped our culture is what we might call the freedom of indifference. On this reading, freedom is the capacity to say "yes" or "no" simply on the basis of one's own inclinations and according to one's own decisions. Here, personal choice is paramount. We can clearly see this privileging of choice in the contemporary economic, political, and cultural arenas. But there is a more classical understanding of liberty, which might be characterized as the freedom for excellence. On this reading, freedom is the disciplining of desire so as to make the achievement of the good first possible, then effortless. Thus I become increasingly free in my use of the English language the more my mind and will are trained in the rules and traditions of English. If I am utterly shaped by the world of English, I become an utterly free user of the language, able to say whatever I want, whatever needs to be said.

In a similar way, I become freer in playing basketball the more the moves of the game are placed, through exercise and discipline, into my body. If I were completely formed by the world of basketball, I could outplay Michael Jordan, for I would be able to do effortlessly whatever the game demanded of me. For the freedom of indifference, objective rules, orders, and disciplines are problematic, for they are felt, necessarily, as limitations. But for the second type of freedom, such laws are liberating, for they make the achievement of some great good possible.

St. Paul said, "I am the slave of Christ Jesus" (cf. Rom 1:1), and "it is for freedom that Christ has set you free" (Gal 5:1). For the advocate of the freedom of indifference, the juxtaposition of those two claims makes not a bit of sense. To be a slave of anyone is, necessarily, not to be free to choose. But for the devotee of the freedom for excellence, Paul's statements are completely coherent. The more I surrender to Christ Jesus, who is himself the greatest possible good, the very Incarnation of God, the freer I am to be who I am supposed to be. The more Christ becomes the master of my life, the more I internalize his moral demands, the freer I am to be a child of God, to respond promptly to the call of the Father.

Finally, human beings are not hungry to choose; they are hungry to choose the good. They don't want the freedom of the libertine; they want the freedom of the saint. And it is precisely this latter freedom that evangelization offers, because it offers Christ. Strange as it is to say, one of the greatest evangelists in the New Testament is Pontius Pilate. Presenting the scourged Jesus to the crowds, he says, "Behold the man" (John 19:15). In the delicious irony of John's Gospel, Pilate is unwittingly drawing attention to the fact that Jesus, completely acquiescent to the will of his Father, even to the point of accepting torture and death, is in fact "the man," humanity at its fullest and most free.

The evangelist today does the same thing. She holds up Christ—human freedom and divine truth in perfect harmony—and she says, "Behold, humanity, behold the best you can be."

Thomas More and
the Bishop of Rome

My favorite movie is *A Man For All Seasons*, a film based on the Robert Bolt play of the same name. I first saw it when I was in high school, and I've watched it at least once a year every year since then. When I was teaching full time at the seminary, I would show it to my students, and on June 22nd I would offer a screening to my fellow faculty members. That date, of course, is not accidental, for it is the feast day of the great St. Thomas More, with whose final years the movie deals.

The drama of *A Man For All Seasons* turns around King Henry VIII's attempt to secure a divorce from his first wife, Catharine of Aragon, who had been unable to produce for the king a male heir. Through the agency of Cardinal Wolsey, his chancellor, Henry sought a dispensation from the pope, but the holy father refused. Upon the death of Wolsey, the King made Thomas More, a man noted for his scholarship, diplomatic skill, and sanctity, his next chancellor, and he continued in his efforts to persuade the pope. When he was met, once again, with a rebuff, Henry took matters into his own hands, breaking with Rome and declaring himself supreme head of a new English church, which promptly granted him the divorce he had so ardently sought. Thomas More had been extremely loyal to Henry VIII and solicitous for the good of the English government, but this was too much. Without explicitly providing a reason to explain his action, he simply resigned his office as chancellor. Some of the most affecting scenes in *A Man For All Seasons* have to do with the years following More's resignation, when Henry tried, by various means, to frighten and cajole his former chancellor into supporting the new religious arrangement. Through it all, More (played by the magnificent Paul Scofield) held steady, even when he was stripped of his freedom, locked up in the Tower of London, and threatened with the rack.

Finally, he was forced to stand trial for high treason. The proceedings took place in a room with which More, a lifelong man of the law, was well acquainted: Westminster Hall. By means of legal chicanery, bribery, and jury tampering, More was convicted. Before they passed sentence, the judges asked if the former chancellor had anything to say. More rose to speak and delivered himself of a speech that is reproduced, almost word for word, in the script of the film. He explained that he had opposed Henry VIII because the king had assumed for himself an authority "that was granted by the mouth of Christ our Savior to St. Peter and the bishops of Rome, whilst he lived and was personally present here on earth"; and he concluded, "it is therefore insufficient in law to charge any Christian to obey it." As he stood condemned to death within the confines of Westminster Hall, Thomas More offered this exquisitely eloquent defense of the primacy and authority of the bishop of Rome. Scofield's reproduction of this speech is perhaps the most thrilling moment in *A Man For All Seasons*.

I couldn't help but think of all of this when a shy German scholar, who was, at the time, also the Bishop of Rome, entered that same Westminster Hall in 2010, in the presence of the representatives of the British political and judicial establishment. After making a few opening remarks, Pope Benedict XVI invoked the name of the man who, five centuries before, had stood condemned in that very place: "In particular, I recall the figure of St. Thomas More, the great English scholar and statesman, who is admired by believers and non-believers alike for the integrity with which he followed his conscience..." How strange and wonderful are the ways of God! In Westminster Hall, More had been a lone voice calling out in defense of the authority of the pope; half a millennium later, the pope came to the same place and vindicated the martyred saint.

But I don't mean this in a religiously jingoistic way, as if Benedict XVI had stripped the Archbishop of Canterbury of his power and reasserted Roman Catholic control over the Church of England. He did it by exercising his considerable moral authority. Before the prime minister and his government, in the presence of the four living former prime ministers, in the hearing of captains of industry and academics, Pope Benedict asserted that ethical principles, discerned through religious and philosophical forms of reasoning, must provide the basis for democratic deliberation and cannot themselves be the subject of that deliberation. He insisted—in his quiet way—that the bracketing or questioning of those moral absolutes leads any government on a short road to chaos. And this is why, the bishop of Rome went on, aggression toward religion—sadly apparent in the West today—is not only a violation of a basic human right, but also a threat to the integrity of the democratic experiment.

Thomas More was condemned in Westminster Hall for defending the authority of the pope. In that same place, a quietly authoritative bishop of Rome subtly rose to More's defense.

Why St. Junípero Serra
Matters Today

The canonization of Blessed Junípero Serra in Washington, D.C. in 2015—the first ever to take place on American soil—generated a good deal of controversy. To his defenders, Padre Serra was an intrepid evangelist and a model of Gospel living, while to his detractors, he was a shameless advocate of an oppressive colonial system that resulted in the deaths of tens of thousands of Indians. Even many who typically back Pope Francis see this canonization as a rare *faux pas* for the Argentine pontiff. What should we make of all this?

It might first be wise to rehearse some of the basic facts of Serra's life. He was born in 1713 on the beautiful island of Majorca off of the Spanish coast, and, as a very young man, he joined a particularly severe branch of the Franciscan order. He quickly became a star in the community, recognized for his impressive intellectual gifts and his profound spirituality. After many years of study, he earned his doctorate in philosophy and commenced a teaching career, which culminated in his receiving the Duns Scotus Chair of Philosophy. But when Padre Serra was thirty-six, he resolved to abandon his relatively comfortable life and promising career and become a missionary in the New World. He undertook this mission out of a sincere and deeply-felt desire to save souls, knowing full well that he would likely never return to his homeland. After spending a few years in Mexico City doing administrative work, he realized his dream to work with the native peoples of New Spain, first in Mexico and later in what was at the time called Baja California (Lower

California). When he was around fifty years old, he was asked by his superiors to lead a missionary endeavor in Alta California, more or less the present day state of California. With the help of a small band of Franciscan brothers, and under the protection of the Spanish government, he established a series of missions along the Pacific coast, from San Diego to San Francisco. He died in 1784, and was buried at the Mission San Carlos Borromeo in Carmel by the Sea.

Much of the disagreement regarding Junípero Serra hinges upon the interpretation of the mission project that he undertook. Though it is certainly true that the Imperial Spanish authorities had an interest in establishing a strong Spanish presence along the Pacific coast in order to block the intrusion of Russian settlers in the region, there is no doubt that Serra's first intention in setting up the missions was to evangelize the native peoples. What fired his heart above all was the prospect of announcing the good news of Jesus Christ to those who had never before heard it, and there is no question that his missions provided the institutional framework for that proclamation. Moreover, the missions were places where the Indians were taught the principles of agriculture and animal husbandry, which enabled them to move beyond a nomadic lifestyle. I find it fascinating, by the way, that there was nothing even vaguely analogous to these missions on the other side of the continent. Though by our standards they treated the native people in a rather patronizing manner, the Spanish evangelized and instructed the Indians, whereas the British settlers in the American colonies more or less pushed them out of the way.

Critics of Serra's project claim that Indians were compelled to join the missions, essentially as a slave labor force, and were baptized against their will. The consensus of responsible historians, however, is that both of these charges are false. In fact, the vast majority of the Indians recognized the advantage of living in connection with the missions, and only about 10% of those who had come to missions opted to leave. To be sure, those who left were hunted down and, upon their return, were sometimes subjected to corporal punishment. Indeed, there is real evidence that Padre Serra countenanced such violence: in one of his letters, he speaks of the need to punish wayward Indians the way a parent would chastise a recalcitrant child, and in another document, he authorizes the purchase of shackles for the mission in San Diego. Certainly from our more enlightened perspective, we would recognize such behavior as morally wrong, and it is no good trying to whitewash the historical record so as to present Serra as blameless.

Having acknowledged this, however, it is most important to note that the lion's share of the evidence we have strongly indicates that Serra was a steadfast friend to the native peoples, frequently defending them against the violence and prejudice of the Spanish civil authorities. Very much in the spirit of Bartolomé de Las Casas, the great sixteenth-century defender of the Indians, Serra insisted again and again upon the rights and prerogatives of the native tribes. In one case, he spoke out against the execution of an Indian who had killed one of Serra's own friends and colleagues, arguing that the whole point of his mission was to save life, not to take it. As Archbishop José Gomez has argued, this represents one of the first principled arguments against capital punishment ever to appear in Western culture.

One might ask why Pope Francis—who certainly knew all of the controversy surrounding Padre Serra—wanted to push ahead with this canonization. He did so, I would speculate, for two reasons. First, he understood that declaring someone a saint is not to declare him or her morally flawless, nor is it to countenance every institution with which the saint was associated. Secondly, and more importantly, he saw Junípero Serra as someone who, with extraordinary moral courage, went to the periphery of the society of his time in order to announce Jesus Christ. Serra could have pursued a very respectable career in the comfortable halls of the European academy; but he opted to go, at great personal cost, to the margins—and this makes him an extraordinary model of a Pope-Francis-style missionary.

Was Padre Serra perfect? By no means. Was he a saint? Absolutely.

Why Having a
Heart of Gold Is Not What
Christianity Is About

Many atheists and agnostics today insistently argue that it is altogether possible for nonbelievers in God to be morally upright. They resent the implication that the denial of God will lead inevitably to complete ethical relativism or nihilism. And they are quick to point out examples of nonreligious people who are models of kindness, compassion, justice, etc. In point of fact, a 2014 article proposed that nonbelievers are actually, on average, more morally praiseworthy than religious people. In this context, I recall Christopher Hitchens's remark that, all things considered, he would be more frightened of a group of people coming from a religious meeting than a group coming from a rock concert or home from a night on the town. God knows (pun intended) that during the last twenty years we've seen plenty of evidence from around the world of the godly behaving very badly indeed.

Though I could quarrel with a number of elements within this construal of things, I would actually gladly concede the major point that it is altogether possible for atheists and agnostics to be morally good. The classical Greek and Roman formulators of the theory of the virtues were certainly not believers in the Biblical God, and many of their neo-pagan successors today do indeed exhibit fine moral qualities. What I should like to do, however, is to use this controversy as a springboard to make a larger point, namely, that Christianity is not primarily about ethics, about "being a nice person," or, to use Flannery O'Connor's wry formula, "having a heart of gold." The moment Christians grant that Christianity's ultimate purpose is to make us ethically better people, they can no longer convincingly defend against the insinuation that, if some other system makes human beings just as good or better, Christianity has lost its *raison d'etre*.

Much of the confusion on this score can be traced to the influence of Immanuel Kant, especially his seminal text *Religion Within the Limits of Reason Alone*. Like so many of his Enlightenment-era confreres, Kant was impatient with the claims of the revealed religions. He saw them as unverifiable and irrational assertions that could be defended not through reason but only through violence. Do you see how much of the new atheism of the post-September-11th era is conditioned by a similar suspicion? Accordingly, he argued that, at its best, religion is not about dogma or doctrine or liturgy but about ethics. In the measure that the Scriptures, prayer, and belief make one morally good, they are admissible, but in the measure that they lead to moral corruption, they should be dispensed with. As religious people mature, Kant felt, they would naturally let those relatively extrinsic practices and convictions fall to the wayside, and would embrace the ethical core of their belief systems. Kant's army of disciples today includes such figures as John Shelby Spong, John Dominic Crossan, James Carroll, Bart Ehrman, and the late Marcus Borg, all of whom think that Christianity ought to be de-supernaturalized and re-presented as essentially a program of inclusion and social justice.

The problem with this Kantianism, both old and new, is that it runs dramatically counter to the witness of the first Christians, who were concerned, above all, not with an ethical program but with the explosive emergence of a new world. The letters of St. Paul, which are the earliest Christian texts we have, are particularly instructive on this score. One can find ethics in the writings of Paul, but one would be hard-pressed indeed to say that the principal theme of Romans, Galatians, Philippians, or first and second Corinthians is the laying out of a moral vision. The central motif of all of those letters is, in fact, Jesus Christ risen from the dead. For Paul, the resurrection of Jesus is the sign that the world as we know it—a world marked by death and the fear of death—is evanescing, and that a new order of things is emerging. This is why he tells the Corinthians that "the time is running out" (1 Cor 7:29) and "the world in its present form is passing away" (7:31); this is why he tells the Philippians that everything he once held to be of central importance he now considers as so much rubbish (3:8); this is why he tells the Romans that they are not justified by their own moral achievements but through the grace of Jesus Christ (3:18-23); and this is why he tells the Galatians that neither circumcision nor uncircumcision means anything (6:15); what counts is the "new creation." The new creation is shorthand for the overturning of the old world and the emergence of a new order through the resurrection of Jesus, the "first fruits of those who have fallen asleep" (1 Cor 15:20).

The inaugural speech of Jesus, as reported in the Gospel of Mark, commences with the announcement of the kingdom of God and then the exhortation to "repent and believe the good news" (1:15) We tend to automatically interpret repentance as a summons to moral conversion, but the Greek word that Mark employs is *metanoiete*, which means, literally, "go beyond the mind you have." On Mark's telling, Jesus is urging his listeners to change their way of thinking so as to see the new world that is coming into existence.

It is indeed the case that Buddhists, Hindus, Christians, Muslims, Jews, atheists, and agnostics can all be "good people." In terms of what we privilege today, they can all be tolerant, inclusive, and just.

But only Christians witness to an earthquake that has shaken the foundations of the world and turned every expectation upside down.

A "No" to a "No"
Is a "Yes"

One of the commonest complaints against Catholicism is that it is the religion of "no," especially in regard to the sexual dimension of life. As the rest of the culture is moving in a progressively more permissive direction, the Church seems to represent a crabbed, puritanical negativity toward sexuality. I think it is important, first, to make a distinction between two modalities of "no." On the one hand, there is "no," pure and simple—a denial, a negation of something good. When a jealous person sees someone else's success, he will say "no" to it, out of resentment. When a racist perceives the object of his irrational hatred, he will say "no" to him and try to undermine him. But on the other hand, there is a "no" which is in service of a "yes," since it represents a "no" to a "no"; it is a double negative that constitutes a positive. Any golf swing coach worth his salt will say "no" much more than he says "yes," because there are a thousand ways to swing a club poorly, but really only one way to swing it properly. So when he says "no," he is negating a series of negatives, trying to move his student onto the narrow path of the right swing. I would suggest that the many "no"s that the Church says to imperfect forms of sexual behavior are of this second type.

Now what, according to the mind of the Church, is the correct or proper expression of sexuality? In order to provide an adequate answer, it would be wise to consult a curious passage in Paul's letter to the Romans. The Apostle to the Gentiles writes: "Think of God's mercy...and worship him...in a way that is worthy of thinking beings, by offering your living bodies as a holy sacrifice, truly pleasing to God" (12:1). Sacrifice, of course, was central to ancient Israelite religion. A Jew would bring an unblemished animal to the Temple in Jerusalem and would then, through the mediation of a priest, offer it to God as a token of gratitude, worship, or penance. In doing so, he would align himself to God, bringing his mind, his will, his very body into right relationship with the Lord. Any pious Israelite would know that Yahweh, the Creator of the universe, had no need of these burnt offerings, unlike the gods of other nations, who seemed to require them. But that faithful Jew also knew that he needed sacrifice, since it brought him into deeper communion with the God who loved him, making him like the God whom he worshiped.

Now, in Jesus Christ, the face of the true God appeared, precisely as a face of love: "God is love and anyone who lives in love lives in God, and God lives in him" (1 John 4:16). To sacrifice to God, therefore, is to become conformed to the love that God is; it is to become love. Paul is telling the Romans (and us) to turn our bodies—our whole selves—into an act of worship of the true God, which is simply another way of saying that we should allow every aspect of our lives to become radical love. Now we can understand the great "yes" of the Church in regard to sexuality. Sex is meant to be completely attuned to love, that is to say, to self-gift. Sex is designed to be a vehicle by which the good of the other is sought and attained. When sex devolves into something less than an expression of love, the Church resolutely and loudly says "no!"

And so it says "no," obviously, to rape, to sexual abuse, to the sexual manipulation of another. But it also says "no" to sexual expression outside of the context of that mutual and radical self-gift that we call marriage. It says "no," furthermore, to a deliberate and conscious frustration of the procreative dimension of sex. In all of these "no's," the Church is fundamentally saying "yes" to sex as a path of love. I realize that many balk at this, arguing that while rape and sexual violence should always be condemned, other forms of sexual expression should be left to the discretion of the individual. But would we settle for this kind of leniency and mediocrity in any other area of life that we take seriously? For example, someone dedicated to having an excellent golf swing will, of course, accepts correction of his most egregious faults, but he will expect his teacher to press forward, righting relatively minor errors, fine-tuning his swing until he reaches real proficiency. I imagine that he would want his teacher to hold up the example not of a middle-level, weekend golfer, not even of a star on the junior tour, but of Rory McIlroy and Fred Couples and Jack Nicklaus. The one thing he would not want his coach to say is, "well, now that you've overcome the major problems, just swing any way you want."

So the Church, which desires to bring human sexuality into full conformity with the love that God is, corrects us, cajoles us, objects to us, encourages us, holds up to us high ideals, and invites us continually into the high and challenging adventure of sexual virtue. Do we often fail? Sure—just as we usually fail to hit the golf ball excellently. Does that mean that the Church should dial down its ideals? Absolutely not. Its "no"s are so strong because its "yes" is so ringing.

Brian Williams, Chris Matthews, and Letting the Fly Out of the Fly Bottle

During the Pope's visit to America in 2015, I had the privilege of commenting for NBC News and for MSNBC. Twice I was on for extended periods with Brian Williams, the former anchor of *NBC Nightly News*, and twice with Chris Matthews, the host of *Hardball*. I must say that both men are very good at what they do, namely, keeping a conversation going among several different people with varying points of view and assuring that things stay sufficiently lively and interesting. Like most gifted people, they make their particular work seem effortless, but it is a delicate and dangerous high-wire act that they are performing—and all on live television. Williams is a cool customer with a sly sense of humor, and, I might add, a surprisingly detailed knowledge of motor vehicles and aircraft, whereas Matthews is more passionate, brash, and unpredictable. I enjoyed spending time with both of them.

A theme to which Chris Matthews returned again and again was the role of women in the Church. Like most liberally minded Catholics, he thinks that women get the short end of the stick most of the time and that simple justice demands that they be given equal opportunity. Once he baldly introduced the subject to me this way: "Bishop, isn't it true that, in the Catholic Church, the management is all male while the women do most of the grunt work? Why can't women be priests?" Another time he wondered, "how come all the bishops are Republicans while all the nuns are Democrats?" I certainly know how complex these questions are and how they stir up such strong feelings on all sides, but in responding to these questions, I tried a technique that the philosopher Wittgenstein referred to as "letting the fly out of the fly bottle." This means to move the discussion into an entirely different register so as to prevent all the disputants from spending a lot of energy only to end up in frustration.

I told Matthews that I thought it was very important to revisit the largely unrealized aspiration of the Vatican II fathers to empower the laity to sanctify the world. Priests, I explained, have as their sole purpose the sanctification of the laity through word and sacrament, to enable great Catholic lawyers, business leaders, writers, journalists, investors, parents, teachers, etc. to make the world a holy place. The book of Revelation holds out to us the image of the heavenly Jerusalem, with its streets of gold and gates of pearl, but with no temple in it. The point is that the city itself has *become* a temple, which is to say, a place of right praise. So what is the role of women in the Church? How can women find more power? By becoming world-transforming saints! Thérèse of Lisieux, Bernadette of Lourdes, Mother Katharine Drexel, Mother Cabrini, Mother Teresa, and Edith Stein all wielded more real power than 99% of the priests and bishops of their time. If we move our attention away from the priesthood and toward sainthood, we let the fly out of the fly bottle.

During our coverage of the Pope's final Mass in Philadelphia, Brian Williams posed a question to all of the commentators: "Isn't it odd," he asked, "that those without families are setting the moral agenda for families?" A number of the contributors chimed in, more or less agreeing with this anomalous thought, and I felt obliged to intervene. "As the only celibate on the panel," I said, "May I offer an opposing point of view?" Borrowing a phrase from the scholastic philosophers, I said, "Brian, in regard to your question, *nego majorem* (I deny the major premise)." Priests, I explained, *have families.* I then indicated the ring that I received upon being ordained a bishop, and I said, "That's a wedding ring, and we are explicitly told never to take it off, for it symbolizes our marriage to the people we serve." Then I quoted my mentor, the late Francis Cardinal George: "Priests are not bachelors; they are married men, and they have spiritual children." Celibacy should never be understood in a purely negative way, as though it amounts simply to the denial of something. The no to marriage and children in the ordinary sense is in service of a far greater 'yes,' the yes to a wider, more inclusive, and more abiding form of marriage and procreation. In point of fact, the very familial implication of the celibate commitment is precisely what makes priests uniquely positioned to help and advise families. Once again, the teaching of Vatican II is apposite. Celibacy and marriage are ordered to one another, since both are ultimately in service of the sanctification of the world. When they are set up as rivals or as mutually antagonistic, we get a fly stuck in the fly bottle.

When Karol Wojtyla was Archbishop of Krakow, he led his people in a careful and prayerful reading of the documents of Vatican II. I am convinced that many of the disputes that we have in the Church in this country are a function of not having done what Wojtyla led his people to do. When the properly theological and spiritual framework falls away, all we are left with is the political or psychological or sociological framework—and this leads to lots of bumping against the side of the bottle.

We've Been Here Before: Same-Sex Marriage and the Room of Tears

I recently had the privilege of spending four hours in the Sistine Chapel with my Word on Fire team. Toward the end of our filming, the director of the Vatican Museums, who had accompanied us throughout the process, asked whether I wanted to see the "Room of Tears." This is the little antechamber, just off of the Sistine Chapel, where the newly-elected Pope changes into his white cassock. Understandably, tears begin to flow in that room, once the poor man realizes the weight of his office.

Inside the small space, there were documents and other memorabilia, but what got my attention was a row of impressive albs, chasubles, and copes worn by various popes across the years. I noticed the specially decorated cope of Pope Pius VI, who was one of the longest-serving Pontiffs in history, reigning from 1775 to 1799. Pius was an outspoken opponent of the French Revolution and its bloody aftermath—and his forthrightness cost him dearly. French troops invaded Italy and demanded that the pope renounce his claim to the Papal States. When he refused, he was arrested and imprisoned in a citadel in Valence, France, where he died six weeks later.

In the room of tears, there was also a stole worn by Pius VI's successor, Pius VII. This Pope Pius also ran afoul of the French, who, under Napoleon, invaded Italy in 1809 and took him prisoner. During his grim exile, he did manage to get off one of the greatest one-liners in papal history. Evidently, Napoleon himself announced to the pope that he was going to destroy the Church, to which Pius VII responded, "Oh my little man, you think you're going to succeed in accomplishing what centuries of priests and bishops have tried and failed to do!"

Both popes find themselves, of course, in a long line of Church people persecuted by the avatars of the regnant culture. In the earliest centuries of the Church's life, thousands—including Peter, Paul, Agnes, Cecelia, Clement, Felicity, Perpetua, Sebastian, Lawrence, and Cyprian—were brutally put to death by officials of the Roman Empire. In the fourth century, St. Ambrose was opposed by the emperor Theodosius; in the eleventh century, Pope Gregory VII locked horns with the Holy Roman Emperor Henry IV; in the nineteenth century, Bismarck waged a *Kulturkampf* against the Catholic Church in Germany, and in the twentieth century, more martyrs gave their lives for the faith than in all the previous centuries combined.

Now, why am I rehearsing this rather sad history? In the wake of 2015's United States Supreme Court decision regarding gay marriage, a not inconsiderable number of Catholics feel beleaguered and more than a little afraid. Their fear comes from the manner in which the decision was framed and justified. Since same-sex marriage is now recognized as a fundamental human right guaranteed by the Constitution, those who oppose it can only be characterized as bigots animated by an irrational prejudice. To be sure, Justice Kennedy and his colleagues assure us that those who have religious objections to same-sex marriage will be respected, but one wonders how such respect is congruent with the logic of the decision. Would one respect the owners of a business who refuse to hire black people as a matter of principle? Would not the government, in point of fact, be compelled to act against those owners? The proponents of gay marriage have rather brilliantly adopted the rhetoric of the civil rights movement, precisely so as to force this conclusion. And this is why my mentor, the late Francis Cardinal George, so often warned against the incursions of an increasingly aggressive secular state, which, he argued, will first force us off the public stage into privacy, and then seek to criminalize those practices of ours that it deems unacceptable.

One reason that this has been rather shocking to American Catholics is that we have had, at least for the last century or so, a fairly benign relationship with the environing culture. Until around 1970, there was, throughout society and across religious boundaries, a broad moral consensus in our country, especially in regard to sexual and family matters. This is one reason why, in the 1950s, Archbishop Fulton Sheen could find such a wide and appreciative audience among Protestants and Jews, even as he laid out fundamentally Catholic perspectives on morality. But now that consensus has largely been shattered, and the Church finds itself opposed not so much by other religious denominations, as it was in the nineteenth century, but by the ideology of secularism and the self-defining individual—admirably expressed, by the way, in Justice Kennedy's articulation of the majority position in the *Obergefell v. Hodges* case pertaining to same-sex marriage.

So what do we do? We continue to put forth our point of view winsomely, invitingly, and nonviolently, loving our opponents and reaching out to those with whom we disagree. As St. John Paul II said, the Church always proposes, never imposes. And we take a deep breath, preparing for what could be some aggression from the secular society, but we take courage from a great cloud of witnesses who have gone before us. The Church has faced this sort of thing before—and we're still standing.

Love, Tolerance, and the
Making of Distinctions

When I wrote a piece on Bruce Jenner's transformation into Caitlyn Jenner, I argued that the manner in which Jenner spoke of his transition reflected a gnostic anthropology, which is repugnant to a Biblical view of the human being. I didn't say a word about Jenner personally; I urged no violence against him/her; I didn't question his/her motives. I simply made an observation that the moral and spiritual context for transgenderism is, from a classically Christian standpoint, problematic.

Not surprisingly, the article garnered a fair amount of attention and inspired a lot of commentary, both positive and negative. Among the negative remarks were a number that criticized me for fomenting "hatred" against Jenner and against the transgender community. Though I've come to expect this sort of reaction, I find it discouraging, and the fruit of some pretty fundamental confusions.

My great mentor Robert Sokolowski long ago taught me—in one of those lapidary remarks that strikes you immediately as right and important—that philosophy is the art of making distinctions. He meant that what brings together Plato, Aristotle, Augustine, Aquinas, Kant, Hegel, and Wittgenstein is a gift for clarifying how this differs from that, how one aspect of an idea profiles itself against another, how seemingly similar concepts are in fact distinct. In executing these moves, the great philosophers made muddy water clear. What strikes me so often, as I listen to the public conversation regarding moral issues, is the incapacity of so many to make the right distinctions.

Some of the muddiest water surrounds the concepts of love/ hate and tolerance/intolerance. In the spirit of Sokolowski, I would like to make what I hope are some clarifying differentiations. For the mainstream of the Catholic intellectual tradition, love is not primarily an emotion, but an act of the will. To love, Thomas Aquinas says, is to want the good of the other. Consequently, hatred is not primarily a feeling, but desiring evil for another, positively wanting what is bad for someone else. Given this, when is hatred called for? When is hatred morally permissible? The simple answer: never. God *is* nothing but love, and Jesus said that we are to be perfect, as our heavenly Father is perfect (Matt 5:48). This is precisely why he told us to love even our enemies, to bless even those who curse us, to pray even for those who maltreat us (Matt 5:44; Lk 6:28). Does this mean that our forebears were obliged to love Hitler and that we are obliged to love ISIS murderers? Yes. Period. Does it mean that we are to will the good of those who, we are convinced, are walking a dangerous moral path? Yes. Period. Should everyone love Bruce/Caitlyn Jenner? Absolutely, completely, unconditionally.

But here is where a crucial distinction has to be made: to criticize someone for engaging in immoral activity is not to "hate" that person. In point of fact, it is an act of love, for it is tantamount to willing good for him or her. Once the sense that there is objective good and evil has been attenuated, as it largely has been in our society, the only categories we have left are psychological ones. And this is why, in the minds of many, to question the moral legitimacy of transgenderism is, perforce, to "attack" or "hate" transgendered people. A very real danger that flows from the failure to make the right distinction in this regard is that moral argument evanesces. If someone who disagrees with you on an ethical matter is simply a "hater," then you don't have to listen to his argument or engage it critically. You are permitted, in fact, to censor him, to shut him down. Sadly, this is what obtains in much of the public arena today: the impugning of motives, the questioning of character, and the imposition of censorship.

Compare this with two Princeton faculty members, Cornel West and Robert George, who had a public debate regarding, in part, same-sex marriage, West arguing for and George against. What was so refreshing was that both men, who are good friends, actually *argued*, that is to say, marshalled evidence, drew reasoned conclusions from premises, answered objections, etc., and neither one accused the other of "hating" advocates of the rival position. May their tribe increase.

Distinctions are called for, furthermore, regarding the word "tolerance," which is bandied about constantly today. Typically, it has come to mean acceptance and even celebration. Thus, if one is anything shy of ecstatic about gay marriage or transgenderism, one is insufficiently "tolerant." In point of fact, the term implies the willingness to countenance a view or activity that one does *not* agree with. Hence, in the context of our wise political system, each citizen is required to tolerate a range of opinions that he finds puzzling, erroneous, repugnant, or even bizarre. There are lots of good reasons for this toleration, the most important of which are respect for the integrity of the individual and the avoidance of unnecessary civil strife, but it by no means implies that one is obliged to accept or celebrate those perspectives. Thus, one should certainly tolerate the right of a person to become transgendered, without feeling, at the same time, obliged to exult in that person's choice.

The ethical conversation has become, in the last fifty years, extraordinarily roiled. It would serve all of us to adopt an intellectual instinct of Thomas Aquinas. When he was confronted with a thorny question, he would typically begin his response with the comment *distinguo* ("I distinguish").

The "Waze"
of Providence

Just after I was named auxiliary bishop of Los Angeles, Archbishop Gomez, my new boss, told me to get the Waze app for my iPhone. He explained that it was a splendid way to navigate the often impossible LA traffic. I followed his instructions and have indeed used the app on practically a daily basis since my arrival on the West Coast. Waze not only gives you directions, but it also provides very accurate information regarding the time to your destination, obstacles on the road, the presence of police, etc. Most importantly, it routes you around traffic jams, which positively abound in the City of Angels.

Especially in my first days and weeks on the new job, I basically had no idea where I was going—and my duties required that I be all over the place: LAX, Pasadena, Inglewood, Granada Hills, Ventura, Oxnard, Santa Barbara, Santa Maria, etc., etc. And often I was required to journey after dark. So I would program an address into the Waze app and then listen to the mechanical female voice as she guided me to my destination. It was often the case that her instructions were counter-intuitive, which was not surprising, given the fact of my disorientation in a new environment. But I gradually learned to trust her as, again and again, she got me where I needed to be.

I'll confess that one particular day, my faith in her was sorely tested. I had left my home in Santa Barbara very early in order to attend a ten o'clock meeting in Los Angeles, and was making pretty good time on the 101 expressway. Suddenly, the Waze lady instructed me to get off the highway a good 25 miles from LA. Though skeptical, I followed her advice. She subsequently sent me on a lengthy, circuitous, and rather slow journey through city streets until finally guiding me back to the 101! I was so frustrated that I pounded my fist on the dashboard and expressed (aloud) my dismay. When I got to the meeting, I laid all of this out to one of my episcopal colleagues and explained that I thought there was a glitch in the system. "Oh no," he quickly responded, "there was a tanker spill this morning on the 101, not far from where she made you exit the road. She probably saved you an hour or two of frustration."

At that point I saw clearly something that had been forming itself inchoately in my mind, namely, that the Waze app is a particularly powerful spiritual metaphor. As Thomas Merton put it in the opening line of his most famous prayer: "My Lord God, I have no idea where I'm going." Spiritually speaking, most of us are as I was when I arrived in Los Angeles: lost, disoriented, off-kilter. But we have been provided a Voice and instructed to follow it. The Voice echoes in the Scriptures, of course, but also in the depth of the conscience, in the authoritative teaching of the Church, in the wise counsel of spiritual directors, and in the example of the saints. Does it often, indeed typically, seem counter-intuitive to us? Absolutely. Do we, as a matter of course, ignore it, presuming that we know better? Sadly, yes. Are there some among us who, in time, learn to trust it, to guide their lives by it, even when it asks them to go by what seem like circuitous routes? Happily enough, yes.

There is another feature of the Waze app worth considering in this spiritual context. When you get lost, or perhaps decide that you know better than the navigator, she doesn't upbraid you or compel you to return to the route she had originally chosen. She calmly recalculates and determines the best way to get to your goal, given the choice you have made. God indeed has a plan for each of us. He has determined, in his wisdom and love, the best way for us to get to our goal, which is full union with him. But, like Israel of old, we all wander from the path, convinced that we are brighter than the Lord of the universe, or perhaps just enamored of asserting our own freedom. But God never gives up on us; rather, he reshuffles the deck, recalculates, and sets a new course for us. Watch this process, by the way, as the Scriptural narrative unfolds. And watch it happening, again and again, in your own life: what looks like a complete dead end turns into a way forward; the wrong path turns, strangely, into the right path.

No matter where you go, Waze can track you and set you on the right road, and this "all-seeing" quality has given us confidence in its direction. As we have learned to trust the mechanical voices of our GPS systems in regard to the relatively trivial matter of finding our way past traffic jams, so may we learn to trust the Voice of the one who, as the Psalmist puts it, "searches us and knows us and discerns our purpose from afar."

What the Hell?

Time and again, as I go about the work of evangelization, I encounter, from both believers and nonbelievers, a fierce objection to the doctrine of hell. In its most radical form, it runs something like this: how could a God who is described as infinitely good create, sustain, and send people to a place of everlasting torment? Many people have directed my attention to a video done some years ago by the comedian George Carlin, a former Catholic. In front of a deeply sympathetic audience, Carlin exposes what he takes to be the silly inconsistency of Catholic belief: "for one mortal sin (usually having to do with sex), God will condemn you to a place where you will suffer forever in unbearable pain...but yet," the comedian goes on in a mocking voice, "He looooves you!" Judging from their hysterical reaction, the audience can't get enough of this. One wonders whether Carlin doesn't have a point. Perhaps we ought to simply jettison this horrifying and apparently illogical doctrine, this superstitious holdover from a primitive time.

Well, I would suggest, not so fast. It might be wise to note first that hell is hardly an ecclesiastical invention of the Middle Ages. In point of fact, "Gehenna" and the "everlasting fire" are mentioned frequently by Jesus himself, and the existence of hell is confirmed by our greatest theologians and spiritual teachers from ancient times to the present day. And one can find a pithy defense of the doctrine in the *Catechism of the Catholic Church* from 1992. The belief is so persistent, I would argue, because it is a corollary of two other essential beliefs, namely, that God is love, and that we are free. Let me say a word about each of these.

In Catholic theology, love is not something that God does, or one attribute among many that God happens to have. Rather, love is what God is. To will the good of the other as other is the very nature, substance, and essence of God. Accordingly, God doesn't love some and hate others; he doesn't fall in and out of emotional states, sometimes loving and sometimes hating. To use Jesus' own metaphor, he is like the sun that shines on the good and the bad alike (Matt 5:45). God doesn't love us because we've been morally upright; rather, whatever moral goodness we have is the result of God having loved us. This is the principle, basic to all Biblical thought, of the primacy of grace.

Now, rocks, trees, planets, animals, and stars all respond to the divine love just by being what they are. But God made human beings in his own image and likeness, which is to say, he endowed them with mind and will, and thereby invited them to respond to his love, not simply by the goodness of their being, but by the integrity of their freedom. He wanted them to have the opportunity to participate personally in the love that he is. But this freedom necessarily carried with it a shadow, namely, the possibility of abuse. We who have been made in God's image can decide not to live in accord with that image; we who have been invited to answer God's love with our love can answer it instead with resistance. To stand athwart the divine love, to run counter to the image of God within us, to turn away from the sun that shines on us whether we like it or not, is to suffer. It is like a furnace; it is a kind of torture; it is to be in a place of tears and the gnashing of teeth. I'm purposely using imagery for hell here, because the definitive state of this resistance to God, the final "no" to God from the depths of one's being, is precisely what the Church means by hell. And perhaps now we can begin to see why this doctrine hasn't a thing to do with God "sending" anyone to a terrible place or "condemning" anyone to an eternal prison. As C.S.

Lewis put it, "the door to hell is always locked from the inside," for it is always our perverse freedom, and not a divine choice, that locks us away from God.

Lewis offered another extremely helpful point of clarification when he said that the love of God lights up the fires of hell. He meant that the suffering of hell is caused by the very same power that produces the delight of heaven, namely, the love that God simply is. The difference between heaven and hell is a function of our freedom: in the first case, it opens itself to God, and in the second case, it turns away from God. A homey image might help. There are two people at the same party. One is caught up in the joy, rhythm, music, and laughter of the gathering, and he's having the time of his life; the other, sunk in moody self-regard, resenting the joy of those around him, sulks in irritation, tortured by the very exuberance of the party itself.

Therefore, if there are any people in hell (and the Church has never obliged us to believe that any human is in that state), they are there, not because God capriciously "sent" them, but because they absolutely insist on not joining in the party.

Pope Benedict as a
Witness to God

Over a period of about 15 years in the 1990s and early 2000s, the German journalist Peter Seewald conducted a number of interviews with Joseph Cardinal Ratzinger, then the prefect for the Congregation of the Doctrine of the Faith. The edited conversations appeared as two rather lengthy books, *The Salt of the Earth* and *God and the World*. Seewald's pointed questions dealt with fundamental matters—God, creation, Incarnation, redemption, sin, grace—and Ratzinger's answers—clear, succinct, illuminating—were marvels of the teacher's art. Perhaps the most extraordinary fruit of these encounters was Seewald's conversion from an unfocused agnosticism to a full embrace of the Catholic faith.

In the summer of 2010, Seewald sat down once again for a lengthy discussion with Joseph Ratzinger, but this time he was dialoguing not with a curial Cardinal but with Pope Benedict XVI. The only-slightly-edited version of that six-hour conversation has appeared as *Light of the World*, and one is happy to see that Ratzinger's elevation to the highest office in the Church did not temper the dynamic quality of their exchange. No question seemed to have been off-limits, as Seewald pressed the pope on everything from the sex abuse scandal, to women's ordination, to AIDS and condoms, to his personal reaction upon being raised to the throne of Peter. Throughout, Benedict's mien is calm and his responses are models of clarity, concision, and insight. However, those who are looking for substantive information about Benedict's psychological and personal life are going to be disappointed. The pope seemed far more comfortable expatiating on matters theological and cultural than exploring his own motivations and inclinations.

I'm quite sure that most of the commentariat—especially in the secular media—will focus on what Benedict has to say concerning the worldwide clergy sex abuse scandal, the dialogue with Islam, women's ordination, and homosexual activity. Thus, I don't feel the need to rehash these matters. I would like to focus instead on what I take to be Benedict's prime concern, which is evident throughout the pages of this book and which provides the proper context for understanding what he says regarding everything else, including the issues mentioned above. Pope Benedict was interested, above all, in God, and he was worried, above all, that God has been marginalized, forgotten, or denied outright in the increasingly secularized Western world. "There are so many problems that all have to be solved but that will not all be solved unless God stands in the center and becomes visible again in the world." The question of God was so central for Benedict, for he was convinced that, once God is denied, human freedom no longer has any limit or standard. And an unfettered freedom is tantamount to license, the rendering permissible of any outrage, any atrocity.

This setting-aside of God can take place both explicitly (as in the musings of the new atheists) or implicitly (as in so much of the secular world, where a "practical" atheism holds sway). In either case, the result is a shutting down of the natural human drive toward the transcendent and, even more dangerously, the elevation of self-determining freedom to a position of unchallenged primacy. The pope elaborated here a theme that was dear to his predecessor, namely, the breakdown of the connection between freedom and truth. On the typically modern reading, truth is construed as an enemy to freedom—which explains precisely why we find such hostility to truth in the contemporary culture. Indeed, anyone who claims to have the truth—especially in regard to moral matters—is automatically accused of arrogance and intolerance. Society will be restored to balance and sanity, Benedict argued, only when the natural link between freedom and truth—especially the Truth which is God—is reestablished.

The pope offered a fascinating analysis of the Enlightenment culture that continues to shape us today. Starting in the seventeenth century, intellectuals began to put a huge premium on scientific progress, advance in knowledge. They furthermore saw a tight connection between knowledge and power: the more we know about nature, the more thoroughly we can master it. However, Benedict argued, along with this stress on progress in knowledge and power there was no commensurate stress on progress in morality. Consequently, we did indeed grow in our capacity to master the world, but we did not know how to handle that mastery or what to do with it. The fruit of this rupture between progress and morality can be seen theoretically in the nihilistic philosophy of Nietzsche, and practically in the murderous and amoral political movements of the last century. In response to Seewald's question about reading the "signs of the times," Benedict had this to say: "I think that our major task now…is first of all to bring to light God's priority again. The important thing today is to see that God exists, that God matters to us, and that he answers us. And, conversely, that if he is omitted, everything else might be as clever as can be—yet man then loses his dignity and his authentic humanity."

Very much in line with his intellectual hero St. Augustine, Benedict XVI characterized the cultural situation today as a kind of battlefield between two "spiritual worlds, the world of faith and the world of secularism." Behind all of our arguments about particular moral and political issues is a fundamental argument about the centrality of God. What became clear to me in the course of reading the wide-ranging conversation between Seewald and Ratzinger is that the pope saw his primary task as witnessing to God, reminding us of God, speaking of God. Everything else, in his mind, was merely commentary.

A Prophetic Pope and
the Tradition of Catholic
Social Teaching

In the wake of the publication of Pope Francis's 2015 encyclical letter *Laudato Si'*, and of his speeches the same year in Latin America, many supporters of the capitalist economy in the West might be forgiven for thinking that His Holiness has something against them. Again and again, Pope Francis excoriates an economy based on materialism and greed, and, with prophetic urgency, he speaks out against a new colonialism that exploits the labor of those in poorer countries. With startling bluntness, he characterizes the dominant economic form in the developed world as "an economy that kills." Moreover, in a speech delivered in Bolivia, a country under the command of a socialist president, the pope seemed, almost in a Marxist vein, to be calling on the poor to seize power from the wealthy and take command of their own lives. What do we make of this?

Well, a contextualization is in order. Pope Francis's remarks, though strong, even a bit exaggerated, in the prophetic manner, are best understood in the framework of Catholic social teaching. One of the most significant constants in that tradition is a suspicion of socialism, which is understood as an economic system that denies the legitimacy of private property, undermines the free market, and fosters a class struggle between the rich and the poor, or, if I can use the more classical language, between capital and labor. The modern popes, from Leo XIII to Benedict XVI, have all spoken clearly against such systems, and it is hard to deny that experience has borne them out. Economies in the radically socialist or communist mode have proven inefficient at best, and brutally oppressive at worst. Robert Sirico, Michael Novak, Arthur Brooks, and many others are therefore right in suggesting that Catholic social teaching does not represent a *tertium quid*, a "third thing" beyond capitalism and socialism; rather, it clearly aligns itself against socialistic arrangements and for the market economy. John Paul II appreciated the free market as the economic concomitant of a democratic polity, since both rest upon the dignity of the individual and his right to self-determination.

But this valorization of the market by no means implies that the Church advocates an unfettered capitalism. The modern popes have consistently taught that the market functions properly only when it is circumscribed both politically and morally—and it is precisely in this context that Pope Francis's remarks should be understood. Let us look first at the political circumscription. Pope Leo XIII and his successors have deeply felt the suffering of those who have been exploited by the market or who have not been given adequate access to its benefits. And this is why they have supported political/legal reforms including child labor laws, minimum wage requirements, anti-trust provisions, workday restrictions, and the right of workers to unionize. All of these legal constraints, they have taught, should not be construed as erosions of the market, but rather as attempts to make it more humane, more just, and more widely accessible. To be sure, people of intelligence and good will can and do disagree regarding the precise application of these principles, debating, for example, just how high the minimum wage should be fixed, just how stringently anti-trust laws should be interpreted, just how the rights of labor and capital should be balanced. And neither popes nor bishops nor priests should get into the nitty-gritty of those conversations, best leaving the details to those expert in the relevant disciplines. But popes, bishops, and priests can indeed call for political reforms if a market has become exploitative and hence self-destructive.

The second circumscription that the Popes speak of—the moral—is even more important than the first. A market economy enjoys real legitimacy if and only if it is set in the context of a vibrant moral culture that forms its people in the virtues of fairness, justice, respect for the integrity of the other, and religion. Indeed, what good are contracts—fundamental to the functioning of a market economy—if people are indifferent to justice? What good is private property if people don't see that stealing is wicked? Won't wealth destroy the rich man who doesn't appreciate the value of generosity or fails to develop sensitivity to the suffering of the poor? Won't the drive for profit lead to the destruction of nature unless people realize that the earth is a gift of a gracious God and is meant to be enjoyed by all? This is precisely why the moral relativism and indifferentism that holds sway in many parts of the West—fostered by the breakdown of the family and the attenuating of religious practice—poses such a threat to the economy.

In light of these clarifications, we can hear the pope's words with greater understanding. He asks, "Do we realize that this system has imposed the mentality of profit at any price, with no concern for social exclusion or the destruction of nature?" He is not speaking here of the market as such, but of a deeply immoral attitude that has seized the hearts of too many who use the market. And he complains, "An unfettered pursuit of money rules. The service of the common good is left behind. Once capital becomes an idol and guides people's decisions, once greed for money presides over the entire socioeconomic system, it ruins society, it condemns and enslaves men and women." These are strong words indeed, but we notice again that the pope's attention is not so much on the mechanisms of capitalism, but rather on the wickedness of those who are using the market economy in the wrong way, greedily making an idol of money and becoming indifferent to the needs of others. In his call for an ethical circumscription of economic life, Francis's language is, if anything, milder than Leo XIII's ("once the demands of necessity and propriety have been met, the rest that one owns belongs to the poor") or St. Ambrose's ("if a man has two shirts in his closet, one belongs to him; the other belongs to the man who has no shirt").

Therefore, we should attend to Pope Francis's prophetic speech, and allow it to bother us. But we should always situate it in the context of the rich and variegated tradition of Catholic social teaching.

The Cleansing of
the Temple

Artistic representations of the Ten Commandments often depict two stone tablets on which there are two tables of inscriptions. This portrayal follows from a classical division of the commandments in which there are two specific categories—those that order humanity's relationship with God and those that order human relationships with one another. If we consider the Bible as a totality, it becomes apparent that the Scriptures give priority to the first tablet, those commands dealing with God.

The Ten Commandments begin with an insistence that the Lord alone is God, and there are to be no other gods besides him. This is not just a principle meant to order humanity's expressions of ritualized worship but a statement about the ethos of the entire moral and spiritual order. Whatever it is that humanity worships, be it the gods of the ancients or the allures of wealth, power, pleasure, or honors, will by necessity give rise to our perceptions and practices concerning the moral life. The God or gods in whom we place our ultimate concern will direct our lives and determine our choices.

Given that the Bible calls humanity over and over again to relinquish its attachment to false gods and embrace the worship of the one true God, we might take that emphasis as a means to interpret Christ's actions in regards to the moneychangers in the Jerusalem Temple, actions that are traditionally referred to as the "cleansing of the Temple" (Matt 21:12–17; Mark 11:15–19; Luke 19:45–48; John 2:13–16). The dramatic scene portrays Christ entering the sacred center of Israel's culture and worship at the height of the Jewish year—the feast of Passover. Christ then raises a ruckus, for he finds the Temple to be not a house of prayer but a "marketplace." He turns over the tables of the moneychangers, disrupts the trade in animals for sacrifice, and cleans the place out.

This scene is often interpreted as testimony against materialism in religious practice. Religion is to remain radically pure in regard to the corruptions of commerce. An idealism emerges from this interpretation that engenders a hair trigger with respect to any and all associations of religion with economics or money. According to this conceit, the only way forward for religion is to maintain its purity by eschewing the corrupting influence of commerce.

While sharing the aversion to using religion as a means to gain material wealth, I think a more fruitful way of understanding Christ's action to cleanse the Temple can be discerned in relation to Israel's aversion to the worship of false gods and the necessity of cleansing our own temple—that is, our lives—of these fallen deities. Remember, St. Paul said that the body of each Christian is "a temple of the Holy Spirit" (1 Cor 6:19). By this he means a place where the one true God is honored and worshiped. The apostle is providing us with an image of the Christian life as one in which a person finds happiness and integration in the measure that she becomes, personally, a place where God is first.

Think, then, that Christ has come to cleanse the Temple of Jerusalem, but also the temple of your own body, your own life. The Lord Jesus comes into your life expecting to find a place ordered to the worship of the one true God, but what he finds is "a marketplace." What does this mean? It means that Christ finds a place where things other than God have become primary. To bring such idolatry closer to our cultural experience, how much of your life is given over to materialism, commercialism, or the accumulation of things? What rivals to the one true God have you allowed to invade the sacred space of your soul? Earlier I referenced wealth, pleasure, power, and honor. How are these things enshrined in the sanctuary of your own heart?

The temple-cleansing Christ is a memorable image with enduring power. We shouldn't relegate that image or the Lord himself to a mere statement about our impatience with the corruptions of religious institutions and miss the point that strikes closer to home: Christ comes to each of us to rid the temple of our own body of the idols to which we have foolishly given power and pride of place.

SUFFERING AND JOY

The whole point of the Christian life is to find joy,
but the attainment of true joy comes, in a sinful
world, at the cost of some suffering.

– BISHOP BARRON

Stephen Fry, Job, and
the Cross of Jesus

The British writer, actor, and comedian Stephen Fry is featured
in a YouTube video interview that quickly went viral, garnering
over 5 million views in the first two weeks. As you may know, Fry,
like his American counterparts Christopher Hitchens and Richard
Dawkins, is a fairly ferocious atheist who has made a name for himself in recent years as a very public debunker of all things religious.
In the video in question, he articulates precisely what he would say
to God if, upon arriving at the pearly gates, he discovered that he
was mistaken in his atheism. Fry says that he would ask God why
he made a universe in which children get bone cancer, a universe in
which human beings suffer horrifically and without justification. If
such a monstrous, self-absorbed, and stupid god exists, Fry insists,
he would decidedly not want to spend eternity with him. Now, there
is much more to Fry's rant—it goes on for several minutes—but you
get the drift.

To those who feel that Stephen Fry has delivered a devastating blow to religious belief, let me say simply this: this objection is
nothing new to Christians. St. Paul, Origen, Augustine, C.S. Lewis,
G.K. Chesterton, and many, many other Christian theologians up
and down the centuries have dealt with it. In fact, one of the pithiest
expressions of the problem was formulated by St. Thomas Aquinas
in the thirteenth century. The great Catholic philosopher argued that
if one of two contraries were infinite, the other would be altogether
destroyed. Yet God is called infinitely good. Therefore, if God exists,

there should be no evil. But there is evil. Thus it certainly seems to follow that God does not exist. Thomas thereby conveys all of the power of Fry's observations without the histrionics. And, of course, all of this subtle theological wrestling with the problem of suffering is grounded in the most devastating rant ever uttered against God, a rant found not in an essay of some disgruntled atheist philosopher but rather in the pages of the Bible. I'm talking about the book of Job.

According to the familiar story, Job is an innocent man, but he is nevertheless compelled to endure every type of suffering. In one fell swoop, he loses his wealth, his livelihood, his family, and his health. A group of friends console him and then attempt to offer theological explanations for his pain. But Job dismisses them all and, with all the fury of Stephen Fry, calls out God, summoning him, as it were, into the dock to explain himself. Out of the desert whirlwind God then speaks—and it is the longest speech by God in the Scriptures: "Where were you when I laid the foundations of the earth? Tell me, if you know…. Who shut within doors the sea…when I made the clouds its garment and thick darkness its swaddling bands? Have you ever in your lifetime commanded the morning and shown the dawn its place?" (Job 38:4, 8-10). God goes on, taking Job on a lengthy tour of the mysteries, conundrums, and wonders of the universe, introducing him to ever wider contexts, situating his suffering within frameworks of meaning that he had never before considered. In light of God's speech, I would first suggest to Stephen Fry that the true God is the providential Lord of all of space and all of time.

Secondly, I would observe that none of us can see more than a tiny swatch of that immense canvas on which God works. And therefore I would urge him to reconsider his confident assertion that the suffering of the world—even the most horrific and seemingly un-justified—is necessarily without meaning. Imagine that one page of Tolkien's *Lord of the Rings* was torn away and allowed to drift on the wind. Imagine further that that page became, in the course of several months, further ripped and tattered so that only one paragraph of it remained legible. And finally, imagine that someone who had never heard of Tolkien's rich and multi-layered story came, by chance, upon that single paragraph. Would it not be the height of arrogance and presumption for that person to declare that those words made not a lick of sense? Would it not be akin to someone, utterly ignorant of higher mathematics, declaring that a complex algebraic formula, coherent in itself but opaque to him, is nothing but gibberish? Given our impossibly narrow point of view, how could any of us ever presume to pronounce on the "meaninglessness" of what happens in the world?

A third basic observation I would make to Mr. Fry is this: once we grant that God exists, we hold to the very real possibility of a life beyond this one. But this implies that no evil in this world, even death itself, is of final significance. Is it terrible that innocent children die of wasting diseases? Well, of course. But is it finally and irreversibly terrible? Is it nothing but terrible? By no means! It might, in fact, be construed as an avenue to something unsurpassably good.

In the last analysis, the best rejoinder to Fry's objection is a distinctively Christian one, for Christians refer to the day on which Jesus was unjustly condemned, abandoned by his friends, brutally scourged, paraded like an animal through the streets, nailed to an instrument of torture, and left to die as "Good Friday." To understand that is to have the ultimate answer to Job—and to Stephen Fry.

God and the Tsunami

On November 1st, 1755, a terrible earthquake struck Lisbon, Portugal. The temblor, which lasted about ten minutes, destroyed most of the buildings in the city and buried thousands of people in rubble. As would be the case with the San Francisco earthquake a hundred and fifty years later, fires broke out in the wake of the Lisbon quake that claimed the lives of many more people and destroyed much of economic infrastructure of the city. Finally, a series of tidal waves ensued, which killed many who had gathered at the shore to escape the flames.

This event, metaphorically speaking, sent shock waves all across Europe, for it called into question the still commonly held belief in a benevolent and providential God. Though they knew about the calamity of Pompeii from their books of ancient history, eighteenth-century Europeans had never directly experienced wanton destruction on the scale of the Lisbon earthquake. How could a gracious, personal God ever have presided over a calamity of that magnitude? Keep in mind that this philosophical and religious crisis occurred at a time when many European intellectuals were, for the first time, calling the narrative of classical Christianity into question. Kant, Rousseau, and Voltaire, among many others, weighed in on the matter of the Lisbon earthquake, and they agreed that such a disaster was reconcilable only with a view of God as an impersonal cosmic force or ultimate cause—and not with the Biblical notion of God as a loving personal presence.

I immediately thought of the Lisbon earthquake and its cultural aftermath when I saw a 2011 CNN report on the earthquake and subsequent tsunami in northeast Japan. It was an eerily similar scenario: temblor, fire, flood, massive destruction, terrible loss of life—and the same inevitable questions about God's involvement or lack thereof. How indeed can religious people make sense of such a disaster? Well, I'm sure we'll find some who will claim, with supreme confidence, that this event is a divine punishment for some offense committed by the people of Japan. (In fact, as I write these words, I am just hearing of a Japanese commentator who claims that it was retribution for the materialism of his country). Of course, the book of Job gives the lie to this kind of facile theologizing about God's purposes when it exposes as frauds the "friends" of Job who endeavor to explain the poor man's sufferings through just this kind of argument. On the other extreme, we will undoubtedly find atheists and agnostics maintaining that the evil unfolding in Japan positively proves that the personal God of the Bible is a childish superstition and a wish-fulfilling fantasy.

The truth of the matter lies beyond these easy options. A first observation to make is this: God can never be construed as the "cause" of evil. This is true for two reasons. First, the God who is nothing but love can never positively will something wicked, and second, the God who is being itself can never be the ground of evil, which is always a lack of being, or a type of non-being. Therefore, we can only say that God "permits" evil within his creation. But why would God ever grant such "permission?" The classical answer is that God allows evil so as to bring about a greater good. Thus we say that God permits the abuse of free will—even in radical cases such as Hitler or Stalin—as a regrettable but inevitable concomitant of the existence of free will itself. And in explaining physical evils such as the Japan tsunami, we might follow the lead of Anglican priest and particle physicist John Polkinghorne and say that the "free will" defense might be accompanied by a "free process" defense. In other words, the same God who allows free will to have its way, with both good and bad consequences, permits the processes of nature to unfold according to their own rhythms, even when this results in states of affairs that are, from our perspective, both good and evil. After all, the recent tsunami was but the natural consequence of an earthquake, which followed upon the shifting of tectonic plates, which followed from the basic structures of the earth, which are the result of the earth's relation to the sun, etc., etc. God desires nature to have its own causal integrity, even though this will result in consequences both good and bad; likewise, evolution pushes forward according to the same dynamic—random genetic mutation—that gives rise to cancer.

Can we clarify any further the reasons for the divine "permission" of evil? I might draw upon an old story from the Eastern spiritual tradition. A farmer's horse ran away, and his friends commiserated with him over his loss; but the farmer responded, "we'll see." A week later, the horse returned with three others, and his friends rejoiced with him over his good fortune; and the farmer said, "we'll see." A week later, his son was riding one of the horses and fell and broke his leg. His friends sympathized with him over this tragedy, and the farmer said, "we'll see." The next week, recruiters for the emperors army came to draft the young man into the army but excused him because of his broken leg; the farmers friends congratulated him on his good luck and the farmer said, "we'll see." The story goes on in this vein, making the simple but significant point that we never ultimately see the good and evil that might come in any set of circumstances. We say that God permits evil so as to bring about a greater good. What possible good could come from the Japanese tragedy? Believers in a provident God and in a life that stretches beyond this one might say, with a serenity born of faith, "we'll see."

Stephen Colbert, J.R.R. Tolkien, John Henry Newman, and the Providence of God

In 2015 Stephen Colbert gave an interview with *GQ Magazine* in which the depth of his Catholic faith was on pretty clear display. Discussing the trauma that he experienced as a young man—the deaths of his father and two of his brothers in a plane crash—he told the interviewer how, through the ministrations of his mother, he had learned not only to accept what had happened but to actually rejoice in it: "Boy, did I have a bomb when I was ten; that was quite an explosion... It's that I love the thing that I wish most had not happened." Flummoxed, his interlocutor asked him to elaborate on the paradox. Without missing a beat, Colbert cited J.R.R. Tolkien: "What punishments of God are not gifts?" What a wonderful sermon on the salvific quality of suffering! And it was delivered, not by a priest or bishop or evangelist, but by a comedian about to take over one of the most popular television programs on late night.

But what particularly intrigued me was the reference to Tolkien, which was culled not from the *Lord of the Rings* or the *Hobbit* but from a letter that the great man wrote to an inquirer, who had wondered whether Tolkien took death with sufficient spiritual seriousness in his literary work. Like Colbert, Tolkien had suffered enormous trauma as a young man. His father died in 1896, when Tolkien was only three, and his mother Mabel took him and his younger brother back to England (the family had moved to South

Africa for economic reasons). Upon their return to her hometown of Birmingham, Mabel decided to become a Roman Catholic, a move that was met with enormous opposition on the part of her family, who essentially disowned her and left her in destitution. During this terrible period, Tolkien's mother turned to the priests of the Birmingham Oratory, who cared for her needs, both spiritual and financial, and who took a keen interest in her fatherless children.

In 1904, Tolkien and his brother became orphans when their mother died of diabetes. Years later, the famous author mused that his mother was a kind of martyr, since she had been in effect hounded to death for her decision to become a Catholic and to raise her sons in the faith. Frightened, alone, and adrift, the boys were taken in by Rev. Francis Xavier Morgan, a priest of the Oratory. The kindly man, whom Tolkien always referred to affectionately as "Fr. Francis," became a father figure, instructing the young men in matters both sacred and secular, and teaching, as Tolkien would later put it, the meaning of "charity and forgiveness." Tolkien named his eldest son for the priest, and many have suggested that there is a fair amount of Fr. Morgan in Gandalf and other wisdom figures in the master's oeuvre. It was assuredly Fr. Francis who taught the young Tolkien, who had endured more trials than any child ought to endure, that "all of God's punishments are gifts."

But where had the priest learned that lesson? The Birmingham Oratory had been established in the mid-nineteenth century by the legendary John Henry Newman, who at the time had just become a Roman Catholic, thereby excluding himself from the institutions of British society. When he set up the Oratory in the industrial city of Birmingham, Newman was passing through a real "Lenten" period, for he was excoriated as a traitor by the Anglican establishment and looked upon with suspicion by Catholics. In time, Newman would reemerge as a cultural leader within British society, and his Oratory would become a center for Catholic evangelism in England. But this would happen only through Newman's dark night experiences. What his Oratorian disciples, including Fr. Francis, would have taken in is the lesson that "punishments" often turn out to be precious gifts.

What this chain of influences teaches us—and here I come to the point of this essay—is that God's providence is a mysterious and wonderful thing. Were it not for John Henry Newman's establishment, through much suffering, of the Birmingham Oratory, there would never have been a Fr. Francis Xavier Morgan, and if there had never been a Fr. Morgan, the young Tolkien boys might easily have drifted into unbelief or spiritual indifference, and if J.R.R. Tolkien had not taken in the lessons he learned from his mentor, he would never have shared the insight about God's gift that brought such comfort to a young Stephen Colbert in his moment of doubt and pain.

One of the most potent insights of the spiritual masters is that our lives are not about us, that they are, in fact, an ingredient in God's providential purposes, part of a story that stretches infinitely beyond what we can immediately grasp. Why are we suffering now? Well, it might be so that, in St. Paul's language, we might comfort someone else with the same consolation we have received in our suffering. And that someone might be a person who has not even been born. St. John Paul II commented that, for people of faith, there are no coincidences, only aspects of God's providence that we have not yet fully understood. The line that runs from Newman to Morgan to Tolkien to Colbert was not dumb chance, a mere coincidence; rather, it was an instance of the slow but sure unfolding of the divine plan.

Hospital-Land and the Divinization of One's Passivities

I once spent six days at a place only about a ten-minute drive from my home, but I had, nevertheless, entered a country as "foreign" to my experience as Botswana or Katmandu. You see, I had taken up residence in Hospital-Land. I will spare you all of the gory details, but I was brought in for an emergency appendectomy, and then had to undergo a second surgery due to complications. As a priest, of course, I had visited Hospital-Land many times, but I had never actually lived in it for an extended period. Hospital-Land has its own completely unique rhythms, customs, language, and semiotic systems. Adjusting to it, consequently, is as complex an undertaking as adjusting to Vienna, Paris, or Tokyo.

For example, the normal rhythm of day and night is interrupted and overturned in Hospital-Land. You are only vaguely aware of the movement of the sun across the sky, and people come barging into your room as regularly at two in the morning as two in the afternoon. I found myself frequently asking visitors not only the time of day, but also whether it was morning or evening. Relatedly, the usual distinctions between public and private simply evanesce in Hospital-Land. As my mother told me many years ago, upon returning from a long visit to that country, "When you enter the hospital, you place your modesty in a little bag and leave it by the door. Then you pick it up when you go home." Nurses, nursing aides, medical students, doctors, surgeons, tech assistants—all of them have license to look over any part of your anatomy, pretty much whenever they want. At first, I was appalled by this, but after a few days, I more or less acquiesced: "Anyone else out there that would like to take a look?" Hospital-Land has its own very distinctive language, largely conditioned by numbers: blood pressure rates, temperature, hemoglobin counts, etc. It was actually a little bit funny how quickly I began to banter with the nurses and doctors in this arcane jargon.

But for me *the* characteristic of Hospital-Land is passivity. When you pass through the doors of the hospital, you simply hand your life over to other people. They transport you, clean you, test you, make you wait for results (an excruciating form of psychological torture, by the way), tell you what you have to undergo next, poke you, prod you, take blood out of you, and cut into you. And when you are at your wits' end, frustrated beyond words, so eager to get home that you can taste it, you have to wait for them to give you permission to leave. You place your modesty in a little bag by the door when you enter the hospital, and you put your autonomy in that same container.

And this is of more than merely psychological interest. It has far-reaching spiritual implications. As I lay on my back in Hospital-Land, a phrase kept coming unbidden into my mind: "the divinization of one's passivities." This is a line from one of the great spiritual works of the twentieth century, *The Divine Milieu* by the French Jesuit Pierre Teilhard de Chardin. In that seminal text, Teilhard famously distinguished between the divinization of one's activities and the divinization of one's passivities. The former is a noble spiritual move, consisting in the handing over of one's achievements and accomplishments to the purposes of God. A convinced Jesuit, Teilhard desired to devote all that he did (and he did a lot) *ad majorem Dei gloriam* (to the greater glory of God). But this attitude,

Teilhard felt, came nowhere near the spiritual power of divinizing one's passivities. By this he meant the handing over of one's suffering to God, the surrendering to the Lord of those things that are done to us, those things over which we have no control. We become sick; a loved one dies suddenly; we lose a job; a much-desired position goes to someone else; we are unfairly criticized; we find ourselves, unexpectedly, in the valley of the shadow of death. These experiences lead some people to despair, but the spiritually alert person should see them as a particularly powerful way to come to union with God. A Christian would readily speak here of participating in the cross of Christ. Indeed how strange that the central icon of the Christian faith is not of some great achievement or activity, but rather of something horrible being done to a person. The point is that suffering, offered to God, allows the Lord to work out his purpose with unsurpassed power.

In some ways, Teilhard's distinction is an echo of St. John of the Cross's distinction between the "active" and "passive" nights of the soul. For the great Spanish master, the dark night has nothing to do with psychological depression, but rather with a pruning away of attachments that keep one from complete union with God. This pruning can take a conscious and intentional form (the active night) or it can be something endured. In a word, we can rid ourselves of attachments, or God can do it for us. The latter, St. John thinks, is far more powerful and cleansing than the former.

I do believe that my stay in the foreign country of Hospital-Land had a good deal to do with the divinization of my passivities and with the passive night of the soul. I certainly wouldn't actively seek to go back to that land, but perhaps God might send me there again. May I have the grace to accept it as a gift.

The Dangers of the
Prosperity Gospel

I once came across an article in the magazine *Atlantic Monthly* that bore the extraordinary title "Did Christianity Cause the Crash?" I realize that much of the mainstream media is ready to blame Christianity for almost every societal ill, but this seemed a bit much. As I read through the article, it became plain that the culprit, in the author's mind, was the so-called "prosperity Gospel," the view, propagated by quite a few extremely popular evangelists, that material prosperity flows from the depth and quality of one's faith in God. His argument was that the willingness on the part of many Christians to risk their savings on questionable investments conduced toward the bursting of the housing bubble and the subsequent economic meltdown. Well, I'm not sure that that particular argument carries much weight, but I'll confess that the article piqued my interest in this influential theology.

In its American incarnation, the prosperity Gospel probably began with the theological speculations of the evangelist Oral Roberts. Roberts encouraged his followers to "expect miracles" and to look forward with confidence to the ways in which God would reward them, materially and financially, for their trust in his providence. One of the most prominent prosperity gospellers on the scene today is Joel Osteen, pastor of the largest church in America, best-selling author, and former student at Oral Roberts University. He tells his millions of readers and listeners that they should not settle for mediocre lives; instead they should trust in the Lord's ability to give them the house that they desire, the job that they deserve, and children that will make them proud. A typical piece of Osteenian advice: "Friend, you have to start believing that good things are coming your way and they will!" Other modern advocates of this position include the very popular televangelists Joyce Meyer and T.D. Jakes.

To give the prosperity gospellers their due, there is some Biblical warrant for their position. The book of Deuteronomy consistently promises Israel that, if it remains faithful to God's commands, it will receive numerous benefits in this world. The Psalmist, too, assures us, "delight yourself in the Lord, and he will give you the desires of your heart" (Ps 37:4) And Jesus himself counsels: "seek ye first the Kingdom of God and his righteousness, and all these things (food, shelter, clothing, etc.) will be added unto you" (Mt 6:33). And there is no doubt that the Bible consistently urges people to trust in the providence of God at all times. Jesus' reminder of the birds, who neither sow nor reap nor gather into barns but who are nevertheless fed by their heavenly Father, is a summation of the Scriptural confidence in God's care for those who have faith in him.

However, we must be attentive to the very subtle way that the Bible itself nuances and specifies these claims. The great counterpoise to the book of Deuteronomy is the book of Job, which tells the story of a thoroughly righteous man who, in one fell swoop, suffers the loss of all of his material prosperity. Job's friends, operating out of a standard Deuteronomistic (or prosperity Gospel) point of view, argue that he must have grievously offended God, but Job—and God himself—protest against this simplistic interpretation. The deepest reason for Job's suffering, we learn, is lost in the infinite abyss of God's permissive will and is by no means easily correlatable to Job's virtue or lack thereof. And Jesus himself, the very archetype of the faithful Israelite, experiences not earthly prosperity but a life of simplicity and death on a brutal instrument of torture. If Joel Osteen and Oral Roberts were right, we would expect Jesus to have been the richest man in Nazareth and a darling of Jerusalem high society.

The resolution of this issue turns on a distinction between a conventional understanding and a divine understanding of the successful life. Deuteronomy is indeed right when it says that "prosperity" will follow from obedience to God's will, but the prosperity in question is spiritual flourishing, not necessarily worldly success. Obeying the divine commands does indeed lead to the right ordering of the self, and therefore to an increase in joy, even if that very obedience leads, in worldly terms, to abject suffering or failure. St. Thomas More followed the voice of his conscience, and this led to the loss of his home, his family, his considerable fortune, his high political status, and eventually his life. But he died, spiritually speaking, a successful man, a saint. St. Thomas Aquinas endeavored to answer a question that many of us ask: why do the wicked often prosper and the righteous suffer? Thomas turned the question on its head by introducing the wider context of God's purposes. Perhaps, he suggested, the good person who is deprived of material goods is actually being rewarded, since that deprivation opens him more and more to the spiritual dimension; and perhaps the wicked person who has every worldly benefit is actually being punished, since those material preoccupations close him to the only good that finally matters.

So embrace the prosperity Gospel, as long as you construe prosperity along properly Gospel lines. Following God's will, abandoning yourself to the divine providence, will indeed give you treasure in heaven, but don't necessarily expect it to give you treasure on earth.

The Lesson of Calcutta

I have been all across the world to film my documentary on Catholicism. With my team, I've traveled to Jerusalem, Rome, Madrid, Mexico City, Warsaw, Krakow, Auschwitz, Cologne, New York, Philadelphia, Istanbul, Corinth, and Athens. But none of these places had a visceral impact to match that of Calcutta, India. We had gone there to film in locales associated with the work of Mother Teresa and her sisters, and therefore we didn't spend much time in the relatively presentable parts of the city. We went to the slums, where, in Mother's famous phrase, "the poorest of the poor" lived. Here are just some of the images that I trust will stay branded in my mind for the rest of my life: a child of about ten gathering horse manure with his bare hands in order to sell it; people bathing in a river filled with raw sewage; a mentally disturbed woman just outside of the Motherhouse of the Missionaries of Charity emitting a blood-curdling, otherworldly scream; garbage absolutely everywhere, as though the entire city were a trash heap; people whose only dwelling was the street or the sidewalk; beggar children surrounding me and gesturing desperately to their mouths; a man at one of Mother's hospitals with a goiter on his neck the size of a pumpkin; a Missionary of Charity sister, having just tended to a man bleeding from one of his ears, saying to me, "maggots again."

When she was still a Loreto nun, Mother Teresa was making her way north of Calcutta by train to Darjeeling for a retreat. While she was riding on that train, she heard a voice inviting her to carry the light of Christ to the darkest places. Upon her return to Calcutta, she commenced the process that led eventually to the founding of the Missionaries of Charity, an order whose purpose would be to respond to that summons. This is the work that is carried on to this day by her sisters, in the meanest streets of Calcutta and in over five hundred establishments around the globe.

On the first day of our filming, we went to the Motherhouse of the community, the international headquarters of the Missionaries of Charity. I met a number of the sisters and had the privilege of speaking to Mother Prema, the current superior of the order. We visited Mother Teresa's tiny cell, a room perhaps 12 feet by 12 feet, decorated by a small table and a bed with an impossibly thin mattress. The greatest joy of that day was to celebrate Mass near Mother's tomb and to see many other pilgrims kneeling by her grave in deep prayer.

On the second day, we filmed in a small hospital where the Missionaries of Charity care for children with mental and physical disabilities. When we arrived, the electricity had just gone out and the room was stiflingly hot, since the fans had stopped. Everywhere the sisters and a large team of volunteers milled about, providing medical assistance, speaking to the kids, teaching some of them to sing simple songs, or just holding them. There was one sister whose name I have forgotten but whose smile I will never forget. She was carrying in her arms a small girl of perhaps a year and half or two years old. The child was blind, her sightless eyes sunken in her head. I asked sister how they had come to care for this girl, and she told me that she had simply been abandoned on the street. "She is my special baby," the sister said, and then she flashed this absolutely radiant smile, which told me that she had found a deep joy precisely in this hot, crowded hospital in the midst of one of the most squalid cities in the world.

We're dealing with a deep mystery here. All of us human beings want joy. Everything we do and say, all of our actions and endeavors, are meant to produce contentment, peace, happiness. Even the most morally corrupt person, ultimately, wants joy. But how do we find it? The most elemental mistake—made consistently across the centuries and up to the present day—is to seek peace by filling up in ourselves something that we perceive to be missing. We tell ourselves that we'd be happy if we just had enough pleasure, enough power, enough security, enough esteem. *But this does not work.* It is the supreme paradox of the Christian spiritual tradition that we become filled with joy precisely in the measure that we contrive a way to make of ourselves a gift. By emptying out the self in love for the other, we become filled to the brim with the divine life. The smile of that Missionary of Charity signaled the presence of a joy that no wealth, no security, no pleasure, no honor could possibly provide, and that can emerge even in the most miserable context. There is the lesson that Calcutta burned deeply into my soul.

A Saint of Darkness

I just finished reading Fr. Paul Murray's astonishing little book on Mother Teresa's interior life, called *I Have Loved Jesus in the Night.* Fr. Murray, a Dominican professor of spiritual theology at the Angelicum University in Rome, was a close confidant of the saint of Calcutta. In this brief and eminently readable text, he has woven together a number of personal reminiscences with an insightful reading of the famous "dark night" undergone for nearly sixty years by the woman who, during her own lifetime, was almost universally acknowledged as a saint. Fr. Murray states the paradox of Mother Teresa succinctly: he had never known anyone more radiantly joyful than this woman who, in hundreds of private letters and notes, admitted to an almost unremitting inner darkness, a practically unrelenting sense of the absence of God.

I've known Paul Murray for many years, and when I was with my team filming in Rome, we all sat down for a lovely, long dinner with him at a cozy restaurant not far from the Pantheon. In time, the conversation turned to Mother Teresa and this puzzle of her dark night. In the course of this exchange, we all got a wonderful sneak preview of the book. A member of our group was a devout Methodist, a woman with a strong Biblical sensibility, and she expressed her bewilderment at this phenomenon of the saint who seemed at times even to doubt the existence of God. "Maybe Mother was just depressed because of her difficult work," she suggested. Fr. Murray immediately clarified that Mother Teresa was not a depressive—as the rich accomplishments of her life and work bear witness—and that the dark night, in the strict sense, has little to do with emotional melancholy. Rather, he said, the dark night of the soul is like the shadow cast by the overwhelming light of the indwelling God. Especially when he deigns to come close, God floods the faculties of the mind and the heart so that they are incapable of processing and understanding in the ordinary sense. The eye can see objects illuminated by the sun, but it becomes dysfunctional, even to the point of blindness, when it turns to gaze at the sun itself. So it is with the soul that has been invaded by God. Perhaps this is why, Fr. Murray hinted, so many of the greatest saints report the experience of the dark night.

Next, someone asked about St. John of the Cross, the Spanish mystic who wrote most extensively about what he called *la noche oscura*. Fr. Paul reminded us that St. John saw the dark night as a cleansing and purifying process, initiated and directed by God himself. We find ourselves, John of the Cross taught, in the midst of a good and beautiful world, but we are meant finally for union with God. Therefore, the soul has to become free from its attachments to finite things so as to be free for communion with God. This purification first involves what John called "the night of the senses," that is to say, the letting go of physical and sensual pleasures, and it continues with the "night of the soul," which is a detachment from the thoughts, ideas, and mental images that one can use as a substitute for God. Like all purifications, this one is painful, especially if one's attachment to these finite things is intense. It will often manifest itself, John of the Cross said, as dryness in prayer and a keen sense of the absence of God, even of God's active abandonment. In this process, God is not toying with the soul; rather, he is performing a kind of surgery upon it, cutting certain things away so that its life might intensify. This aspect of the dark night, Paul Murray said, was present in Mother Teresa as well.

Toward the end of the evening, after lots of give and take, our Dominican friend offered another interpretation of Mother Teresa's experience. It was perhaps, he said, a vivid participation in the desolation that Christ Jesus felt on the cross when he said, "My God, my God, why have you forsaken me?" We can say, blithely enough, that the spiritual life consists in allowing Christ to live his life in us. But this means that he will live his passion in us, that he will permit us fully to feel what he felt at the bitter end of his earthly life. In Mother Teresa's case, this participation was particularly intense, precisely because her ministry was to the lonely, the poor, the hopeless and the abandoned. She identified with their physical and psychological suffering, but her terrible sense of isolation from God allowed her to identify even with their spiritual suffering. And from that solidarity flowed her compassion.

I'm just giving you a sense of Paul Murray's wisdom in regard to Mother Teresa. Do buy his book if you want to understand more fully the woman who said, "If I ever become a saint, I will be a saint of darkness."

The Lesson of
Lough Derg

Our *Catholicism* film crew arrived at the shores of a large lake in far northwest Ireland, in the county of Donegal. We stepped onto a ferry and were taken to an island in the middle of the lake. On the island was a collection of buildings, which in both architecture and color reminded me vividly of Alcatraz prison. The weather that day was horrific: temperature around 50, heavy winds, and a steady cold rainfall. Our hosts offered us tea and scones and then we made our way onto the island to begin our work. Out of the mists and the rain emerged the figures that we had come to film. They were swathed in raincoats, hoods, and jackets, but their feet were bare. Most of them carried rosaries in their hands, and some of them were praying aloud. A few were making their way, on their knees, around rude "beds" of stone, and one woman was standing against a wall in the attitude of the crucified Christ. Some of the more elderly denizens of the island were walking with a halting, pained gait. We had come to Lough Derg, otherwise known as St. Patrick's Purgatory.

I had wanted to find a place that would be a fitting visual accompaniment to the section of our *Catholicism* series dealing with purgatory—and I wasn't disappointed. I don't know any other place on earth that better exemplifies the idea and practice of purgative suffering than Lough Derg. Tradition has it that St. Patrick himself came to this island in the fifth century in order to spend a penitential retreat of forty days and forty nights. And from the Middle Ages to the present day, pilgrims have journeyed there, in imitation of Patrick, to do penance and to pray. When the retreatants arrive, they are instructed to immediately take off their shoes and socks, and they endure the three day process barefoot, regardless of the weather. That first day, they fast (eating nothing but dry bread and a soup composed of hot water and pepper), and they move through a series of prayers and spiritual exercises. The first night, they are compelled to stay awake, fasting from sleep. If someone dozes off, his fellow pilgrims are expected to wake him up. The following day, they continue with their fast and their exercises, but they are allowed to sleep that night. The third day involves still more prayer, and culminates with confession and Mass. After the liturgy, the pilgrims put their shoes back on and are ferried across to the mainland. Though we didn't want to disturb the prayer of the retreatants, a few of the pilgrims approached us. One, a man in his mid-seventies, told us that he has made the Lough Derg retreat every year since 1957; and another, a woman in her sixties, told us that the feeling of freedom and inner peace that she has upon leaving the retreat is incomparable.

Now I'm sure that many people, especially in our largely secularized culture, would raise a number of questions about a place like Lough Derg. Why would anyone willingly endure such suffering? Why would a gracious God expect this of any of his children? Isn't all of this a sign of neurosis, the fruit of low self-esteem and the product of a sick culture? Well, I know lots of people who quite willingly go through an hour or more of intense physical exercise every day—running on treadmills, climbing on stairmasters, lifting heavy weights—in order to assure the health of their bodies. Professional football teams commence grueling two-a-day workouts in the late summer sun in order to prepare for the rigors of the NFL season. And young people all across the country regularly move through hours and hours of practice in order to master the guitar, the flute, or the violin. No one accuses these people of neurosis or low self-esteem, or construes their exercises as the fruits of a dysfunctional culture. The point is this: whenever we take something to be of great importance, we are willing to suffer in order to achieve it or participate in it.

Those who come to Lough Derg take their spiritual lives with utter seriousness, and that is precisely why they are willing to endure hardship—even imposing it on themselves—in order to deepen their communion with God. They know that there are certain tendencies within their bodies and souls that are preventing the achievement of full friendship with God and therefore they seek, quite sensibly, to discipline themselves. John Henry Newman commented that the ascetical principle is basic to a healthy Christianity. He meant that Christians, at their best, understand that our sinful nature has to be chastised, disciplined, and rightly ordered. When the ascetical instinct disappears (as it has in much of Western Christianity), the spiritual life rapidly becomes superficial and attenuated, devolving into an easy "I'm okay and you're okay" attitude.

The whole point of the Christian life is to find joy, but the attainment of true joy comes, in a sinful world, at the cost of some suffering. That's why I, for one, am glad that a place like Lough Derg exists.

A Tale of Two Skulls

I once spent five wonderful days in the diocese of Leeds in the Yorkshire district of England. I was the guest of Bishop Arthur Roach, who had invited me to give a series of talks to his priests and lay leaders. While I was in the area, I was taken to see two of the greatest of the English cathedrals, Durham and York, and I was duly impressed by their stateliness and spiritual power. But the York and Durham cathedrals were not the most beautiful things that I saw on my journey. Bishop Roach took me to the far more modest cathedral of Leeds, led me to the main altar, and then invited me to examine a treasure.

We crouched down and the bishop pulled out two heavy stones from the front of the altar, revealing a pair of well-preserved human skulls. These, he explained, were the remains of Blessed Peter Snow and Blessed Ralph Grimston. Peter Snow was a Yorkshireman who had left Elizabethan England in order to study for the Catholic priesthood in France. At the time, of course, it was an offense to be a Catholic and a capital crime to be a priest. Peter Snow had been ordained in Reims and subsequently smuggled into England, where he had successfully ministered for two or three years, clandestinely celebrating the Mass, encouraging Catholics in their faith, and instructing children in their catechism. Like many other priests in England at that time, he was protected by Catholic families who hid him away in cellars, attics, and hiding-holes concealed behind walls. In May 1598, he was making his way to York in the company of Ralph Grimston, a layman who was travelling with him for protection. The two Catholics were waylaid by the authorities. Grimston drew his sword and shouted at the young priest to ride off, but they were captured. A trial was held in York, and Snow was convicted of being a priest, and Grimston of harboring an enemy of the state. On June 15th, they were executed. Grimston was hanged and then beheaded; Fr. Snow suffered the far worse fate of being hanged, slowly eviscerated, and then cut into four pieces. Afterward, their heads were placed on pikes over the gate of the city in order to dissuade any who might be tempted to imitate them.

The heads were taken down, and for many centuries were hidden away, eventually coming to rest at a Carmelite monastery. When that monastery was sold, Bishop Roach, who knew of the existence of the skulls, asked that they be transferred to the Leeds cathedral and placed in the new altar. Before they were ensconced in the altar, the bishop allowed them to be examined by a forensic scientist in London, who was able to reconstruct facsimiles of the faces, letting us see, after all of these centuries, what these men looked like. When I saw the photographs, I was deeply moved, especially by the face of the young priest (only 32 when he was killed). He looked for all the world like one of the students that I taught at the seminary. It just broke my heart to think that this courageous kid could have been treated with such brutality and inhumanity, simply for saying Mass and administering the sacraments. I mused on the depths of human cruelty, on a wickedness that beggars the imagination and is, nevertheless, on full display up and down the centuries to the present day.

But above all, I found myself edified by his witness. During his years of study in France, he knew that he was preparing for a desperately dangerous mission. He was fully aware that many of his colleagues had already been arrested or killed, and yet he persevered. His ministry in his home country was grim, haunted, and fearsome. How many terrible days and nights he must have endured, and yet he pressed on. Looking at his placid face, I thought about the transforming quality of God's amazing grace, what God's love can do with our frail and deeply compromised humanity.

Part of the genius of Catholic theology is that it clearly articulates both sides of the human condition. There is nothing naïve or blandly optimistic in Catholic anthropology. It takes original sin and its consequences with utter seriousness, arguing that human beings are weakened, twisted, even, in both body and soul. No moral outrage—Auschwitz, Hiroshima, the Cambodian killing fields, or Elizabethan totalitarianism—really surprises the Catholic mind, for as Chesterton said, "we're all in the same boat and we're all seasick." At the same time, Catholic teaching holds that we are made in the image and likeness of God, and are destined, ultimately, to share in the very dynamics of the divine life, loving as effortlessly and radically as God himself. This Catholic hope outstrips even the fondest dreams of any humanist philosophy.

Those two skulls in the altar at Leeds silently speak of the best and the worst in us human beings. Peter Snow and Ralph Grimston, pray for us.

The Fire at Namugongo

In 1879, the first Catholic missionaries arrived in the heart of Africa, in what is now the nation of Uganda. They catechized and preached, and in a few years had made a number of converts, especially among the young. The most prominent of these were a group of men and boys who served as pages of the court of King Mwanga II. This king had initially been supportive of the missionaries, but his attitude quickly changed when he discovered how seriously his Christian pages took the moral demands of their new faith. Accustomed to getting whatever he wanted, Mwanga solicited sexual favors from several of his courtiers. When they refused, he presented them with a terrible choice: either renounce their Christian faith or die. Though they were new converts, and though they were very young, the pages, to a man, refused to deny their Christianity.

Joseph Mukasa Balikuddembe was killed outright by the king himself, and the rest were led off on a terrible death march to the place of execution, many miles outside the capital city. On the way, the condemned passed the home of the priest who had baptized and catechized many of them. One can only imagine the profoundly conflicting feelings of pride and anguish that the priest must have experienced as he watched this procession. Witnesses said that the young men showed enormous resolution on the march and that the youngest, a boy named Kizito, actually chattered and laughed with this friends as he walked. When they arrived at the place of execution, a spot called Namugongo, they were put to death, some by spear but most by fire. The leader of the group, Charles Lwanga, all of twenty-five years old, asked permission to prepare the pyre himself. After arranging the wood, he lay down and endured a slow torture in silence, crying out "Oh God!" only at the very end.

I'm sure that practically any objective observer of that terrible scene would have concluded that Christianity was finished in that part of Africa. The remaining Christians—a tiny minority surrounded by hostile enemies, including the king himself—would be terrorized by what happened at Namugongo, and many of them undoubtedly would surrender whatever allegiance they had to the new faith brought by the white missionaries. But there is a peculiar logic that obtains in matters supernatural, a logic of paradox, reversal, and surprise. That which should stifle Christianity in point of fact makes it grow stronger, precisely because the faith is correlative to a reality that transcends nature and the dynamics that govern ordinary experience. The Church father Tertullian caught this in his famous adage to the effect that the blood of martyrs is the seed of Christians. I'm sure that some who saw or heard of the executions at Namugongo abandoned their faith, but many others were galvanized by the courage of those young witnesses. And as the story was passed on, people came not only to admire the valor of those who died but more importantly, to understand that, as Evelyn Waugh would put it, "the supernatural is the real." The Catholic Church in Africa didn't die at Namugongo; it came to life there.

On June 3rd, the feast of the Ugandan martyrs, a festive liturgy attended by over 500,000 people takes place at Namugongo, just adjacent to the site where Charles Lwanga uttered his plaintive, "Oh God." It was one of the great privileges of my life to have assisted at that Mass, as part of the filming for my series on Catholicism. As the massive crowd assembled, choirs from many different parts of Africa sang and swayed, and a tremendous spirit of prayerfulness obtained. About fifteen minutes before the formal commencement of the Mass, a liturgical procession—the most wonderful I've ever witnessed—took place. It began with three dignified young men, wearing the formal garb of acolytes, and just behind them came a parade of female dancers, dressed in the traditional tribal costumes of Africa, and dancing and gyrating joyfully to the music. Then came a team of male dancers, wearing leopard skins and feathers, and jangling ankle bells as they stepped. Behind them came a long line of priests and bishops, swathed in red chasubles, evocative of the blood shed by the young martyrs. The general mood that this created—almost overwhelming in its power—was joy, triumph, victory. As I watched all of this unfold, I confess that several times tears came to my eyes, for I could see, beyond the procession and beyond the crowd, the top of the basilica constructed on the site of Charles Lwanga's execution. As that brave young Christian uttered his dying "Oh God" on that spot so many years before, could he ever have imagined that one day a half a million African Catholics would gather there in festive celebration of the faith for which he gave his life? Could he ever have imagined that, in the year 2016, there would be 400,000,000 Christians in Africa?

The blood of the martyrs is indeed the seed of Christians. Charles Lwanga, you won!

A Persecuted Church
and Its Heroes

A recent survey has indicated something that should lift the hearts of Christians everywhere, namely, that the fastest-growing religion on the planet is Christianity. This explosive growth is on particularly clear display in Africa and Asia, where churches and seminaries can't be built fast enough to accommodate the need. It is especially important that we in the West become cognizant of this state of affairs, for with the rise of secularism and the falloff in church attendance in Europe, Canada, Australia, and America, we can far too easily assume that Christianity is in a state of permanent decline. Au contraire, in point of fact.

But other studies carry the dark truth that the fastest-growing religion in the world is also the most persecuted. Again, this might surprise many in the post-September 11th West, who presume that Islam is the religion most in danger, and hence most in need of special protection. But all over the world, particularly in Asia, Africa, and the Middle East, Christians are, by far, the most threatened religious group. Indeed, Vatican research shows that 75% of those killed around the world for religious reasons are Christians.

We're all aware of the shocking and brutal attacks by ISIS. But who can also forget the horrendous attack on a Catholic Church in Baghdad? Islamist militants burst into the church while Mass was in progress and proceeded to open fire indiscriminately on men, women, and children. As they finished up their grisly work, the killers found themselves trailed by a toddler who asked plaintively, "why are you doing this?" In time, they turned on the child and killed him, too. In the wake of that assault, huge numbers of Catholics and other Christians left their country. Estimates are that in the last ten years somewhere between six hundred thousand and a million Christians have been forced to flee Iraq. In Saudi Arabia, no Christian is allowed to worship publicly, and no church of any kind can be built. Many were cheered by the "Arab Spring" that saw the expulsion of dictators from Libya, Yemen, and Egypt, and the shaking of the Assad regime in Syria, but Christians in those countries are far from encouraged. The secularist proclivities of those dictators at least allowed for a rough toleration of non-Islamic religions; thus the collapse of the tyrants has made possible the tyranny of radical Islamic factions, resulting in an aggressive campaign against Christianity. Egyptian Copts—members of one of the oldest Christian communities in the world—were publicly assaulted in the streets of Cairo by representatives of the Islamic brotherhood. The *Wall Street Journal* reported on an Egyptian Christian mother of two young girls, who was blithely informed by her Muslim physician that, according to a prescription of sharia law, her daughters would have to be circumcised. Convinced that the government would no longer protect them, mother and children fled the country.

At the beginning of 2012, Nigeria's president declared a state of emergency in sections of his country due to a series of unprovoked attacks on Christian churches. Boko Haram, a militant Islamist sect, has claimed credit for the assaults, including attacks on Christmas day that left 42 people dead. One of the most troubling stories of Christian persecution comes out of Pakistan, where fierce anti-blasphemy laws are in effect. A Christian woman named Asia Bibi was imprisoned on trumped-up charges of speaking against the prophet Muhammad. Despite protests from around the world, she was tried, convicted, and sentenced to death. Currently she languishes in prison, awaiting her execution and praying for her jailers.

Now, God knows that Christians have far from a spotless record when it comes to tolerating religious diversity, but the fact remains that Christians are, by far, the most victimized religious group in the world. From Pakistan to Nigeria, from Egypt to Iraq, ordinary Christians routinely risk their lives simply by declaring their faith and worshiping according to their conscience. They are walking in the footsteps of great martyrs of the tradition, from Stephen, Peter, and Paul to Charles Lwanga and Edith Stein.

A Message in Blood:
ISIS and the Meaning
of the Cross

In February 2015, the attention of the world was riveted to a deserted beach in northern Libya, where a group of twenty-one Coptic Christians were brutally beheaded by masked operatives of ISIS. In the wake of the executions, the militant Islamist group released a gruesome video entitled "A Message in Blood to the Nation of the Cross." I suppose that for the ISIS murderers the reference to "the Nation of the Cross" had little sense beyond a generic designation for Christianity. Sadly, for most Christians, too, the cross has become little more than an anodyne, a harmless symbol, a pious decoration. I would like to take the awful event on that Libyan beach, as well as the ISIS message concerning it, as an occasion to reflect on the still-startling distinctiveness of the Cross.

In the time of Jesus, the cross was a brutal and very effective sign of Roman power. Imperial authorities effectively said, "If you cross us (pun intended), we will affix you to a dreadful instrument of torture and leave you to writhe in agonizing, literally excruciating (*ex cruce*, from the cross) pain until you die. Then we will make sure that your body hangs on that gibbet until it is eaten away by scavenging animals." The cross was, basically, state-sponsored terrorism, and it did indeed terrify people. The great Roman statesman and philosopher Cicero once described a crucifixion, but only through a convoluted circumlocution, for he couldn't bring himself to characterize it directly. After putting down the great slave uprising of Spartacus, the Roman government lined the Appian Way with hundreds of crosses so as to dissuade any other would-be revolutionaries. Pontius Pilate had much the same intention when he nailed dozens of Jewish rebels to the walls of Jerusalem. That same Pilate arranged for Jesus to be crucified on Calvary hill, a promontory situated close to one of the gates of ancient Jerusalem, guaranteeing that his horrific death would not be missed by the large Passover crowds moving into and out of the city.

From the crucified Jesus, all of the disciples, (save John) fled, precisely because they wanted with all their hearts to avoid his dreadful fate. After Good Friday, the friends of Jesus huddled in terror in the Upper Room, petrified that they might be nailed up on Calvary as well. The disciples on the road to Emmaus were, understandably, heading out of Jerusalem, away from danger, and they were utterly convinced that Jesus' movement had come to naught. In a word, the cross meant the victory of the world, the annihilation of Jesus and what he stood for.

And this is why it is surpassing strange that one of the earliest Apostles and missionaries of the Christian religion could write, "I preach one thing, Christ and him crucified!" (1 Cor 2:2). How could Paul possibly present the dreadful cross as the centerpiece of his proclamation? He could do so only because he knew that God had raised the crucified Jesus from the dead, proving thereby that God's love and forgiveness are greater than anything in the world. This is why his exaltation of the cross is a sort of taunt to Rome and all of its brutal descendants down through the ages: "You think that scares us? God has conquered that!" And this is why, to this day, Christians boldly hold up an image of the humiliated, tortured Jesus to the world. What they are saying is, "We are not afraid."

How wonderful this is, by the way, in light of the Charlie Hebdo tragedy and the controversy over the Dutch cartoonist's mocking depictions of the prophet Muhammad. Christians don't fuss particularly about insults to Jesus, for we reverence a depiction of the insulted Christ as our most sacred icon. We can say, with Paul, "I am certain that neither death nor life, neither angels nor principalities, neither height nor depth, nor any other creature will be able to separate us from the love of God in Christ Jesus our Lord" (Rom 8:38-39), for we know that the world killed Jesus but God raised him from the dead.

Just before their throats were cut, many of the murdered Coptic Christians could be seen mouthing the words "Jesus Christ" and "Jesus is Lord." The first of those phrases is a rendering of the Aramaic *Ieshouah Maschiach*, which means "Jesus the anointed one" and which hearkens back to King David, the paradigmatic anointed figure of the Old Testament. The second phrase is one that can be traced to St. Paul's kerygmatic cry *Iesous Kyrios* (Jesus is Lord!), which was intended to trump a watchword of the time, *Kaiser Kyrios* (Caesar is Lord). In short, both declarations assert the kingship of Jesus, but what a strange kingship! The new David reigns not from a throne but from a cross; the one who trumps Caesar doesn't lead an army, but embodies the divine forgiveness.

The ISIS barbarians were actually quite right in entitling their video "A Message Written in Blood." Up and down the centuries, tyrants and their lackeys have thought that they could wipe out the followers of Jesus through acts of violence. But, as Tertullian observed long ago, the blood of the martyrs is the seed of the Church. Furthermore, they were right in sending their message to "the Nation of the Cross." But they should know that the cross taunts them.

The Joy of Evangelizing

An emergency tends to focus one's mind and energies and to clarify one's priorities. If a dangerous fire breaks out in a home, the inhabitants thereof will lay aside their quarrels, postpone their other activities, and together get to the task of putting out the flames. If a nation is invaded by an aggressor, politicians will quickly forget their internal squabbling and put off their legislative programs in order to work together for the shared purpose of repulsing the enemy.

Christianity is grounded in what its earliest proponents called "good news," *euangelion*. There is, therefore, something permanently fresh, startling, and urgent about the Christian faith. It is not a bland spirituality or generic philosophy; it is news about something amazing and unprecedented, namely, that a carpenter from Nazareth, who declared himself the Son of God, has been raised from the dead. This is why there is a "grab you by the lapels" quality about the early Christian witnesses: the authors of the New Testament are not trading in generalities and abstract principles; they are telling the world about a revolution, an earthquake, an emergency. Jesus is risen from the dead, and therefore he is the king. And because he is the king, your whole life has to be rearranged around him.

This evangelical urgency, which Pope Francis gets in his bones, is the leitmotif of the pope's 2013 Apostolic Exhortation *Evangelii Gaudium* (The Joy of the Gospel). He knows that if Catholicism leads with its doctrines, it will devolve into an intellectual debating society, and that if it leads with its moral teachings, it will appear fussy and puritanical. It should lead today as it led two thousand years ago, with the stunning news that Jesus Christ is the Lord, and the joy of that proclamation should be as evident now as it was then.

The pope helpfully draws our attention to some of the countless references to joy in the pages of the New Testament: "Rejoice!" is the angel's greeting to Mary (Luke 1:28); in her Magnificat, the Mother of God exults, "My spirit rejoices in God my savior" (Luke 1:47); as a summation of his message and ministry, Jesus declares to his disciples, "I have said these things to you so that my joy may be in you and your joy may be complete" (John 15:11); in the Acts of the Apostles, we are told that "wherever the disciples went there was great joy" (8:8). The pope concludes with a wonderfully understated rhetorical question: "Why should we not also enter into this great stream of joy?" Why not indeed? Displaying his penchant for finding the memorable image, Pope Francis excoriates Christians who have turned "into querulous and disillusioned pessimists, 'sourpusses,'" and whose lives "seem like Lent without Easter."

Once this basic truth is understood, the rest of the Church's life tends to fall more correctly into place. A church filled with the joy of the Resurrection becomes a band of "missionary disciples," going out to the world with the good news. Ecclesial structures, liturgical precision, theological clarity, bureaucratic meetings, etc. are accordingly relativized in the measure that they are placed in service of that more fundamental mission. The pope loves the liturgy, but if evangelical proclamation is the urgent need of the Church, "an ostentatious preoccupation with the liturgy" becomes a problem; a Jesuit, the pope loves the life of the mind, but if evangelical proclamation is the central concern of the Church, then a "narcissistic" and "authoritarian" doctrinal fussiness must be eliminated; a man of deep culture, Pope Francis loves the artistic heritage of the Church, but if evangelical proclamation is the fundamental mission, then the Church cannot become "a museum piece."

If there is one thing that bothers Pope Francis above all it is the endless bickering within the Catholic Church itself: "how many wars take place within the people of God and in our different communities!" Elitists on both the left and the right want to establish a church of the pure, of those who hold all the right positions on the key issues, and they are none too shy about critiquing, attacking, and excommunicating those who don't agree with them. But the Church is meant to be a countersign to the divisiveness and violence of the world, a place where love, compassion, and mutual understanding hold sway. When we become but an echo of the fallen world, then we are like salt that has lost its savor (cf. Matt 5:23; Luke 14:34), and our evangelical persuasiveness is fatally compromised. Again, keep in mind the metaphor of the emergency: when a threat or a great moment of opportunity appears, we ought to lay aside our petty (and even not-so-petty) differences and make common cause.

Twice in the course of the apostolic exhortation, Pope Francis references the ancient principle *bonum diffusivum sui* (the good is diffusive of itself). When we find something that is good or beautiful or compelling—whether it is a movie, a work of art, a book, or even a person—we don't keep it to ourselves. Rather, we are filled with a missionary fervor to share it. This principle applies, par excellence, to our experience of Christ Jesus, risen from the dead. We want, with reckless abandon, to give this supremely good news away. This energy, this compulsion—"woe to me if I do not evangelize" (1 Cor 9:16)—is, for Pope Francis, the beating heart of the Church.

What Are You
Waiting for?

Advent is the liturgical season of vigilance or, to put it more mundanely, of waiting. During the four weeks prior to Christmas, we light the candles of our Advent wreaths and put ourselves in the spiritual space of the Israelite people who, through many long centuries, waited for the coming of the Messiah ("How long, O Lord?" [Ps 13:2]).

In the wonderful avant-garde German movie *Run Lola Run*, a young woman finds herself in a terrible bind: she needs to gather an enormous amount of money in a ridiculously short period of time. Throughout the movie she runs and runs, desperately trying through her own frantic efforts to make things right, but nothing works. Finally, at the moment when she finds herself at the absolute limit of her powers, she slows to a trot, looks up to heaven, and says, "Ich warte, ich warte" ("I'm waiting, I'm waiting"). Though she does not explicitly address God, and though there has been no hint throughout the movie that Lola is the least bit religious, this is undoubtedly a prayer. And in the immediate wake of her edgy request a rather improbable solution to her problem presents itself.

Lola's prayer has always reminded me of Simone Weil, that wonderful and mysterious twentieth-century French mystic whose entire spirituality is predicated upon the power of waiting, or, in her language, of expectation. In prayer, Weil taught, we open our souls, expecting God to act even when the content of that expectation remains unclear. In their curious vigilance and hoping against hope, both Lola and Simone are beautiful Advent figures.

Their attitude is, of course, deeply rooted in Biblical revelation. From beginning to end, Scripture presents us with stories of people who are compelled to wait.

The patriarch Abraham received the promise that he would become, despite his old age, the father of a son, and through that son the father of descendants more numerous than the stars in the night sky. But the fulfillment of that promise was a long time in coming. Through many years, as he and his wife grew older and older, as the likelihood of their parenthood became increasingly remote, Abraham waited. Did he doubt? Did he wonder whether he had misconstrued the divine promise? Did he waver in his faith? Did he endure the taunts of his enemies and the pitying glances of his friends? Probably. But he waited, and in time the promise came true.

Abraham's great-grandson Joseph, the wearer of the multi-colored coat, saw in a dream that he would be a powerful man and that his brothers would one day bow down to him in homage. But the realization of that dream came only after a long and terrible wait. He was sold into slavery by those very brothers, falsely accused of sexual misconduct, humiliated, and finally sent to prison for seven years. Imagine what it must have been like to endure years in an ancient prison—the discomfort, the total lack of privacy, the terrible food in small amounts, the sleeplessness, the torture, and, above all, the hopelessness. This is what Joseph had to wait through before his dream came true in a most unexpected way.

The people of Israel were miraculously delivered from slavery in Egypt, led across the Red Sea by the mighty hand of Moses—and then they waited. A journey that normally would have taken only a few weeks stretched to 40 years as they wandered rather aimlessly through the desert. The book of Exodus frequently gives us indications of what this time of vigil was like: "The people grumbled against Moses, 'We are disgusted with this wretched food... Why did you lead us out into this desert to die? Were there not graves enough in Egypt?'" (Exod 16:2-3) They were hardly models of patience.

Even poor Noah had to wait, cooped up in the ark with his irritable family and restless animals while the waters slowly retreated.

In the course of the Christian tradition, there is much evidence of this spirituality of waiting. Relatively late in life, Ignatius of Loyola realized he was being called by God to do great things. But before he found his path he passed through a wide variety of experiences in the course of many years: a time of stark asceticism and prayer at Manresa, wandering to the Holy Land and back while living hand-to-mouth and sleeping in doorways, taking elementary courses in Paris alongside young kids, gathering a small band of followers and leading them through the Spiritual Exercises. Only at the end of this long sojourn—founding the Company of Jesus—did he realize the great thing God called him to do.

In Dante's *Purgatorio*, the theme of waiting is on prominent display. Dante and Virgil encounter a number of souls who slouch at the foot of the mountain of purgatory, destined to make the climb to heaven but compelled for the time being to wait. How long? As long as God determines.

All of this, I submit, is very hard for most of us. I suppose we human beings have always been in a hurry, but modern people especially seem to want what they want when they want it. We are driven, determined, goal-oriented, fast-moving. I, for one, can't stand waiting.

As an Angelino (and before that, as a Chicagoan) I find myself unavoidably in a lot of traffic jams, and nothing infuriates me more. Usually stuck behind a line of cars, you have no idea when you will get where you want to be, and there is nothing you can do about it.

I hate waiting at doctors' offices; I hate waiting in line at the bank; I hate waiting for the lights to come back on when the electricity fails.

So when I'm told that waiting seems to belong to the heart of the spiritual life, I'm not pleased, for here, too, I want answers, direction, clarity—and I want them pronto. I desire to feel happy and to know what God is up to; I need my life to make sense—now. I'm pleased to live a spiritual life, but I want to be in charge of it and to make it unfold according to my schedule: Run, Barron, Run. All of this is profoundly antipathetic to the mood and spirit of Advent.

So what sense can we make of the countercultural and counterintuitive spirituality of vigilance? The first thing we have to realize is that we and God are, quite simply, on different timetables. The second letter of Peter states this truth with admirable directness: "To you, O Lord, a thousand years are like a day" (3:8).

To the God who stands outside of space and time and who orders the whole of creation, our hours, days, years, eons have a radically different meaning. What is a long time to us is an instant for God, and hence what seems like delay to us is no delay at all to God. What seems like dumb and pointless waiting to us can be the way that God, in a unique and finally mysterious manner, is working out God's purposes.

Theologian Richard Rohr summed up the spiritual life in the phrase "your life is not about you," and this insight is particularly important in terms of the present question. "Why isn't God acting how I want and when I want?" Perhaps because your life is part of a complex whole, the fullness of which only God can properly grasp and fittingly order.

But we can make things even more specific. Is it possible that we are made to wait because the track we are on is not the one God wants for us? Author G.K. Chesterton said that if you are on the wrong road, the very worst thing you can do is move quickly. And there is that old joke about the pilot who comes on the intercom and says, "I have good news and bad news, folks: The bad news is that we're totally lost; the good news is that we're making excellent time!" Maybe we're forced to wait because God wants us to seriously reconsider the course we've charted, to stop hurtling down a dangerous road.

Or perhaps we are made to wait because we are not yet adequately prepared to receive what God wants to give us. In his remarkable letter to Proba, Saint Augustine argued that the purpose of unanswered prayer is to force expansion of the heart. When we don't get what we want, we begin to want it more and more, with ever greater insistency, until our souls are on fire with the desire for it. Sometimes it is only a sufficiently expanded and enflamed heart that can take in what God intends to give.

What would happen to us if we received, immediately and on our own terms, everything we wanted? We might be satisfied in a superficial way, but we wouldn't begin to appreciate the preciousness of the gifts. After all, the Israelites had to wait thousands of years before they were ready to receive God's greatest gift.

Even if we are on the right track, and even if we desire with sufficient intensity what God wants to give, we still might not be ready to integrate a particular grace into our lives or to handle the implications of it. Joseph the dreamer clearly wanted to be a great man, but if he had been given political power and authority when he was an arrogant kid, the results would have been disastrous both for himself and for those under his control. His many years of suffering—his terrible wait—made him a ruler with both wisdom and deep compassion. And so, when his brothers did indeed finally bow down to him, as he had foreseen in his dream, he was able to react not in vengeance, but in love: "I am Joseph, your brother" (Gen 45:4).

The entire Bible ends on a note not so much of triumph and completion as longing and expectation: "Come, Lord Jesus" (Rev 22:20). From the very beginning of the Christian dispensation, followers of the risen Jesus have been waiting. Paul, Augustine, Chrysostom, Agnes, Aquinas, Clare, Francis, Newman, and Weil have all waited for the Second Coming, and hence have all been Advent people. Let us join them, turning our eyes and hearts upward and praying, "Ich warte, ich warte."